HOLIDAY FALDERAH

by Jackie Olden

THE KNAPP PRESS
LOS ANGELES

Library of Congress Cataloging-in-Publication Data

Olden, Jackie, 1934-
    Jackie Olden's Holiday Falderah.

    Includes index.
        1. Holiday Cookery.   2. Entertaining.   I. Title.
TX739.044 1987   641.5'68   87-3968
ISBN 0-89535-188-9

JANUARY

Should auld acquaintance be forgot and resolution time is here, the rebirth, off with the old and on with the new. New Year's Eve and the fun of a new beginning with someone you love. Diets and Super Bowl Sunday. Snowball fights and hot chocolate. This is the quiet time of the year.

CHEESE BALL

> 1 (8-ounce) package cream cheese
> 1 (4-ounce) package bleu cheese
> ⅛ teaspoon Tabasco sauce
> ¼ teaspoon Worcestershire sauce
> ¾ cup chopped nuts

Cream together softened cheeses. Blend in seasonings and ¼ cup of the nuts. Shape into a ball and roll in the remaining nuts. Wrap in clear plastic and chill.

Serve on tray surrounded by crackers or sliced party bread.

ONION HORS D'OEUVRES

Cut rounds of stale bread, and butter lightly.
Cut thin slices of small white onions to fit bread rounds. Top with about ½ teaspoon mayonnaise. Spread over onions. Sprinkle with Parmesan cheese and a dash of paprika. Place under broiler for about 10 minutes or until mayonnaise bubbles and edges brown a little.

This is very easy and sooo tasty—Anyone can.

Happy Holidays . . . .

MARINATED SHRIMP

Marinade:
> 1⅓ cups olive oil
> ⅔ cup tarragon vinegar
> ½ teaspoon salt
> ¼ teaspoon freshly ground black pepper
> ¼ teaspoon paprika
> 1 large onion, coarsely chopped
> 1 clove garlic, mashed
> 3 tablespoons Dijon mustard
> 1 tablespoon German style mustard
> 2 tablespoons prepared horseradish
> 1 tablespoon powdered thyme
> 1½ to 3 pounds jumbo shrimp

Place all ingredients except the shrimp in a blender or food processor. Blend until onion is finely minced. Cook the shrimp in boiling salted water about 3 minutes, then rinse under cold running water to stop the cooking process. Remove shells and chill in the marinade until icy cold. To serve, drain off the marinade and serve it separately as a dip for the shrimp.

Serves 8 to 12

MEATBALLS FOR A CROWD

  9 pounds lean ground beef
  9 cups finely chopped onions
  1 quart milk or cream
  2 tablespoons M.S.G. (optional)
  9 eggs, beaten
  3 tablespoons salt
  1 tablespoon white pepper
  1 teaspoon nutmeg

Combine all ingredients. Roll into marble sized balls. May be sauteed in small batches or dropped into boiling sauce and simmered till done. This recipe makes 225 meatballs and they freeze beautifully. You may also reduce this recipe with no problem.

SOPA DE LIMA

  2 corn tortillas
    oil for frying
  2 teaspoons vegetable oil
 ⅓ cup chopped onion
  1 California chili, roasted, peeled, chopped or ¼ cup canned
    chopped green chilies
  4 cups chicken broth
  1 cup shredded cooked chicken
    salt
  1 tomato, chopped
  1 tablespoon lime juice
  4 large lime slices

Cut tortillas in 2 × ½-inch strips. Pour oil for frying ½ inch deep into a small saucepan or skillet. Heat to 365°. Fry tortilla strips in hot oil until browned and crisp. Drain on paper towels.

Heat 2 teaspoons vegetable oil in a large saucepan. Add onion and chili. Saute until onion is tender but not browned. Add broth, chicken and salt to taste. Cover and simmer 20 minutes. Add tomato; simmer 5 minutes longer. Stir in lime juice. Taste and add more lime juice if desired.

To serve, ladle soup into bowls and add some fried tortilla strips. Float a lime slice in the center of each serving.

Yield 4 servings

JULIENNE TURKEY SALAD

    1 pound turkey breast, cooked and cut into julienne strips
    2 hard cooked eggs, sliced
    2 boiled potatoes, peeled and sliced thin
    2 tablespoons green onion, minced
    2 tablespoons chopped pickle, can use sweet or dill
    2 boiled beets, sliced
    4 sprigs fresh tarragon (½ teaspoon dry)
    1 cup dry white wine
    1 cup olive oil
    2 tablespoons wine vinegar

Combine the first 6 ingredients in a salad bowl. Combine remaining ingredients in a jar and give a good shake. Pour over salad in bowl, chill 3 to 4 hours. Drain off excess dressing, toss again and serve with a few lettuce leaves.

Serves 4

JACKIE'S LASAGNA

    1 pound ground beef
    1 pound Italian sausage (sweet or hot)
    2 packages spaghetti sauce mix
    2 large cans herbed tomato sauce
    3 cans water
  ½ cup dry red wine
    1 tablespoon wine vinegar
    1 tablespoon chopped parsley
    1 pound Ricotta cheese
    1 pound Mozzarella cheese, shredded
    1 pound lasagna noodles
        Parmesan cheese

Brown beef and sausage that has been removed from the casing. When browned drain off grease. Add spaghetti mix, tomato sauce, water, wine, vinegar and parsley. Simmer for 1 hour, stirring frequently. Cook lasagna according to package instructions adding a little oil to the water. Layer in a baking pan, noodles, sauce, dot Ricotta by the tablespoon and Mozzarella. Repeat layers saving enough sauce to cover top layers of noodles. Dust with Parmesan. Bake at 350° until hot and bubbly about 35 to 45 minutes.

Serves 8 to 10

SALAD NICOISE

   2 (16-ounce) cans whole new potatoes, drained and thickly sliced
   1 (16-ounce) can cut green beans, drained
   1 (14-ounce) can water-packed artichoke hearts, drained and
      halved
   1 large onion, thinly sliced
   3 cups garlic dressing
      Salad greens torn into chunks
   3 (6½-ounce) cans water-packed tuna, drained and flaked
   ¼ cup chopped fresh parsley
   1 pint cherry tomatoes, halved
   1 (4½-ounce) can sliced black olives, drained
   6 hard-boiled eggs, quartered
   ½ cup canned or bottled red peppers, cut in strips
   1 large green pepper, cut into thin rings
   2 (2-ounce) cans anchovies rolled with capers, drained
      Salt and freshly ground black pepper

Combine potatoes, beans, artichoke hearts and onion in a bowl. Pour dressing over them. Refrigerate for a minimum of 3 hours, turning occasionally. Line a very large salad bowl, preferably one with sloping sides, with salad greens, covering both the bottom and sides. Mound tuna in center of the bottom of bowl.

Drain refrigerated vegetables as well as possible, reserving the dressing. Arrange vegetables on top of greens. Arrange tomatoes on top of vegetables and tuna. Arrange olive slices in same manner, then the eggs, red peppers, green pepper rings and last the anchovies. Sprinkle with parsley. Sprinkle with salt and pepper. Pour dressing over all. Do not toss.

Must be served by reaching deep into salad at sides and middle in order to get some of every ingredient. Salad can be arranged in bowl at last possible minute. Do not pour dressing on until ready to serve. Should be refrigerated until ready to serve.

Garlic Dressing

   2 cups olive oil
   ½ cup tarragon vinegar
   ¼ cup fresh lemon juice
   2 medium cloves garlic, minced
   1 tablespoon dry mustard
   1 teaspoon salt and pepper

Combine all ingredients in covered jar. Shake well. Refrigerate.

BACK TO BASIC DILL POT ROAST

   3 to 5 pound chuck roast of your choice
   1 teaspoon garlic salt
  ½ teaspoon dill weed
   1 teaspoon paprika
  ¾ cup beef bouillon
   2 small onions, sliced
   6 to 8 large carrots, peeled and cut
   2 tablespoons cornstarch
   2 tablespoons water

Place meat in a roasting pan, sprinkle with the herbs and bouillon. Put sliced onions on top. Put peeled and cut carrots around the meat. Roast at 350°, covered, for 3 hours. Make gravy by adding cornstarch and water mixture to drippings after roast is cooked.

Serves 6 to 8

THE GREAT PUFFY PANCAKE

  ½ cup flour
  ½ cup milk
   2 eggs, slightly beaten
    Pinch of nutmeg
   4 tablespoons butter
   2 tablespoons confectioners sugar
    Juice of ½ lemon

Preheat oven to 425°. Mix flour, eggs, milk and nutmeg together, leaving batter a bit lumpy. Melt butter in a large frying pan and add the batter. Bake 15 to 20 minutes until golden brown. Sprinkle with confectioners sugar and return briefly to oven. Sprinkle with lemon juice. Cut into wedges.

Serves 3. Double this for 6 and use two skillets.

IT'S BETTER TO GET LAUGH WRINKLES THAN WORRY WARTS

QUICHE MEAL IN A DISH

   24 ounce bag frozen hash brown potatoes.

Shape thawed potatoes into a 10-inch pie plate. Press out extra moisture with a clean paper towel.

   ⅓ cup butter or margarine.

Melt and drizzle evenly over potatoes. Bake 20 minutes at 425°.

   1 tablespoon butter or margarine

Add:

   1½ cups zucchini, sliced
   ½ cup green onions, sliced
   2 medium fresh tomatoes, chopped
   1 teaspoon basil
   1 teaspoon parsley flakes
   ½ teaspoon garlic salt

Saute vegetables and herbs until al dente.

   2 cups grated cheese (can vary with any cheese mixture of your choice)
   ⅔ cup diced cooked ham, bacon, chicken, turkey etc.

Sprinkle the meat and ½ the cheese in the cooked potato crust. Top with the vegetables.

Beat together:

   4 eggs
   ½ cup milk

Pour over quiche and top with remaining cheese. Bake 30 minutes at 350°.

Serves 6

WINE MAYONNAISE

   1 cup mayonnaise
   3 tablespoons Chablis, Sauterne or Rhine wine
   ½ tablespoon fresh lemon juice

Blend together and chill. Excellent served over molded fruit or vegetable salads, tossed with mixed greens or spooned over tomato slices and garnished with chopped parsley. Wine mayonnaise is also delicious served as a sauce for fish, shellfish and with cold meats.

HUEVOS RANCHEROS

  6 cans Ortega Green Chile Salsa
  1 (15-ounce) can tomato sauce
  4 chorizo sausages, skinned and broken into pieces
  1 bunch green onions, chopped
  1 (4-ounce) can sliced ripe olives
  2 teaspoons ground cumin
  ½ teaspoon garlic powder
 12 corn tortillas
    Oil for frying
 12 eggs

Heat ½-inch of oil in a small skillet. Dip each tortilla into hot oil for about 5 seconds, just to soften. Drain on paper towels. Set aside. Brown sausages, drain off grease and add green chile salsa, tomato sauce, green onions, sliced ripe olives, cumin and garlic powder. Simmer covered for 1-hour.

    Pour sauce into a large electric frying pan or top-of-the-stove skillet and heat through. Poach eggs in sauce, cooking as many as will comfortably fit in the pan at one time. Remove eggs carefully from sauce and place one on each softened tortilla. Spoon some sauce over each egg and sprinkle with garnishes, ending with a squeeze of lime over all. NOTE: This sauce could also be used in omelettes.

Makes 12 Servings

Garnishes

    chopped green onion tops
    chopped ripe olives
    grated Monterey Jack cheese
    chopped avocado
    lime wedges

PRACTICALLY PERFECT EASY HASH BROWNED POTATOES

  2 medium sized baking potatoes
  1 tablespoon dry minced onion
  4 tablespoons margarine
  1 tablespoon oil

Boil the potatoes whole and unpeeled in a covered saucepan with just enough water to cover, about 25 minutes or till fork tender. Remove from water and chill till cool enough to handle. Peel off skins and crumble potato in bowl, add onion, salt and pepper to taste. Mix well. Melt margarine and oil in a 9-inch skillet. Pack crumbled potato mixture into pan to cover bottom of it. Brown gently on med-low about 6 to 8 minutes or until crispy brown.

Serves 2, or 1 can pig out

SUPERBOWL SUNDAY CASSEROLE

 2 tablespoons oil
 2 cloves garlic, crushed
 1 onion, chopped
 1 pound lean ground beef, chicken or turkey
 1 (1 pound) can stewed tomatoes
 1 cup chicken bouillon
 1 (7-ounce) can tomato sauce
   Salt and pepper to taste
 ¼ teaspoon cinnamon
 ¼ cup raisins, prunes, dates or grapes
 1 (8-ounce) carton low-calorie cottage cheese or ricotta
 1 egg
 ¼ pound Monterey jack cheese, grated
 4 corn tortillas
 1 (7-ounce) can green chilies, chopped

Saute garlic and onion in the oil. Add ground meat and cook until meat loses its pink color; drain off grease. Add tomatoes, bouillon, tomato sauce, salt, pepper, cinnamon, raisins and simmer for about 20 minutes, or until sauce is thick. .

Combine cottage cheese with egg in a small bowl. Grease a 2-qt. casserole dish. Heat tortillas in a teflon skillet, about 20 seconds per side. Place two tortillas on bottom of casserole, cover with half the chilies, half the cottage cheese mixture, then half the meat sauce. Repeat the layers and top with the grated jack cheese. Bake at 350° until hot and bubbly, about 25 to 30 minutes.

Serves 4

OVEN MEATBALLS WITH BAR-B-QUE SAUCE

 2 pounds ground round
 ½ cup instant cream of
   wheat, uncooked

 1 (10-ounce) can cream of
   onion soup
 3 large eggs

Combine all 4 ingredients thoroughly. Using a melon scoop, measure out mixture, shaping into balls, and place in a single layer in a large shallow roasting pan, with just enough oil in the bottom to coat it evenly. Bake meatballs, without turning them, at 350° for 30 minutes, uncovered. Remove from pan with a slotted spoon and place in a deep dish or casserole. Prepare sauce.

MEATBALL BAR-B-QUE SAUCE

 1 pound jar spaghetti sauce
 1 cup grape jam

 1 cup port wine
 1 (6-ounce) can V-8 juice

Heat all ingredients together gently in a saucepan. Spoon over meatballs. Return to oven covered. Bake at 350° for 40 minutes.

Serves 6

ONE DISH PASTA FOR A CHURCH GROUP

This is a great casserole for any type of large get together. It can be assembled a day ahead of time and would need just a salad and some type of bread.

2 large onions
Oil
2 pounds lean ground beef
¼ pound sausage
Salt and pepper to taste
4 (8-ounces each) cans tomato sauce
1 can corn niblets, drained
1 can mushrooms (use any size you like) drained
1 can pitted black olives, drained
1 teaspoon Worcestershire sauce
1 pound spaghetti, cooked to al dente
½ to 1 pound cheddar cheese, grated

Saute onions in oil add the meat and brown. Pour off any excess fat. Add remaining ingredients except the spaghetti and simmer 10 minutes. Combine with the cooked spaghetti in a greased casserole. Top with the cheese. Bake at 300° for 1 hour.

Easy and good

Serves 16

CAN SIZES

8 ounce can   = 1 cup (serves 2)
No. 1 can   = 1¼ cups (serves 3)
No. 303 can   = 2 cups (serves 4)
No. 2 can   = 2½ cups (serves 6)
No. 2½ can   = 3½ cups (serves 7-8)
No. 3 cylinder = 5¾ cups (serves 10-12)

CHICKEN A LA KING NEW ORLEANS STYLE

2 tablespoons butter
1½ tablespoons flour
1 cup heavy cream
½ cup dry sherry
3 eggs, lightly beaten
1 teaspoon salt
¼ teaspoon pepper

¼ cup finely chopped pimientos
½ cup chopped mushrooms
¼ cup grated carrot
½ cup finely chopped scallions
½ teaspoon paprika
2 cups diced cooked chicken
2 eggs, hard-cooked and sliced

Melt butter in top of double saucepan. Stir in flour. Gradually stir in cream and sherry. Cook over hot water, stirring constantly, until thickened and smooth. Stir in beaten eggs, salt, pepper, green pepper, pimientos, mushrooms, carrot, scallions, paprika and chicken. Cook over hot water, stirring frequently, for 15 minutes. Arrange in serving dish. Garnish with egg slices and parsley.

Yield 4 servings

SHRIMP-CRABMEAT CASSEROLE

1 pound shrimp, peeled and deveined
1 package frozen artichoke hearts
¼ cup butter or margarine
½ pound fresh mushrooms, sliced
2 cloves garlic, crushed
2 tablespoons shallots, finely chopped
¼ cup flour
½ teaspoon white pepper
1 tablespoon dill weed
¼ teaspoon curry
¾ cup milk
1 cup sharp cheddar cheese, grated
⅔ cup dry white wine
1 pound cooked crab meat
2 tablespoons cornflake crumbs
1 tablespoon butter

Cook shrimp in boiling, salted water for 3 minutes and drain. Cook artichoke hearts according to package directions and drain. Preheat oven to 375°. Saute mushrooms in 2 tablespoons butter; and shallots and garlic. Remove from heat. Stir in flour, pepper and dill. Remove from heat; add half the cheese and stir until melted. Stir in the wine, dill and curry, and add the seafood. Pour into a greased 2-quart casserole; sprinkle with cheese, crumbs and dot with butter. Bake for 30 minutes, until mixture is bubbly and browned on top.

Serves 6

CHINESE NEW YEAR'S CHICKEN

    3 large chicken breasts, boned and skinned
    1 egg white, lightly beaten
    2 teaspoons cornstarch
      Salt to taste
    2 tablespoons bean sauce
    1 tablespoon hoi-sin sauce
    1 tablespoon chili paste (or Szechwan paste)
    2 teaspoons sugar
    1 tablespoon red wine vinegar
    5 cloves garlic, crushed
    6 dried red peppers, cut in half and seeded
    1 cup raw unsalted peanuts
    2 cups peanut oil

Cut chicken into cubes. Combine with the egg white, cornstarch and salt. Chill for 30 minutes. Combine the bean sauce, hoi-sin, chili paste with garlic, sugar and wine vinegar. Set aside.

Heat two cups of oil in wok. When it is almost boiling hot, but not smoking, turn off heat and add the peanuts. They should turn a light brown. If not, you can turn on the heat briefly, watching carefully, as they cook fast.

Heat one cup of oil in the wok (you can save the rest), and cook chicken for 45 seconds, but do not brown. Now pour off all but two tablespoons of oil from the wok. Add peppers and cook until dark (approximately 15 seconds). Add sauce and the chicken and cook for one minute more. Serve sprinkled with peanuts. This is great with rice and stir-fried vegetables.

Serves 6

BARBECUED BRISKET

     8 to 10 pounds brisket (1st cut)
     8 ounces bottled barbecue sauce
     1 quart catsup
    ¾ cup wine vinegar
     3 ounces Worcestershire sauce
     2 tablespoons liquid smoke
     2 tablespoons prepared mustard
     3 tablespoons lemon juice
     6 bay leaves
     1 clove garlic, mashed
    12 peppercorns
     1 cup beef consomme
    16 sour dough rolls

Mix sauce. Pour over brisket. Bake 3½ to 4 hours at 350°, basting often. Serve on sliced, toasted, buttered sourdough rolls.

Serves 16

BRAN MUFFINS

Combine and stir well:

 2 cups all-purpose or whole-grain flour
 1½ cups bran
 2 tablespoons sugar
 ¼ teaspoon salt
 1¼ teaspoons soda
 1 to 2 tablespoons grated orange rind (optional)

Beat:

 2 cups buttermilk
 1 beaten egg
 ½ cup molasses
 3 tablespoons melted butter

Combine the dry and the liquid ingredients with a few swift strokes. Fold in, before the dry ingredients are entirely moist:

 1 cup nut meats or nut meats and raisins combined
 ½ cup mashed bananas (optional)

Bake about 25 minutes at preheated 350° oven.

Yield 22 (2-inch) muffins

GLUTEN-FREE BREAD

 1 cup unsifted rice flour
 ½ teaspoon salt
 3 teaspoons baking powder
 4 tablespoons vegetable shortening
 4 tablespoons sugar
 2 egg yolks
 ½ cup milk
 2 egg whites, beaten stiff

Combine dry ingredients. Cream shortening and sugar, stir in yolks. Add flour with milk into the shortening mixture. Fold in egg whites. Place batter in well-greased 8-inch bread pan. Let rise until doubled in bulk. Bake in a preheated oven at 325° for 45 minutes. For a darker crust, increase oven temperature to 450° the last 5 minutes of baking.

Yield 1 loaf

BIENENSTICH "BEE'S STING" COFFEECAKE

½ pound farmer cheese
½ cup milk
½ cup cooking oil
½ cup sugar

Topping

½ cup butter or margarine
1 cup sugar
1 teaspoon vanilla extract
⅛ teaspoon salt
3½ cups sifted all-purpose flour
2 teaspoons baking powder
2 tablespoons milk
1 cup slivered blanched almonds

Press farmer cheese through a sieve. Add milk, oil, sugar and salt. Blend well. Sift flour with baking powder and beat it into the cheese mixture. Roll out dough on a lightly floured board to ¼-inch thickness and spread in a greased jelly roll pan 15½ × 10½ × 1-inch. Melt butter and stir in remaining ingredients. Cook until mixture starts to bubble. Cool. Spread mixture evenly over the dough. Bake in a preheated moderate oven (350°) for about 20 minutes, or until cake is golden brown. Cut in squares or bars.

PARTY BUTTER HORNS

2 cups flour
1 (8-ounce) carton sour cream
1 egg yolk
2 cubes butter or margarine

Work these ingredients together with your hands. Chill 2 hours or over-night.

Filling

¾ cup sugar
1 teaspoon cinnamon
1 cup chopped walnuts

Divide dough into 8 balls. Roll each into an ⅛-inch circle. Cut into 8 wedges. Spread filling on each wedge and roll starting at wide end. Bake on a ungreased cookie sheet at 350° for 20 to 25 minutes.

Makes about 4½ to 5 dozen horns. . . . . .

This is a listener's recipe that is sooo easy and will be a favorite of yours as well.

ECLAIR CAKE

1 large instant vanilla pudding mix
1 (8-ounce) package cream cheese
1 cup water
1 stick butter or margarine
1 cup flour
4 eggs
1 large Cool Whip
1 small can Hershey's syrup or fudge sauce (will be less messy)

Mix pudding according to directions on the box. Set aside. Soften cream cheese to room temperature. Set aside. Combine water and butter. Let melt, come to a boil and simmer. Add flour and mix 1 minute. Let cool. Add eggs, one at a time to flour mixture. Spread mixture into a greased $15 \times 10 \times \frac{1}{2}$-inch cookie sheet. Bake at 425° for 20 minutes or until lightly browned. Will be light and airy. Cool. Take palm of hand and press out air bubbles. Beat cream cheese until light and fluffy. Add pudding and beat. Spread over crust. Spread Cool Whip over pudding mixture. Drizzle with chocolate syrup or fudge sauce.

PINEAPPLE MILLIONAIRE PIE

2 cups sifted powdered sugar
¼ pound (1 stick) margarine or butter, softened
2 large fresh whole eggs
⅛ teaspoon salt
¼ teaspoon vanilla extract
2 baked 9-inch pie crusts
1 cup heavy cream
½ cup sifted powdered sugar
1 cup crushed pineapple, well drained
½ cup chopped pecans

Cream together powdered sugar and butter on electric mixer. Add eggs, salt and vanilla. Beat until light and fluffy. Spread mixture evenly into baked pie crusts then chill.

Whip cream until stiff. Blend in powdered sugar. Fold in pineapple and pecans. Spread this mixture on top of base mixture and chill thoroughly.

Yields: two 9-inch pies

GOOEY BUTTER CAKE FROM ST. LOUIS

One of our listeners wrote this in as it was featured in the St. Louis papers an easy way to make this wonderful cake. Yummy!

1 box Duncan Hines Butter Recipe cake mix
2 eggs
1 stick butter softened
1 (8-ounce) package Philadelphia cream cheese, softened
2 eggs
1 (1-pound) box powdered sugar

Mix together cake mix, eggs and butter. Spread in a greased 9 × 13-inch cake pan. Mix together cream cheese, eggs and powdered sugar. Pour over cake batter. Bake 1 hour at 350°. Cool. Refrigerate. Cut into squares.

Easy and good.

NEW HAMPSHIRE BLUEBERRY CAKE

⅓ cup butter
1 cup sugar
1 large egg
2 cups sifted all purpose flour
1 teaspoon baking soda
½ cup sour milk or buttermilk
3 cups fresh blueberries

Cream the butter until light, add sugar and beat until fluffy. Beat in egg. Mix dry ingredients and add alternately with the milk, beginning and ending with the dry ingredients. The batter will be very stiff. Fold blueberries into the batter. Spread into a 9 × 9 × 2-inch baking pan. Bake at 350° for 45 to 50 minutes.

According to the legend of this cake they say "The cake begins to smell so good it is done".

A home is built of peace and love
And not of wood and stone
A place where understanding lives
And memories are sown

OLD FASHIONED OATMEAL COOKIES

    2 cups old fashioned oatmeal
    1 cup shortening, melted
    2 eggs
    1 cup sugar
    ¼ cup milk
    2 cups all purpose flour
    1 teaspoon soda
    1 teaspoon baking powder
    1 teaspoon cinnamon
    1 teaspoon cloves
    1 teaspoon vanilla
    ½ cup walnuts
    1 cup raisins (optional)

Melt shortening and pour over oatmeal. Add sugar, eggs, milk and vanilla. Stir well and add sifted dry ingredients. Add nuts and raisins and drop by spoonfuls on an oiled cookie sheet. Bake 15 minutes at 350°.

CINNAMON GRAHAM CRACKERS

    2 cups whole wheat flour
    1 cup all-purpose flour
    1 teaspoon baking powder
    ½ teaspoon baking soda
    ¼ teaspoon salt
    ¾ cup packed brown sugar
    ½ cup shortening
    ⅓ cup honey
    1 teaspoon vanilla
    ½ cup milk
    3 tablespoons granulated sugar
    1 teaspoon ground cinnamon

Stir together first 5 ingredients. Cream together the brown sugar and shortening until light. Beat in honey and vanilla until fluffy. Add flour mixture alternately with milk to creamed mixture, beating well after each addition. Chill dough several hours or overnight. Divide chilled mixture into quarters. On well-floured surface, roll each quarter to 15 × 5-inch rectangle. Cut rectangle crosswise into 6 small rectangles measuring 5 × 2½-inches. Place on ungreased baking sheet. Mark a line crosswise across center of each small rectangle with tines of fork. Combine granulated sugar and cinnamon; sprinkle over crackers. Bake at 350° for 13 to 15 minutes. Remove from sheet at once.

Makes 24 crackers

FEBRUARY

Send me no paper flowers, no cupids, bows or darts, but the truest of all Valentine's is the one that's from the heart.

CURRIED CHICKEN BITES

    1 (8-ounce) package cream cheese, softened
    3 tablespoons mayonnaise
    2 cups finely, chopped cooked chicken
1½ cups finely chopped walnuts
    3 tablespoons chutney, chopped
    2 teaspoons curry powder
    2 cups flaked coconut

Beat cream cheese and mayonnaise until light and fluffy. Stir in the next 5 ingredients, mixing well. Shape mixture into 1-inch balls, roll in coconut. Chill several hours.

Yield 4½ dozen

Super party fare—From a listener—great appetizer.

JACKIE'S FAVORITE BUFFET PATE

    1 cup pistachio nuts
   ½ pound chicken livers
    3 tablespoons green onion, minced finely
    2 cloves garlic crushed
    3 tablespoons butter
   ½ teaspoon Hungarian paprika
   ½ teaspoon curry powder
   ½ cup dry vermouth
     Salt and pepper to taste
    1 pound cream cheese, softened

Toast nuts in a 350° oven for 5 minutes. Saute chicken livers, onion and garlic in butter or margarine for 7 minutes. Remove from heat and discard garlic. Add seasonings and wine. When cooled slightly place mixture in food processor or blender and mix until smooth. Add cream cheese broken into chunks and blend briefly. Stir in nuts. Chill in crock or favorite serving dish overnight. Serve with small rye or French rounds.

Serves 20

MOCK LIVER PATE

   ½ pound fresh liver sausage
    1 (3-ounce) package cream cheese
    2 to 4 tablespoons mayonnaise
    2 hard-boiled eggs, finely chopped
    1 teaspoon minced onion
     Sieve egg yolk or minced parsley for garnish

Combine first five ingredients and shape into a ball. Garnish with additional sieved hard-boiled egg yolk or minced parsley. Serve with crackers.

LUNCHEON PASTA SALAD WITH ITALIAN SAUSAGE

½ cup olive oil
½ cup tarragon vinegar
1 teaspoon oregano
1 teaspon rosemary
Salt and pepper to taste
1 pound spaghettini, broken into 3 inch lengths, cooked and drained
4 to 5 sweet Italian Sausages

Combine oil, vinegar, oregano and rosemary. Season to taste with salt and pepper. Toss with spaghettini. Chill. Remove sausage casings and place sausage on broiler pan. Broil, turning to cook on all sides, about 15 to 20 minutes. Cool. Cut sausage into ¼ inch slices. Add to salad just before serving. Salad is best if brought almost to room temperature before serving. You can spiff it up with Parmesan cheese or sweet sliced gherkins for a different taste.

Serves 8

SPAGHETTI AL PESTA

4 bunches parsely—soaked clean and rinsed.
Use "flowers" not the heavy stems; small stems okay!
*Liquefy in 2 cups olive oil, one handful to one ounce at a time.

Add 2 heaping tablespoons basil (whole), 1 tablespoon thyme (whole), 1 teaspoon oregano (whole), 1 tablespoon fresh ground pepper, and 1 tablespoon seasoned salt

½ pound butter
2 pounds spaghetti—cook 12 minutes.

Pour blended ingredients in skillet, with butter. When butter is melted, sauce is finished. Don't overcook—5 minutes. Toss with spaghetti, top with Parmesan cheese at table.

*If you want to use less oil, (one cup), liquefy the parsley in water, then pass through a fine mesh strainer (shake dry). Blend the seasonings in the cup of oil, add to the parsley in skillet, add the butter. Heat low until butter melts. That's all.

Serves 8—for 4 people, cut in half.

KNISHES
Dough
    2½ cups sifted flour
    1 teaspoon baking powder
    ½ teaspoon salt
    2 eggs
    ⅔ cup salad oil
    2 tablespoons water

Sift the flour, baking powder and salt into a bowl. Make a well in the center and drop the eggs, oil and water into it. Work into the flour mixture with the hand and knead until smooth.

There are two ways to fill the knishes. In either case, divide the dough in two and roll as thin as possible. Brush with oil. Now you can spread the filling on one side of the dough and roll it up like a jelly roll. Cut into 1½-inch slices. Place in an oiled baking sheet cut side down. Press down lightly to flatten. Or you can cut the rolled dough in 3-inch circles. Place a tablespoon of the filling on each; draw the edges together and pinch firmly. Place on an oiled baking sheet, pinched edges up. In either case, bake in a 375° oven 35 minutes or until browned.

Makes about 24

FILLINGS FOR KNISHES
Potato
    1 cup chopped onions
    6 tablespoons chicken fat or butter
    2 cups mashed potatoes
    1 egg
    1 teaspoon salt
    ¼ teaspoon pepper

Brown the onions in the fat or butter. Beat in the potatoes, egg, salt and pepper until fluffy.

Cheese
    1½ cups diced scallions or onions
    4 tablespoons butter
    2 cups pot cheese
    1 egg
    1½ teaspoons salt
    ⅛ teaspoon pepper
    2 tablespoons sour cream

Scallions are better than onions for this, so try to get them. Brown the scallions in the butter and beat in the cheese, egg, salt, pepper and sour cream until smooth.

POTATO-DOUGH KNISHES

  ¾ cup minced onions
  6 tablespoons chicken fat or butter
  4 cups mashed potatoes
  ½ cup potato flour
  3 eggs
  1 teaspoon salt
  ¼ teaspoon pepper

Brown the onions in 4 tablespoons chicken fat or butter. Cool.

Knead together the remaining fat or butter, the potatoes, potato flour, eggs, salt and pepper. Break off pieces (about 2 inches long) and flatten slightly. Place a teaspoon of browned onions on each and cover by pinching the edges together. Place on a greased baking sheet.

Bake in a 375° oven 25 minutes. Makes about 20.

SCOTCH EGGS

  6 hard cooked eggs, peeled
  1 pound lean pork sausage
  1 raw egg
  1 cup bread crumbs

Divide sausage into 6 portions. Roll into balls and flatten. Form sausage around each egg, covering completely. Dip coated eggs in raw egg, mixed with a little water. Roll in bread crumbs. Deep fat fry until coating is brown and sausage is cooked (about 4 to 5 minutes in 375° oil). Slice and serve on toast points or croutons.

No matter what
No matter where
It's always home
If love is there

DEVILED EGGS BECHAMEL

  8 hard boiled eggs
  ¼ cup butter or margarine, melted
  ¼ teaspoon Dijon mustard
  1 cup cheddar cheese, grated
  1 teaspoon parsley, minced
  1 tablespoon onion, grated
  ⅓ cup chipped beef, chopped

Halve eggs lengthwise! Remove yolks and mash, mix all the ingredients except the cheese. Stuff egg whites and arrange in a greased flat baking dish. Pour Bechamel sauce over eggs and sprinkle with grated cheese. Cover with foil and bake in a 325° oven for 20 minutes.

Bechamel Sauce:

  3 tablespoons butter, melted
  ¼ cup flour
  1 cup boiling chicken broth
     Salt and paprika to taste
  ¾ cup light cream

In a saucepan, combine melted butter and flour. Gradually add boiling chicken stock. Stir with a whisk until combined. Season to taste! Add cream and cook over low heat stirring constantly, until thick and smooth.

OLIVE CHOW YUK

  2 tablespoons olive oil
  1 medium green pepper, cut into strips
  2 medium onions, sliced
  1 stalk celery, cut into 1-inch slices
  1 cup beef consomme
  1 tablespoon cornstarch
  1 tablespoon soy sauce
  2 cups sliced pitted ripe olives
     Cooked rice

Heat oil in large skillet. Saute green pepper, onions and celery over medium heat for 10 minutes. Add consomme, bring to a boil. In a small bowl combine cornstarch and soy sauce to a smooth paste. Stir in vegetables. Cook over low heat, stirring constantly, until thickened and clear. Stir in olives. Serve over cooked rice.

Yield 4 servings

NEBRASKA CARROTS

　　2 bunches carrots, sliced
　　1 large onion, diced
　　1 (10½-ounce) can condensed tomato soup, undiluted
　　¾ cup vinegar
　　1 teaspoon dry mustard
　　½ cup salad oil
　　1 cup sugar

Cook carrots and onion in salted water until tender; drain and cool. Cover and refrigerate.

Place remaining ingredients in a saucepan, bring to a boil, stirring constantly. Simmer for 5 minutes. Add carrots and onions, toss to mix. Cool, cover and refrigerate at least overnight.

Note
This will keep in the refrigerator for several weeks. Good for buffets, potluck dinners . . . men love them.

Makes 1 quart

COMPANY FLANK STEAK

　　2 pounds flank steak
　　½ pound Italian sausage
　　1 (15-ounce) can tomato sauce
　　1 cup green onion, chopped with tops
　　¼ cup parsley, chopped
　　2 tablespoons flour
　　　Salt to taste
　　3 tablespoons oil
　　½ cup beef stock or wine
　　1 bay leaf

Tenderize steak. Remove casing from sausage and crumble into a bowl. Mix in ½ cup of the tomato sauce, onions and parsley. Spread over steak, roll up jelly roll fashion. Tie with string or secure with skewers. Sprinkle with flour and salt if you wish. Brown in skillet in oil. Mix remaining tomato sauce, beef stock or wine and bay leaf. Pour over steak. Bake at 350 degrees for 1½ hours, covered, or until tender. Baste with sauce often. Can serve with a side of noodles and a steamed green vegetable.

Serves 4

EASY ONE DISH MEAL

4 medium chops of your choice
6 tablespoons raw rice
1 can consomme
1 pinch marjoram
1 pinch thyme
1 onion, sliced
2 tomatoes (you may use canned)
1 green pepper, cut into rings

Brown the chops in a skillet. Place rice in the bottom of your favorite greased casserole. Lay the chops on top of the rice. Top each chop with a slice of onion, tomato and pepper ring. Pour over the consomme, add a pinch of marjoram and thyme, and cover and bake at 350° for 1 hour.

Serves 2

SWEETHEART STEAK DINNER

2 pounds round steak
Salt and pepper to taste
Flour
2 tablespoons butter
2 large onions, thinly sliced
1 garlic clove, minced
1 cup white wine
1 tablespoon olive oil
1 cup beef broth
1 teaspoon Worcestershire sauce
1 teaspoon soy sauce
⅛ teaspoon pepper
1 cup cheddar cheese, grated
½ cup sour cream or yogurt

Cut steak into serving pieces. Dredge steak with flour and season to taste. Brown on both sides in the butter and oil in a heavy skillet. Remove steak from the pan, add onions and saute until golden. Stir in garlic, wine, broth, soy sauce, Worcestershire sauce and pepper, being very careful to get all the darling part from the bottom of the pan. Return the steak to the pan, cover and simmer very slowly for 1½ hours, or until the meat is very tender. Remove the meat to a heated platter and keep warm.

Stir in the cheese into the onions and pan juices. Stir until melted; now stir in the sour cream or yogurt. Heat but do not boil. Pour the sauce over the meat and garnish the platter with watercress.

With this, add a little rice or buttered noddles, some nice steamed asparagus and a fruit salad with greens to complete a terrific evening. Not fancy, just delectable. If you gals are working on a guy, this will definitely get him thinking very seriously.

Serves 4

MAKE-AHEAD STUFFED CABBAGE SURPRISE

Wash one medium head of cabbage. Cover with boiling water and boil for 20 minutes; drain and cool. With kitchen shears or sharp knife, remove core and enough of the center part of cabbage to make a cavity for the stuffing mixture.

Stuffing

- ½ cup onion, chopped
- 2 tablespoons green pepper, diced
- 1 pound ground beef
  Salt and pepper to taste
- ¼ cup green olives, sliced
- ½ teaspoon Worcestershire sauce
- 1 egg, well beaten
- ½ cup bread crumbs

Saute the first 3 ingredients. Remove from heat and combine with remaining ingredients. Stuff cabbage with mixture. Place cabbage upright in a baking dish; cover and bake for 30 to 40 minutes at 350°. To serve, cut cabbage into wedges. Serve with a little rice and a fruit salad.

Serves 4 to 6

HAWAIIAN HAM SUPPER

- 1⅓ cups raw rice
- ⅛ teaspoon ground cloves
- 2⅔ cups boiling water
- 2½ cups cooked ham, cubed
- ⅓ cup green pepper, chopped
- 2 tablespoons shortening
- 1½ tablespoons vinegar
- 2 tablespoons brown sugar
- 1½ teaspoons Dijon mustard
- ½ cup pineapple tidbits

Cook rice and cloves in boiling water until tender and liquid is absorbed. Let stand 10 minutes. Lightly brown ham and green pepper in shortening. Mix vinegar, brown sugar, mustard and add to ham mixture. Stir well and cook until sauce is transparent. Add pineapple tidbits. Heat thoroughly. Place rice in serving dish, and pour over ham mixture.

This can be made ahead and reheated in the microwave.

Serves 4 to 6

BASTILA

     2 whole chicken breasts, skinned and boned
     3 cups chicken stock
     1 cup finely chopped onions
     1 cup butter, softened
     7 tablespoons olive oil
     1 tablespoon fresh coriander, finely chopped
     2 tablespoons parsley, finely chopped
     1 teaspoon ground ginger
    ½ teaspoon cumin
    ¼ teaspoon cayenne pepper
    ¼ teaspoon turmeric
    ⅛ teaspoon saffron threads
     4 teaspoons cinnamon
     6 eggs, plus 2 egg yolks
     2 tablespoons sugar
  1½ cups coarsely chopped and toasted almonds
    10 sheets phyllo pastry
     3 tablespoons powdered sugar
    12 whole almonds, toasted and reserved for garnish

Preheat oven to 375°. Poach chicken breasts in stock for 30 minutes or until tender. Reserve stock. Cool chicken and coarsely chop. Set aside.

In a heavy skillet, saute the onion in 4 tablespoons of the butter and 4 tablespoons of oil until golden. Stir in coriander, parsley, ginger, cumin, cayenne, turmeric, saffron and ¾ teaspoon cinnamon. Add the reserved stock, mix well and bring to a boil. Simmer for 15 minutes. Add the chicken and cook for another 10 minutes. Pour 1½ cups of the liquid from the skillet into a bowl. Reduce remaining liquid in skillet to about ¼ cup. Remove the chicken mixture to a bowl and set aside.

In a separate bowl, beat together the 6 eggs and 2 yolks. Return the 1½ cups of the liquid to the skillet, add the beaten eggs, stirring over moderate heat until the mixture forms soft creamy curds. Remove from heat and set aside.

In a small bowl, combine the sugar, 1¼ teaspoons cinnamon and the chopped almonds. Melt remaining 12 tablespoons butter with remaining 3 tablespoons olive oil. Lightly brush a 10-inch round baking dish or 10-inch iron skillet with the butter-oil mixture. Working quickly, overlap 6 sheets of phyllo pastry in a circle in the baking dish. Fold 2 sheets of phyllo in half separately. Place them, one on top of the other, in the center of the circle. Brush the phyllo with butter, then sprinkle the almond mixture over the pastry. Spread with half the egg mixture, top with chicken mixture, then cover with remaining egg mixture. Coat all exposed edges of phyllo with butter and fold a few over the filling. Add remaining 2 sheets of phyllo, folded in half separately, and brush with butter. Bring up all the edges of phyllo to enclose the chicken filling and brush the entire surface with butter. Bake for 30 to 40 minutes.

To serve, invert onto a serving plate. Combine powdered sugar and remaining 2 teaspoons cinnamon. Sprinkle the mixture on top. Draw a diamond pattern across the top, and center each diamond with a whole toasted almond. Cut in wedges.

Yield 10 to12 servings

CHALUPAS

    1 boiled chicken, cooked and boned
    1 dozen flour tortillas, medium sized

Mix together

    2 cans cream of chicken soup
    1 pint sour cream
    ¾ cup Jack cheese, grated
    1 (7-ounce) can green chilies, chopped
    1 small can black olives, sliced
      Sliced green onions to taste
      Cheddar cheese for garnish
      Sliced black olives for garnish

Reserve 2 cups of soup mixture. Add chicken to the remaining mix. Butter a 9 × 13-inch pan. Fill flour tortillas with chicken mix sauce and place in pan seam side down. Cover with reserved 2 cups of sauce. Sprinkle over cheddar cheese and sliced olives.

Bake in a 350° oven for 30 minutes or until hot and bubbly.

Great with a pitcher of margaritas a fruit salad and some steamed corn tortillas. Que Sobroso!

Serves a family

LOBSTER AU WHISKEY

    2 (1½-pound each) lobsters
    ⅛ cup clarified butter
    5 shallots, minced
    2 tablespoons chives, minced
    1 teaspoon parsley, chopped
    ½ cup heavy cream
    ¼ cup of your favorite bourbon
    Salt and pepper to taste

Plunge lobsters into boiling water and cook for a minute or two or until the shells turn red. Chill. Remove meat from the tail and claws, leaving the shell intact for serving. Saute the shallots, chives and parsley in the clarified butter for 1 minute. Add lobster, cream and whiskey and heat thoroughly, do not boil. Season to taste with salt and pepper. In the lobster shell, place a bed of rice pilaf, now top with lobster. Garnish with chopped parsley and lemon.

Serves 2

CINNAMON STICKY BUNS

    1 package dry yeast
   ¼ cup warm water
    1 cup milk, scalded
    4 tablespoons shortening
    1 tablespoon sugar
    1 teaspoon salt
    1 egg, beaten well
  3½ to 4 cups flour
    4 tablespoons butter, melted
    1 cup light corn syrup
  1½ pounds light brown sugar
       Additional melted butter
    2 teaspoons cinnamon
    1 cup nuts, chopped

Soften yeast in warm water. Pour scalded milk over shortening, sugar and salt in a large bowl. Cool to lukewarm. Add softened yeast and beaten egg. Gradually stir in flour to form a soft dough. Beat vigorously, cover and let rise until doubled in bulk (about 2 hours).

Prepare three 8-inch round pans. In each, put 2 tablespoons melted butter, ⅓ cup corn syrup and ⅓ box brown sugar. Mix and melt over low heat.

Turn out dough onto a lightly floured board and divide dough in half. Roll into an oblong about ¼-inch thick. Brush with melted butter, and sprinkle with ¼ cup brown sugar, 1 teaspoon cinnamon and ¼ to ½ cup chopped nuts. Roll up like a jelly roll and seal edges; cut into slices about ¾-inch thick. Repeat on second half of the dough. You should have about 18 rolls from each half.

Place rolls in pans. Cover and let rise until double (about 1½ hours). Bake at 375° for 25 to 30 minutes or until done. Remove immediately from pan by inverting onto aluminum foil or serving plate. Let pan remain over rolls for a few minutes so all of the syrup will run down onto the rolls. This freezes well.

Yields 3 dozen

Keep your temper
No one else wants it

CHERRY PECAN BREAD

¾ cup sugar
½ cup butter or margarine
2 eggs
2 cups sifted flour
1 teaspoon baking soda
½ teaspoon salt
1 cup buttermilk
1 cup chopped pecans or walnuts
1 (10-ounce) jar maraschino cherries, drained and chopped (1 cup)
1 teaspoon vanilla

In large mixer bowl, cream together sugar, butter and eggs until light and fluffy.

Sift together flour, soda and salt; add to creamed mixture with buttermilk. Beat until blended. Stir in nuts, cherries and vanilla. Pour batter into greased 9 × 5 × 3-inch loaf pan. Bake in 350° oven for 55 to 60 minutes. Remove from pan; cool. Glaze with confectioners' sugar icing.

PINEAPPLE-ZUCCHINI CAKE

2 cups sugar
3 eggs
2 teaspoons vanilla
1 cup oil
2 cups shredded zucchini, coarsely grated
3 cups flour
1 teaspoon baking powder
1 teaspoon salt
1 teaspoon baking soda
1 cup drained pineapple
1 cup chopped nuts

Cream sugar, oil, eggs and vanilla until creamy. Add zucchini and beat again. Add dry ingredients to creamed mixture. Mix well. Stir in pineapple and nuts. Pour into greased and floured 9 × 13 pan. Bake 1 hour at 325°. Frost with favorite frosting or dust with powdered sugar.

Better to be silent and be thought a fool
Than to speak up and remove all doubts

SOUR CREAM POUND CAKE

    1 cup butter
 2¾ cups sugar
    6 eggs
    3 cups flour sifted
  ½ teaspoon salt
  ¼ teaspoon baking soda
    1 cup sour cream
  ½ teaspoon lemon extract
  ½ teaspoon orange extract
  ½ teaspoon vanilla extract

Cream butter and sugar until light and fluffy. Add eggs, one at a time, beating well after each addition. Sift flour, salt and soda together; add to butter mixture alternately with sour cream, beating after each addition. Add extracts and vanilla; beat well. Pour batter into greased and floured 10-inch tube pan or bundt pan. Bake at 350° for 1¼ hours or until cake tests done. Cool 15 minutes, remove from pan to cool on rack. When cool, glaze or sprinkle with confectioners sugar, if desired.

RICH CHOCOLATE DESSERT FOR YOUR VALENTINE

    1 cup semi-sweet chocolate bits, melted
    3 tablespoons strong coffee
    1 teaspoon vanilla
    1 cup whipping cream, whipped
    2 to 3 pieces English toffee, crushed

Add coffee to the melted chocolate blend well and let cool. Fold chocolate mix into the whipped cream. Add vanilla and crushed candy. Spoon into 6 small dessert dishes or 4 medium size ones or if you like 2 great big ones depending on how you like chocolate. Happy Valentine's Day.

CASTOR OIL COOKIES

    1 cup sugar
    1 cup molasses
    1 cup milk
  ½ cup castor oil
  ½ teaspoon salt
    1 teaspoon baking soda
    2 teaspoons ginger
      sifted flour to make dough

Mix ingredients, using enough sifted flour to make a dough that can be rolled. Roll out, cut and bake in a hot oven (400°). Two of these cookies are equal to a dose of castor oil.

(This recipe is at least 70 years old and comes from Cherokee, Iowa.)

MARY TODD LINCOLN'S VANILLA-ALMOND CAKE

1½ cups sugar
1 cup butter or margarine
1 teaspoon vanilla
2¼ cups sifted cake flour
1 tablespoon baking powder
1⅓ cups milk
1 cup finely chopped almonds
6 stiffley beaten egg whites
White frosting of your choice

Cream together sugar, butter and vanilla. Stir together the dry ingredients. Add to the creamed mixture alternately with the milk. Stir in the nuts and gently fold in the beaten egg whites.

Pour into 2 greased and lightly floured 9-inch cake pans. Bake in a preheated oven at 375° for 30 minutes. Frost with your favorite white icing.

HEAVENLY CHOCOLATE PIE FOR MY VALENTINE

2 egg whites
½ teaspoon vinegar
¼ teaspoon cinnamon
¼ teaspoon salt
¾ cup sugar
1 (6-ounce) package chocolate chips
2 egg yolks
¼ cup water
1 cup whipping cream
½ teaspoon cinnamon
1 (9-inch) pie shell, baked

Beat egg whites, vinegar, cinnamon, and salt until stiff, but not dry. Gradually add ½ cup of the sugar and beat until very stiff. Spread on bottom and sides of baked pie shell. Bake at 325° for 15 to 18 minutes until lightly browned. Cool. Melt chips over hot water. Blend in egg yolks and water, stir until smooth. Spread 3 tablespoons of chocolate mixture on bottom of cooled meringue. Chill remaining chocolate until it begins to thicken. Beat together cream, ¼ cup sugar, and cinnamon until stiff, and spread half of this over chocolate layer in pie shell. Fold remaining chocolate into remaining cream mixture and spread over top of pie. Refrigerate at least 4 hours before serving.

Serves 8

MARCH

There are two kinds of people on St. Patricks's day. Those who are Irish and those who wish they were. In this chapter I am including some of the wonderful folklore from my grandmother, Harriett Love, County Cork, Ireland.

March is a wonderful month for family get togethers and great soup dinners in front of the fireplace; they're all here in this chapter.

STEAK TARTARE

  ½ cup fresh parsley leaves
  1 pound filet of beef, trimmed and cut in 1-inch pieces
  1 small onion, quartered
  2 egg yolks
  2 or 3 dashes of Worcestershire sauce
  1 teaspoon Dijon mustard
  2 tablespoons capers, drained
  1 teaspoon lemon juice
  2 teaspoons Cognac
     Salt and freshly ground pepper
     Watercress for garnish (optional)
     Warm toast triangles (optional)
     Thinly sliced dark bread (optional)
     Sour cream (optional)

Using STEEL BLADE, chop parsley fine. Reserve.

Using STEEL BLADE, with on/off turns, chop filet fine, 1 cup at a time. Transfer to medium mixing bowl.

Using STEEL BLADE, with on/off turns, chop onion fine. Drain and add to chopped filet. Clean work bowl.

Using STEEL BLADE, process egg yolks, Worcestershire sauce, mustard, capers, lemon juice and Cognac until blended. Combine thoroughly with chopped filet, onion and parsley, using your hands. Season with salt and pepper to taste.

To serve as a main dish, shape into 2 large ovals, place on serving plate, and decorate with watercress. Serve with warm toast triangles.

To serve as an appetizer, shape into 1 large mound, place on serving plate and cover with sour cream. Surround with thinly sliced dark bread.

Do not prepare in advance and do not freeze.

Variation: To basic recipe, add 2 tablespoons tomato ketchup, 2 tablespoons chopped anchovy fillets, and 1 mashed clove garlic.

Note
Additional chopped onions, capers and chopped egg may be served if desired.

Serves 2 as main dish, or 4 to 6 as appetizer

SPANAKOPITA

(Spinach and cheese appetizer)

A most attractive dish—delicious and excellent with lamb. This freezes very well. Tasty and different

   ½ pound feta cheese
   4 ounces cream cheese
   2 eggs
   2 tablespoons dried parsley
   1 teaspoon nutmeg
   4 ounces Monterey Jack cheese
   1 (10-ounce) package frozen chopped spinach, thawed and
       squeezed dry
   1 medium onion, chopped
   2 tablespoons butter
   ½ pound phyllo pastry (about 30 sheets or layers)
   12 tablespoons butter, melted

Preheat oven to 350°. Blend feta cheese, cream cheese, eggs, parsley, nutmeg and Monterey Jack cheese, a little at a time, in a blender or food processor. Combine with spinach. Saute onion in the two tablespoons butter until transparent. Add to spinach mixture.

Cut the phyllo sheets to fit a 9 × 12-inch baking dish. Butter the dish and place 12 layers of phyllo in it, brushing each with melted butter. Spread cheese-spinach mixture over phyllo layers and top with 10 or 15 more phyllo sheets, buttering each as you layer. To make cutting easier, place the dish in the freezer for approximately 20 minutes. Cut into squares or diamonds and bake for 45 minutes or until brown and crisp. May be made ahead and reheated. It may also be frozen unbaked; thaw and bake as directed.

Serves 8

BANANA RUMAKI

   8 to 10 slices bacon, cut in half
   5 bananas, slightly underripe
   ½ cup brown sugar
   1 tablespoon curry powder

Blanch bacon in boiling water for 10 minutes. Drain and dry thoroughly. Cut bananas into 1½-inch chunks and wrap in bacon, securing it closed with a toothpick. Combine brown sugar and curry powder and sprinkle on wrapped bananas. Back on rack for about 10 minutes at 350° until bacon is crisp and sugar is lightly caramelized.

Serves 8

CHEESE POPCORN

2 quarts of popped corn
¼ cup butter (cut in pieces)
1 cup shredded cheese
1 teaspoon salt

Combine popcorn, butter, cheese and salt in deep baking dish and bake at 300° 12 to 15 minutes.

Toss well, serve hot.

CHOCOLATE PUNCH

4 (1-ounce) squares semi-sweet chocolate
½ cup sugar
2 cups hot water
2 quarts milk
2 teaspoons vanilla
1 quart vanilla ice cream
1 quart club soda
½ pint heavy cream, whipped
Cinnamon

In a large saucepan, combine chocolate and sugar with hot water. Bring to a boil, stirring for two minutes. Add milk and continue heating. When hot, whisk in vanilla. Remove from heat and chill.

Pour over club soda, ice cream, and top with whipped cream and dust top with cinnamon.

Serves 12

MONROE'S MOCK TURTLE SOUP

2 cups dry black beans
¼ cup onion, chopped
¼ cup butter or margarine
2 stalks celery, chopped
¼ cup dry sherry
2 hard cooked eggs finely chopped
1 lemon, thinly, sliced

Cover beans with water. Soak overnight. Drain, rinse well. In a large sauce pan cook onion, in butter, until tender, do not brown. Add beans, celery and 10 cups water. Cover, simmer till beans are soft 3 to 3½ hours. Place part of the bean mixture a little at a time in the blender and puree until smooth. Return all to the saucepan. Season to taste with salt and pepper. Heat soup to just boil. Stir in sherry. Garnish each serving with chopped eggs and lemon slices.

Serves 8

ZUCCHINI SOUP

  6 small zucchini, trimmed and cubed or shredded
    Salt
  2 medium onions, finely minced
  1 clove garlic, minced
  1 tablespoon oil
  2 tablespoons sweet butter
  5 cups chicken stock
  2 tablespoons fresh herbs (combination of oregano, basil, parsley
    and chives)
  2 tablespoons lemon juice
    Salt and freshly ground pepper to taste

Place cubed or shredded zucchini in a colander, sprinkle with salt, and allow to drain for about 30 minutes. In a large pot or dutch oven saute onions and garlic in oil and melted butter until the onions are golden. Dry zucchini on paper towels and add to onions and cook over low heat 5 minutes. Add chicken stock and simmer for 15 minutes. Puree soup in a blender or food processor. Return to pot and season with herbs, lemon juice and salt and pepper. Reheat and serve.

Yield 8 servings

BROCCOLI AND CHICKEN SOUP

     1 bunch broccoli
  1½ cups boiling water
     2 cans (10½-ounces each) cream of chicken soup
     1 cup light cream
       Salt, pepper, cayenne

Cut off and discard large leaves and tough parts of stalks. Wash and chop broccoli coarsely. Add boiling water. Boil rapidly until tender. Using all the liquid, chop broccoli very fine in blender or force through coarse sieve. In saucepan mix soup, cream and broccoli; season to taste. Heat to simmering. Top with croutons and grated Parmesan cheese.

Yield 1 quart

Love is like a butterfly
It goes where it pleases
It pleases where ever it goes

BUFFET HOT CURRIED COLE SLAW

1 can consomme	4 tablespoons butter
1 cup water	2 tablespoons flour
1 bay leaf	1 tablespoon curry powder
3 cloves	Salt and pepper to taste
3 pounds cabbage, shredded	1½ cups sour cream
1 medium onion, chopped	½ cup bread crumbs
1 clove garlic, crushed	

In a large saucepan simmer consomme, water, bay leaf and cloves for about 5 minutes. Remove bay leaf and cloves. Add cabbage, cover and simmer 10 minutes. Drain cabbage and reserve ½ cup broth. In another saucepan, saute onion and garlic in butter for 3 minutes. Blend in flour and seasonings. Stir in sour cream and reserved broth. Cook over low heat, stirring constantly until sauce simmers and thickens. Combine sauce with the cabbage. Place in a 2 quart casserole. Sprinkle with the crumbs. Bake at 425° 15 to 20 minutes.

This can be made ahead and just heated before putting on buffet table. This is just terrific and a real different way to serve slaw. Elegant with pork, chicken, beef or lamb.

Serves 10

RICE AND SEAFOOD SALAD

    1 cup uncooked rice
    ¼ cup salad oil
    1 tablespoon vinegar
    1½ teaspoons salt
    ½ teaspoon pepper
    1 cup cooked green peas
    ¼ cup each of chopped pimiento, chopped parsley and minced
      onion
    2 tablespoons chopped green pepper
    1 cup cooked flaked crabmeat
    1 cup shelled and deveined cooked shrimps
    1 cup cooked flaked lobster
    ⅔ cup mayonnaise
    1 tablespoon fresh lemon juice
      Salad greens   Black olives

Cook rice until tender according to package directions.

In the meantime, combine oil, vinegar, salt and pepper to make a French dressing. Drain rice and toss immediately with French dressing; cool. Gently mix in vegetables, crabmeat, shrimps and lobster; chill.

Just before serving, combine mayonnaise with lemon juice. Fold into salad. Pile pyramid fashion on salad greens and decorate with black olives.

Makes 8 servings

LIME-PEAR GELATIN MOLD

    1 can (1-pound) pear halves
    1 small package lime gelatin
    2 tablespoons lemon juice
    ½ cup crumbled bleu cheese
    1 cup creamed cottage cheese
      Paprika
    ½ cup finely chopped delicious apple
    ½ cup mayonnaise

Drain pears well and add enough water to syrup to make 1¾ cups. Heat liquid and pour over gelatin, stirring until dissolved. Add lemon juice and cool. Pour small amount (about ½-inch deep) into 8-inch cake pan. Chill until set.

Meanwhile, combine bleu cheese with 2 tablespoons cottage cheese and blend well. Divide mixture evenly into hollows of pear halves. Sprinkle with paprika and arrange cheese side down, in gelatin, 6 in a circle and 1 in center. Fold remaining cottage cheese, apple and mayonnaise into remaining gelatin. Pour over pears and chill until firm. Unmold on greens.

Serves 6

So pretty for St. Paddy's day or for any family do!

INSTANT SALSA FOR MEXICAN DISHES OR DIPS

    1 (14½-ounce) can stewed tomatoes
    1 (8-ounce) can tomato sauce
    1 package onion soup mix
    ½ teaspoon Tabasco sauce
    2 tablespoons Jalapeno peppers (this is optional, makes it hot)
      Dash cayenne pepper
      Cilantro, chopped (go easy if it is your first experience)

Put it all in the blender give it a few whirs and keep it in a covered container in fridge. Use within 3 weeks. You can use this warmed or cold. Super!

Makes 3 cups

LENTEN CHEESE-CLAM FETTUCINI

    6 ounces green spinach noodles, cooked al dente
    ½ cup butter or margarine
    4 cloves garlic, crushed
    1 (6½-ounce) can minced clams
    1 cup Parmesan cheese, grated
      Ripe olives

Melt butter, add garlic and clams. Toss hot drained noodles into the clam mixture. Add cheese. Toss thoroughly. Pour onto a serving platter and garnish with black olives.

Serves 4—Easy and fast

GEORGE WASHINGTON'S FAVORITE APPLE OMELET

1 cup cooked or canned apples, diced (drained)
10 eggs
¼ cup milk
½ teaspoon salt
2 tablespoons clarified butter or oil
Cinnamon
Nutmeg
Powdered sugar or Honey

Beat eggs together with a fork. Add milk and salt and beat again until smooth.

Heat butter or oil in an 8-inch skillet or omelet pan. Pour in ⅓ the egg mixture. Cook over medium heat until egg is set but still shiny. Top with ⅓ the apple mixture. Sprinkle with cinnamon and nutmeg. Fold one side of the egg over the apples and roll omelet over to close. Cook just a moment to seal and slide onto a warm plate. Repeat to make 3 omelets.

When last omelet is done, return the other two to the pan to reheat. Add a little butter if needed and turn each once again. Sprinkle with powdered sugar or honey and serve hot.

Note
Canned peaches, pears or other fruit may be substituted or blended with apples.

Makes 3 omelets

CELERY PARMIGIANA

1 large bunch celery
Boiling water
1 onion, sliced
2 cloves
1 teaspoon salt
4 slices bacon, cooked and crumbled (optional)
1½ cups tomato or spaghetti sauce
½ cup grated Parmesan cheese

Clean celery and remove top leaves. Cut stalks and heart into 4-inch lengths. Place celery in saucepan and cover with boiling water. Add onion, cloves and salt. Simmer 15 minutes, or until celery is tender. Drain. Layer half the celery in a greased baking dish and pour over half the sauce. Sprinkle with half the bacon and Parmesan cheese. Repeat layers, ending with cheese topping. Bake 15 minutes at 375°, or until sauce is bubbly.

Makes 4 servings

BROCCOLI CASSEROLE

1 can (10¾-ounces) cream of mushroom soup
1 cup mayonnaise
1 small onion, chopped, or a few onion flakes to taste
1 cup grated American cheese
2 eggs, beaten
2 packages (10-ounces each) chopped broccoli, cooked 5 minutes
and drained
Ritz cracker crumbs
Margarine

Mix soup, mayonnaise, onion, cheese and eggs together. Then add broccoli and mix very well. Put in buttered casserole. Top with Ritz cracker crumbs. Dot with margarine. Preheat oven to 350° and bake for 45 minutes.

Serves 6 to 8

PORK NOODLE CASSEROLE

1 pound pork, diced
2 tablespoons oil
1 (10½-ounce) can chicken with rice soup
¾ cup green pepper, chopped
¼ cup pimiento, chopped
½ cup celery, chopped
1 (15-ounce) can cream style corn
2 cups sharp cheddar cheese, grated
1 teaspoon salt or to taste
Pepper
1 (4-ounce) package egg noodles, cooked and drained

In a medium saucepan, brown pork on all sides in hot oil. Add soup, peppers, pimiento and celery, cover and simmer for ½ hour. Stir in remaining ingredients. Pour into a 2 quart casserole, cover and bake at 350° for 45 minutes, or until pork is tender.

Serves 6

To be rich is no longer a sin
It's a miracle

WORLD'S BEST CORNED BEEF

5 to 6 pounds corned beef
 brisket
½ cup celery tops (leaves)
2 onions, quartered
1 turnip, quartered

1 parsnip, sliced
5 whole allspice
6 whole peppercorns
1 bay leaf

Rinse corned beef under cold running water. Place in a large kettle along with seasonings. Cover with cold water; bring to a boil and simmer 10 minutes. Skim, if necessary. Reduce heat to low; simmer and cook 4 to 5 hours, or until corned beef is fork-tender. Remove from liquid and slice thin.

SERVING SUGGESTIONS—Boiled cabbage, potatoes and carrots.

Hot mustard sauce.

COUNTRY BAKED BEEF PIE

1 pound ground beef
1 carrot, grated
1 clove garlic, crushed
1 tablespoon Worcestershire sauce
1 tomato, chopped
1 medium potato, grated
1 tablespoon A-1 sauce
 Salt and pepper to taste
1 package cornbread made according to package instructions

Brown meat, and add remaining ingredients. Cover with cornbread batter. Bake until browned at 400° about 30 to 40 minutes.

Serves 4

CHILE RELLENO CASSEROLE

1 large can Ortega green chiles (whole)
6 eggs
1½ pounds Monterey Jack cheese, grated
 Flour
1 large can evaporated milk

Cut chiles into long, thin strips. Line a square pan with the chiles. Sprinkle flour on top. Layer with some grated cheese. Repeat layers until you use up all the chiles.

In a bowl, whisk together the eggs, milk and season to taste with salt and pepper. Pour liquid over top of casserole. Dust top with paprika. Microwave on High for 10 to 15 minutes. Casserole should be cooked through, not watery. Then place under broiler to brown for about 3 to 5 minutes.

If you don't have a microwave, bake at 325° for 40 to 50 minutes, or until a knife inserted in the center comes out clean.

Serves 8

OSSOBUCO

   4 meaty veal shanks, about 2-inches thick
       All-purpose flour
       Salt and pepper to taste
  ¼ cup olive oil
   1 clove garlic, minced
  ½ cup dry white wine
  ½ cup tomato puree
   1 anchovy fillet, minced
       Few sprigs of parsley, chopped
       Grated rind of 1 lemon
       Hot cooked rice
       Pinch of saffron

Dredge veal shanks with flour seasoned with salt and pepper. Brown on all sides in hot olive oil. Add garlic, wine and tomato puree. Bring to boil, cover and simmer 1 hour or until meat is tender. Add anchovy, parsley and lemon rind. Heat well and serve on rice lightly mixed with saffron.

Yield 4 servings

CHALUPAS

    2 pounds lean pork, cubed
    3 tablespoons shortening
    2 tablespoons flour
    1 cup water
    1 to 2 teaspoons ground cumin
    1 (14-ounce) can tomatoes
    2 (7-ounce) cans chopped, mild green chiles
    8 crisply fried corn tortillas
    2 whole chicken breasts, poached and shredded
    3 cups refried beans
    2 cups guacamole
 1½ cups grated Cheddar cheese
    1 cup sour cream

Brown pork cubes in shortening. Stir in flour. Add water, cumin, garlic salt, tomatoes and green chiles. Simmer until thick, stirring occasionally. To assemble each chalupa, begin with a crisp tortilla and layer on refried beans, chicken, sauce, cheese, guacamole and sour cream.

Note
This is a very spicy dish

Yield 8 servings

BROILED CHICKEN

2 (2½-pounds) broiling chickens cut into halves

Marinade
½ cup soy sauce
⅓ cup peanut oil
⅓ cup Grand Marnier
2 garlic cloves, finely chopped
2 teaspoons fresh ginger root
1 tablespoon orange zest
Garnish with parsley

Arrange the chickens in a shallow pan. Combine all the marinade ingredients and pour over the chicken. Marinate for 3 to 4 hours, turning 2 to 3 times. Arrange the chicken on a broiling rack cut side up. Place the chicken under the broiler 5-inches from the heat. Broil 12 to 14 minutes, brushing once or twice with the marinade from the dish. Turn the chicken over and broil for another 12 to 14 minutes, brushing with the marinade. Remove the chicken to a warmed platter and garnish with the parsley.

Serves 4

CHICKEN BREASTS WITH WALNUTS AND LEMON SAUCE

Seasoned flour
1 ounce sweet butter
2 whole chicken breasts, skinned, boned and cut into half
½ cup strong chicken broth
⅓ cup walnuts
½ cup light cream
Grated rind of ½ lemon
2 teaspoons lemon juice

Lightly flour chicken breasts with the seasoned flour. Heat butter in a frying pan. Add chicken and saute to a golden brown. Add the walnuts and saute until golden brown. Sprinkle in 1 teaspoon flour, add the stock, lemon rind and lemon juice. Simmer 3 minutes. Remove the chicken to a heated platter. Slowly stir in the cream, reheating the stock, season to taste and pour the sauce over the chicken. Garnish with watercress.

Serves 2

SHRIMP AND GRAPEFRUIT

    3 grapefruits
    1 carrot, blanched and diced
    ¼ cup peas, blanched
    ¼ cup onion, finely chopped
    1 pound shrimp, shelled and deveined

Stand grapefruit upright and with a sharp knife, make notches in a saw-toothed effect to the center of the grapefruit to make two halves. With a sharp paring knife, ream out the flesh and remove the fibers from between the fruit. Set fruit aside.

Court Bouillon

    2 quarts water
    ½ cup white wine
    ½ cup vinegar
    1 onion, chopped
    1 bay leaf
    1 carrot, chopped
    1 clove garlic, crushed
    3 pepper corns

Place all ingredients in a saucepan and bring to a boil. Simmer for 30 minutes. Add shrimp and simmer 3 to 4 minutes. Drain and cool shrimp.

Mayonnaise

    2 egg yolks
    1 teaspoon vinegar
    ½ teaspoon salt
    ¼ teaspoon white pepper
    ½ cup oil
      Lemon juice to taste
    1 to 2 tablespoons boiling water

With a whisk, mix egg yolks, salt, pepper and vinegar. Gradually add the oil drop by drop, whisking vigorously. As sauce thickens, add progressively more oil. Finish the sauce with additional lemon juice, if necessary, and add the boiling water to lighten the sauce.

Combine the mayonnaise with the shrimp, carrots, peas, onion and grapefruit sections. Fill the grapefruit halves with the mixture and garnish with a shrimp, sprig of parsley and slices of stuffed green olives.

Serves 6

IRISH OATMEAL BREAD WITH SWEET BUTTER

      3 cups, sifted flour
1¼ cups quick-cooking rolled oats
1½ tablespoons baking powder
      1 tablespoon salt
      ½ cup honey
1½ cups milk
      1 tablespoon butter, melted
      1 egg, beaten

Preheat oven to 350°. Mix the first 4 ingredients. In another bowl add honey, milk and butter to the beaten egg. Pour egg mixture into oat mixture, stirring until dry ingredients are moistened. Mixture will be lumpy. Spread into 2 greased and floured loaf pans. Bake 1 hour. Turn out of pans onto a wire rack. Brush with more melted butter while warm.

Makes 2 loaves

IRISH BRAN BREAD

12 ounces bran
   4 ounces flour
   ¾ teaspoon baking soda
   ½ teaspoon cream of tartar
   ½ teaspoon salt
   1 teaspoon powdered sugar
   1 ounce of margarine
11 ounces buttermilk

Sift together dry ingredients; stir in bran and mix well. Cut in margarine. Make a well in the center and pour in buttermilk. Mix well. Place dough in a greased 9-inch round springform pan. Smooth top with a knife dipped in milk and make a cross on top with the knife. Bake at 425° for 15 minutes, then lower temperature to 325° and bake for 1 hour.

FROZEN GRASSHOPPER SURPRISE

    24 Oreo cookies
    ¼ cup butter, melted
     2 cups heavy cream
    ¼ cup creme de menthe
     1 (7-ounce) jar marshmallow fluff

Place cookies in a blender and spin until all are crumbled. Combine with melted butter. Line a 9-inch springform pan with cookie mixture, saving ¼ cup for trim. Mix together rest of ingredients. Pour into pan and top with remaining crumbs. Freeze. When firm, remove from pan and wrap in aluminum foil and stick back in the freezer until ready to serve.

This is so easy to double as many times as you wish for church doings, family get togethers etc.

Serves 6 to 8

CHERRY CRUNCH DESSERT

     1 cup sifted flour
    ½ teaspoon salt
    ½ teaspoon cinnamon
    ½ cup butter or margarine
    ½ cup brown sugar, packed
     1 teaspoon vanilla
     1 cup coconut
     1 cup oatmeal
    ½ cup chopped walnuts
     1 (1-pound, 4-ounce) can cherry pie filling

Sift together the flour, salt and cinnamon. Cream butter and add brown sugar gradually, creaming until fluffy. Add vanilla, then sifted dry ingredients, blend well. Stir in coconut, oatmeal and nuts. Press 2½ cups crumb mixture into bottom of ungreased baking dish and bake at 350° for 15 to 18 minutes until lightly browned. Chill before serving. Top with ice cream.

Makes 9 to 12 servings

BUTTERNUT CRUST

     1 cup flour
    ½ cup brown sugar, packed
    ½ cup butter
    ½ cup chopped pecans

Spread on 2 cookie sheets. Bake at 350° for 12 to 15 minutes or until golden, stirring occasionally. Immediately turn out onto cool cookie sheets; break into fine crumbs if necessary. Press into 9-inch pie plate, reserve ⅓ cup for garnish. Chill until firm.

MOUTH-WATERING CHOCOLATE CAKE

2¼ cups sifted cake flour
2 teaspoons baking soda
½ teaspoon salt
½ cup butter or regular margarine
2¼ cups brown sugar, packed
3 eggs
1½ teaspoons vanilla
3 (1-ounce) squares unsweetened chocolate, melted and cooled
1 cup dairy sour cream
1 cup boiling water
Butter Cream Frosting

Sift together cake flour, baking soda and salt; set aside.

Cream together butter and brown sugar in mixing bowl until light and fluffy, using electric mixer at medium speed. Add eggs, one at a time, beating well after each addition. Beat in vanilla and chocolate.

Add dry ingredients alternately with sour cream to creamed mixture, beating well after each addition. Stir in boiling water. (Batter is very thin.) Pour batter into greased 13 × 9 × 2-inch baking pan.

Bake in 350° oven 35 minutes or until cake tests done. Cool in pan on rack. Frost with Butter Cream Frosting. Cut in squares. Makes 16 servings.

Butter Cream Frosting
Sift 1 (1-pound) box confectioners sugar into mixing bowl. Add ½ cup soft butter or regular margarine, 1 teaspoon vanilla and 2 to 3 tablespoons hot water. Beat until smooth.

STRAWBERRY JAM
(Microwave Oven)

4 (10-ounce) packages frozen strawberries, defrosted
2 tablespoons lemon juice
5 cups sugar
3 ounces liquid pectin

Place thawed strawberries in a 4-quart casserole. Sitr in lemon juice and sugar. Cover. Cook on high 10 to 12 minutes, or until mixture boil rapidly. Stir. Cover. Cook on high 3 to 5 minutes stirring several times. Skim. Pour into hot sterilized jars and seal at once.

Variation: Frozen raspberries or peaches may be substituted for strawberries.

Yield 3 half pints

CHAMPION CHERRY PIE

    1 cup sugar
    ⅛ teaspoon salt
    ¼ cup cherry juice
      Red food coloring
    4 cups pitted, canned cherries
    1 tablespoon butter
    ¼ cup cherry juice
    3 tablespoons cornstarch
    1 tablespoon lime juice
    ¼ teaspoon almond extract
      Pastry crust

Combine sugar, salt, ¼ cup cherry juice and food coloring in a saucepan. Cook over medium heat until mixture comes to a full boil. Add cherries and butter; bring to a boil again. Boil 2 minutes. Make a paste of ¼ cup cherry juice and cornstarch. Add to hot mixture and cook, stirring constantly, until thickened. Remove from heat. Add lime juice and almond extract. Cool. Pour cooled filling into pastry. Top with remaining pastry. Flute edges and make slits or cut cherry designs in crust. Bake at 400° for 50 to 55 minutes or until crust is golden brown.

Pastry Crust

    2 cups sifted flour
    1 teaspoon salt
    ½ cup oil
    ¼ cup milk

Combine flour and salt in bowl. Blend oil and milk; add all at once to flour mixture. Stir lightly with fork until blended. Roll out between two thicknesses of waxed paper to ⅛-inch thickness. Line 9-inch pie plate with pastry. Fill. Top with remaining crust.

SHAM ROX

(Irish Coffee Flavored Cookies)

    ½ cup maple syrup
    2 cups crushed vanilla wafers
    1 cup chopped blanched almonds
    1 cup powdered sugar
    ½ cup Irish whiskey
    ¼ cup Continental style sweetened coffee mix

Simmer syrup until it has reduced to ¼ cup (4 or 5 minutes). Cool syrup. Combine crushed cookies, nuts, sugar, syrup and whiskey. Let stand 15 minutes. Roll into small balls and dust with coffee mix.

Makes 4 Dozen

APRIL

April showers bring May flowers. This is a very busy month
with the Easter Holidays and Passover. Spring is here and it is
reflected in our special party menus. I hope you will enjoy this
chapter as much as I did in our home.

MARDI GRAS PUNCH

3 cups water
3 cups sugar
3 cups boiling water
¼ cup tea leaves
3 cups orange juice

1 cup lemon juice
3 cups pineapple juice
2 quarts ginger ale
Sliced fruit (oranges, lemons, strawberries)

Combine the 3 cups water and sugar in a saucepan. Heat and stir until sugar is dissolved. Boil 7 minutes. Chill. Combine 3 cups boiling water with the tea leaves. Steep 5 minutes. Strain and cool. When ready to serve combine all ingredients in a punch bowl and garnish with fresh fruit.

Makes 3½ quarts

Handy hint: To keep punch from becoming diluted, freeze ginger ale in favorite ice mold.

SAM'S "FAMOUS RAMOS" GIN FIZZ

1½ ounces gin or vodka
1 ounce lemon juice
1 tablespoon orange juice
1 teaspoon sugar
1 whole egg
2 ounces heavy cream
Dash of orange flower water
½ cup cracked ice

Pour all ingredients into a blender and blend well.

Serves 1

Now that you know the secret for a great "Gin Fizz" make them by the blender full.

PUNCH BOWL BLOODY MARYS

2 (18-ounce) cans or 4½ cups tomato juice
2 cups vodka
4 teaspoons Worcestershire sauce
Ice cubes
½ teaspoon coarsely ground pepper
1 teaspoon salt
Few dashes hot pepper sauce
4 limes, quartered lengthwise

In a large pitcher, combine tomato juice, vodka, Worcestershire sauce, salt, pepper and hot pepper sauce. Cover and refrigerate if made ahead of time. Pour over ice cubes in highball glasses. Squeeze a lime wedge into each glass; stir.

Serves 6 to 8

COFFEE CONTINENTAL

⅔ cup instant cocoa mix
8 cups boiling water
½ cup instant coffee
Whipped cream, sweetened

Mix all the ingredients except the whipped cream in a heatproof container. Pour into coffee mugs and top with sweetened whipped cream.

Serves 12

CHEESE PUFFS

1 loaf unsliced white bread
½ cup butter
3 ounces cream cheese
¼ pound sharp Cheddar cheese, grated
2 egg whites, stiffly beaten

Preheat oven to 400°. Trim crust from bread and cut loaf into 1-inch cubes. In the top of a double boiler over simmering water melt butter, cream cheese and Cheddar cheese, then beat until smooth. Fold in egg whites. Line a cookie sheet with foil. Dip bread cubes into cheese mixture and place on cookie sheet. Refrigerate overnight or freeze. Bake in a 400° oven for 10 to 12 minutes or until browned. May be baked directly from the freezer.

Makes about 4 dozen

GREEN BEAN SOUP WITH BEEF

4 cups very strong beef stock
1 cup chopped cooked beef
2 medium potatoes, diced
2 carrots, sliced thin
1 stalk celery, sliced thin
1½ cups green beans, cut into 1-inch pieces
1 small onion, chopped
1 teaspoon chopped fresh or ¼ teaspoon crumbled dried rosemary
1 teaspoon salt
¼ teaspoon freshly ground black pepper
1 cup heavy cream or evaporated milk

Bring the beef stock to a boil in a 2½ quart saucepan, add the chopped beef, potatoes, carrots, celery, beans, onion, thyme, and rosemary. Taste before adding salt and pepper. If the beef stock is salty, less seasoning will be needed. Simmer for 30 minutes. Add the cream or evaporated milk and heat through. Taste before serving. If necessary, adjust seasoning.

Note: You may use canned green beans. In this case, add the beans when the soup has cooked for about 20 minutes.

Yield 6 servings

MOLDED SPINACH SALAD FOR EASTER

 4 (10-ounces each) packages frozen spinach
 ½ cup celery, chopped
 1 cup small curd cottage cheese
 1¼ cups sour cream
 ¼ cup cream style horseradish
 6 tablespoons mayonnaise
   Salt to taste
   Watercress
   Sliced cucumbers
   Grated carrots

Cook spinach according to package directions; drain, pressing out moisture through sieve. Chop spinach, add celery, cottage cheese, ¼ cup sour cream, 3 tablespoons horseradish, 4 tablespoons mayonnaise and salt to taste. Place in an oiled 1½ quart ring mold; chill until firm. Unmold salad; garnish with watercress and cucumbers sprinkled with carrots. Blend remaining sour cream, horseradish and mayonnaise for dressing.

Serves 10

LUNCHEON TOSTADA SALAD

 1 pound ground beef, chicken or turkey
 1 onion, chopped
 1 (14-ounce) can kidney beans, drained
 1 package taco seasoning mix
   Salt to taste
 1 head lettuce, cut into pieces
 4 ounces cheddar cheese, grated
 1 cup Thousand Island dressing
 1 (6-ounce) package tortilla chips
 1 large avocado, sliced
 4 tomatoes, cut into small wedges
   Sour cream garnish

Brown meat and add onions. Add beans, taco seasoning and salt. Cover and simmer 10 minutes. Combine lettuce, cheese, dressing, chips, avocado and tomato wedges, reserving some chips for garnish. Add meat mixture and toss lightly, garnish with sour cream.

Serves 6 to 8

CRAB LOUIS SALAD

    1 cup mayonnaise
    2 tablespoons wine vinegar
  ¼ cup olive oil
      Salt and pepper to taste
  ¼ cup chili sauce
    2 tablespoons minced chives (if your strapped can use green
      onions, chopped)
    1 teaspoon horseradish sauce
    1 teaspoon Worcestershire sauce
      Chilled lettuce
    3 cups flaked crabmeat
    4 hard boiled eggs, quartered
      Capers

Combine the first 9 ingredients, mix well. Chill. Tear lettuce into bite-sized pieces. Arrange lettuce in a salad bowl or individual plates. Mound crab meat on lettuce. Spoon dressing over crab. Garnish with eggs, tomatoes and capers.

Serves 4

SEAFOOD RICE SALAD

  ½ pound cooked bay shrimp
    1 (6½-ounce) can albacore, drained and flaked
    3 cups cooked and chilled brown rice
  ½ cup onion, chopped
 1½ cups celery, chopped
  ¼ cup pimiento, chopped
    1 tablespoon lemon juice
    1 cup mayonnaise
  ½ cup sweet pickles, chopped

Combine everything in a large bowl. Toss and chill. Serve on salad greens. Garnish with tomato wedges.

Serves 8

FINES HERBS

This classic phrase denotes a delicate blend of fresh herbs suitable for savory sauces and soups, and for all cheese and nonsweet egg dishes. Use equal parts of parsley, tarragon, chives and chervil.

These herbs added at the last minute to your dish being cooked, give up the essential oils and add a lovely freshness to your dish.

If dry herbs are being used follow the recipe but as a rule they are added when the sauce is being made.

PASSOVER DERMA

½ cup grated carrots
1 large onion, chopped
½ cup finely chopped celery
2 cloves garlic, crushed
3 cups crushed egg matzos
2 eggs, beaten

1 cup pareve margarine,
  melted
1 teaspoon salt
¼ teaspoon pepper
¼ teaspoon poultry seasoning
Aluminum foil

Pre-heat oven to 350°. Combine all ingredients in a large bowl; mix well. Place a 20-inch piece of aluminum foil on a cookies sheet. Shape mixture into a 16-inch roll. Bring two sides up over derma; fold down loosely in a series of locked folds, allowing for heat circulation and expansion. Fold short ends up and over again; crimp to seal. Cook for 45 minutes. Unwrap and cut while hot into ½-inch thick slices.

Makes: one 16-inch roll

EASTER HOLIDAYS WILD RICE STUFFING

½ cup wild rice cooked in chicken broth
½ cup brown rice, cooked in chicken broth
4 tablespoons butter or margarine
1 medium onion, chopped
½ pound mushrooms, sliced
¼ cup celery, chopped
½ cup pecans, chopped
2 tablespoons parsley, chopped
¼ teaspoon thyme
¼ teaspoon marjoram
  Salt and pepper to taste

Saute vegetables in butter or margarine until al dente. Add cooked rice and seasonings. Can be baked in a greased casserole at 350° for 35 to 45 minutes or can be used to stuff game hens, chicken or small turkey.

Serves 4

SHEEPHERDER'S DIP

4 (8-ounce) packages
  cream cheese
1 (5-ounce jar) dried beef
14 dashes garlic salt
14 dashes pepper

6 green onions, chopped
3 tablespoons mayonnaise
2 teaspoons lemon juice
1 loaf sheepherder's bread

Cut a 5 or 6 inch top off of bread. Pull out soft insides. (Can save for making bread dressing). Soften cream cheese. Combine with remaining ingredients. Fill shell with mixture. Replace top of bread. Cover bread with foil. Bake for 1½ hours at 300°.

Use fresh vegetables as well as top of bread for dipping.

Rabbi Yale Butler's
VEGETABLE KUGEL FOR PASSOVER
2 tablespoons margarine ("Mother's Passover" brand)
3 carrots, grated
½ cup chopped celery
½ cup chopped parsley
1 onion, chopped
½ cup chopped green pepper
⅓ cup water
1 package frozen chopped spinach
3 eggs, beaten thick
½ teaspoon garlic powder
¼ teaspoon pepper
½ teaspoon salt (optional)
¾ cup matzo meal

Melt margarine in large frying pan. Add all vegetables and water; cook over low heat until vegetables are tender—approximately 10 to 12 minutes. Place vegetables in large bowl, add beaten eggs, salt, garlic powder, pepper and matzo meal.

Using ½ teaspoon oil on waxed paper, lightly grease 10-inch pie plate or 9 × 9-inch square pan. Pour in mixture. Bake in a preheated 350° oven for 45 to 50 minutes, until firm.

Cut into 10 equal servings.

1 serving equals 105 calories; ½ fat exchange, ½ bread exchange, 2 vegetable exchanges.

CARROT TSIMIS
1 bunch of carrots (about 7)
2 large sweet potatoes (optional)
1 tablespoon onion (cut fine)
Pinch of ginger
1½ pounds brisket or plate meat (brust or flanken)
½ tablespoon cornstarch
2 tablespoons sugar (preferably brown)
Salt to taste

Cover the meat with boiling water, add the onion, and cook for three quarters of an hour. Add the carrots, scraped and cut into small cubes, the potatoes which have been peeled and cut into large cubes, the sugar and ginger. Pack these vegetables closely over the meat and have just enough water to cover when it starts boiling. Cook at least an hour, until the meat and carrots are tender and the water boiled down considerably.

Mix the cornstarch with a little cold water until smooth and then add some of the carrot water. Pour this down the side of the kettle, stirring carefully so as not to mash the tsimis. Cook slowly for another ten minutes. The meat may be omitted and a teaspoon of butter or chicken fat substituted.

GREEN BEANS WITH MUSHROOMS FOR EASTER

    1 pound sliced mushrooms
    1 medium onion, sliced
    ½ cup butter
    ¼ cup flour
    2 cups warm milk
    1 cup light cream
    ¾ pound cheddar cheese, diced
    ⅛ teaspoon Tabasco
    2 teaspoons soy sauce
    ½ teaspoon pepper
    3 packages French green beans, cooked and drained
    1 (5-ounce) can water chestnuts, sliced
    ½ to ¾ cup toasted slivered almonds

Saute mushrooms and onion in butter. Add flour and cook until smooth. Add milk and cream and stir until smooth. Add cheese, Tabasco, soy sauce, pepper and simmer until cheese is melted. Add beans and water chestnuts. Pour in shallow casserole and cover with almonds. Bake 20 minutes at 375°. If prepared ahead, allow 35 minutes. Good with ham, corned beef, or anything.

Serves 10 to 12

ASPARAGUS WITH SAUCE MALTAISE

    2 pounds asparagus

Sauce Maltaise

    3 egg yolks
    Salt to taste
    1 tablespoon orange juice
    1 stick butter, cut into small pieces
    2 teaspoons orange zest
    2 tablespoons Grand Marnier
    Watercress to garnish

Wash and trim asparagus. Lay flat in a skillet, barely cover with water. Bring to a boil and simmer until tender, about 6 to 8 minutes. Drain.

Put the egg yolks, salt and orange juice in a small pan over low heat. Beat with a wire whisk until well blended and the egg yolks have thickened to the consistency of heavy cream. Add the butter piece by piece until it has been absorbed. Blend in the orange zest and Grand Marnier. Arrange asparagus on a serving platter and spoon sauce over. Garnish with watercress.

Serves 4

PORK BURGERS

1 pound bulk sausage
1 cup soft bread crumbs
¼ cup green pepper, chopped
¼ cup green onion, finely chopped
1 (6½-ounce) can water chestnuts, chopped
1 egg
2 tablespoons dry sherry
2 tablespoons soy sauce
2 cloves garlic, crushed
¼ teaspoon ginger
6 large sesame seed hamburger buns
1 cup bean sprouts, rinsed and drained
Sweet and sour sauce

Combine pork sausage, bread crumbs, green onions, green peppers, water chestnuts, egg, dry sherry, soy sauce and ginger. Mix well. Shape into patties and pan fry until done, turning once.

BAKED HAM

"This is contributed by a friend of the Junior League from Georgia and is often served at Colonial Dames Meetings at the Powder Magazine in Charleston. It is superlative for Country—not Smithfield ham—but good for any standard ham."

The ham is baked in a dough blanket, made as follows:

4 cups flour
1 cup brown sugar
2 tablespoons ground cloves
2 tablespoons powdered cinnamon
2 tablespoons dried mustard
1 teaspoon black pepper
Peach pickle juice or apple cider

Cut rind off ham. Combine dry ingredients and add enough juice to make a dough which can be rolled. Cover fat part of ham with the dough, put in a cold oven and bake at 325°, about 20 or 25 minutes per pound—four or five hours for a 15 pound ham—basting every 30 minutes. Take dough off and finish with brown sugar or any favorite way of browning ham.

ROAST LOIN OF PORK WITH ARTICHOKE SAUCE

    1 3-pound center cut pork loin, boned
      Salt, pepper, thyme

Sauce

    1 can artichoke hearts
    1 medium onion, chopped fine
    1 tablespoon olive oil
    ½ cup dry white wine
    ½ tablespoon Dijon mustard
    1 clove garlic (pressed or chopped fine)
    1 teaspoon nutmeg
    ⅔ cup heavy cream
      Salt and pepper to taste

To marinate pork, trim off the fat on top leaving just a thin layer to secure the juices while roasting. Sprinkle the top first with salt, then thyme and finally white pepper and allow to set in the refrigerator for 5 to 6 hours or overnight, if possible. Roast for 30 to 45 minutes at 350°.

Sauce

While roast is in the oven saute the onion gently for five minutes, add garlic and saute for another minute. Cut the artichoke hearts in half and add to the onions with the juice from the can. Add the white wine, mustard, nutmeg, salt and pepper and allow to reduce until the mixture has thickened. Add the cream and allow to simmer and reduce to desired texture. Remove roast from the oven and let stand for 3 to 4 minutes. Cut into thin slices and arrange down the center of a serving platter with rice pilaf on both sides. Mask with the sauce and serve.

BAKED HAM SLICE SAUTERNE

    1 (3-pound) ham slice
    ½ cup firmly packed brown sugar
    3 tablespoons cornstarch
    1 tablespoon butter or margarine
    ½ cup raisins
    ½ cup sauterne or any dry white wine

Cover ham with cold water, bring to a boil. Remove ham to a greased baking dish. Place cornstarch and brown sugar in a saucepan, add 1½ cups water and butter. Cook for 5 minutes, stirring constantly. Remove from heat, stir in raisins and wine. Pour sauce over ham and bake uncovered, at 350° for 45 minutes, or until ham is tender.

Serves 4

ROAST LEG OF LAMB WITH ROSEMARY STUFFING

    1 to 1¼ cups fresh bread crumbs
    2 tablespoons milk
    3 tablespoons shallots, minced
    2 tablespoons butter
1½ cups ground lamb
    2 garlic cloves, mashed
    ⅓ teaspoon crushed or ground rosemary
    Salt and pepper to taste
    8 to 9 pounds butterflied leg of lamb

Make paste from bread crumbs and milk. Saute shallots in butter. Combine paste, shallots, ground lamb, garlic, rosemary, salt and pepper. Open out butterflied leg of lamb and spread mixture over, then roll and tie roast securely. Place roast on rack in roasting pan and coat with herb and mustard sauce (below). Insert meat thermometer in thickest part of roast and bake at 325° to 350° for 2½ to 4 hours or until thermometer reads 150° for rare.

Herb and Mustard Sauce

    3 to 4 garlic cloves, mashed
    ½ teaspoon ground rosemary
1½ teaspoons soy sauce
    ½ cup Dijon mustard
    4 to 5 tablespoons olive oil

Combine garlic, rosemary, soy sauce and mustard with a wire whisk. Beat in oil by droplets to make a very thick viscous sauce.

Serves 8 to 12

CHICKEN WITH CHERRY WINE SAUCE

    1 (3-pound) fryer cut into parts
    ¼ cup flour
    Salt and pepper to taste
    3 tablespoons butter and margarine
    1 cup dry red wine
    1 tablespoon sugar
    1 teaspoon cinnamon
    ½ teaspoon allspice
    2 cups pitted sweet red cherries

Dredge chicken in flour and season to taste. Brown in butter or margarine. Stir in wine, sugar, cinnamon, allspice and cherry juice. Cover and simmer until tender. Five minutes before serving add cherries to heat.

Serves 4

CHICKEN WITH MUSHROOMS (Moo Goo Gai Pan)

    1 chicken breast, boneless and skinless—frozen
    ¼ pound fresh mushrooms
    8 water chestnuts
    2 ounces fresh snow peas or ½ package defrosted snow peas
    1 clove garlic, peeled and crushed
    4 tablespoons cooking oil

Marinade

    1 teaspoon cornstarch
    ½ teaspoon salt
    2 teaspoons dry sherry

Sauce

    ¼ cup chicken broth
    1 tablespoon soy sauce
    1 tablespoon dry sherry
    ½ teaspoon sugar
    1½ teaspoons cornstarch

Cut partially frozen chicken breast crosswise into halves. Pack breasts cut side down in feed tube and slice with medium slicing disk. Mix chicken with the marinade. Replace the medium slicing disk.

Slice mushrooms, then water chestnuts. Remove the ends and strings of fresh snow peas. Place all vegetables in the same bowl with crushed garlic on top. Combine the sauce ingredients.

Have ready before cooking: bottle of cooking oil; bowl with chicken; bowl with vegetables; bowl with sauce; serving platter. Heat wok on high heat until very hot. Add 3 tablespons oil and heat until oil is hot. Add chicken, stirring constantly until chicken just turns white, about 2 minutes. Remove from wok.

Heat 1 tablespoon oil over medium heat. Fry garlic, and discard when it turns golden. Add vegetables to garlic-flavored oil, stirring over medium-high heat for 2 to 3 minutes. Return chicken to wok, and turn heat to high, stirring to mix. Give the sauce mixture a good stir and pour into wok, stirring to mix until the sauce becomes translucent. Transfer to the serving platter and serve immediately.

Variations: Toast ⅓ cup slivered almonds in 325° oven for 8 to 10 minutes or until golden. Let them cool; sprinkle on chicken before serving. Or substitute 1 cup cut up broccoli, asparagus, or Bok Choy for snow peas.

Yield 2 servings

STRAWBERRY SPICE LOAF
Loaf
    3 cups sliced strawberries
    3 cups all-purpose flour
    2 cups sugar
    1 teaspoon salt
    3 teaspoons cinnamon
    1 teaspoon nutmeg
    1 teaspoon soda
 1¼ cups oil
    4 eggs, beaten

Let strawberries stand at room temperature while preparing the batter so the juice can settle. Combine dry ingredients in a large bowl and mix thoroughly. In a separate bowl, combine oil and eggs. Drain the berries, reserving the juice, and mash. Add oil and egg mixture to the berries and mix well. Make a center well in the dry ingredients and pour in the strawberry mixture. Mix until thoroughly combined.

Grease and flour two 9-inch loaf pans. Divide the batter equally between the two pans. Bake at 350° for 1 hour or until a cake tester inserted into the center of the loaf comes out dry. Cool slightly before removing from the pan. Spread with cream cheese frosting.

Cream Cheese Frosting
    12 ounces cream cheese
    ½ cup strawberry juice

Soften cream cheese and beat in reserved juice from the berries. Spread on cooled strawberry loaves.

Makes 2 loaves

NO KNEAD ROLLS FOR EASTER
    3 eggs
    3 tablespoons sugar
    ½ teaspoon salt
    1 package dry yeast
    1 cup warm water
    ½ cup cold margarine
    4 cups flour

Dissolve yeast in warm water and let it stand 5 minutes. Beat eggs with mixer until light in color. Add sugar, salt and dissolved yeast. Stir to combine. Cut cold margarine into small chips and gently stir into the egg mixture. Stir in flour until thoroughly combined. Cover bowl with plastic wrap. Let rise 2 hours. Shape into rolls of desired shape. Place on a greased baking sheet. Cover with tea towel. Let rise 1 hour more. Bake at 350° until lightly browned.

Makes approximately 50 rolls

NUT CAKE—PESACH

    6 eggs, separated
1½ cups walnuts, ground fine
  ¾ cup sugar
    4 ounces bittersweet chocolate, melted
      Pinch of salt

Beat egg whites and add sugar. Then add the egg yolks and other ingredients. Bake in two sheets about 9 × 12 each for 20 minutes at 350°.

BEST STRAWBERRY CHEESECAKE

Crust

    4 tablespoons butter, melted
    1 cup graham cracker crumbs
    1 tablespoon sugar
  ½ teaspoon cinnamon

Combine all ingredients. Press onto bottom only of a 10-inch springform pan. Chill pan in refrigerator until ready to fill it.

Cheese Filling

1½ pounds cream cheese (three 8-ounce packages)
    6 large eggs, separated
1⅓ cups sugar
    2 tablespoons flour
1¾ cups sour cream
    2 teaspoons grated lemon rind
    2 teaspoons lemon juice (fresh if possible)
1½ teaspoons vanilla extract

Combine cheese and egg yolks and beat with an electric mixer until completely blended and perfectly smooth. When cheese is smooth, add, beating all the time, 1 cup of the sugar, the flour, sour cream, lemon rind, lemon juice and vanilla extract. Beat until light and smooth.

Now beat the egg whites until they form soft peaks. Add in the remaining ⅓ cup sugar and beat until the whites form stiff peaks. Fold, do not mix, egg whites into the cheese mixture. Pour into prepared pan.

Bake in preheated 325° oven for 70 to 75 minutes. Turn off oven, let cake cool in oven with door open for 1 hour, then let cake finish cooling on kitchen counter. Don't top with fruit until cake is completely cooled, which means letting it sit in refrigerator overnight after cooling on kitchen counter.

Fruit Topping and Glaze

Wash, hull fresh strawberries and place around the chilled cheesecake top. Use 1 pint or 1½ pints for making a big impression. Melt ½ cup strawberry jelly (not jam) over low heat and brush over berries for glaze.

STRAWBERRY FANTASIA

2 baskets raspberries
2 baskets strawberries, sliced
2 whole peaches, sliced
2 tablespoons Grand Mariner
8 long-stemmed strawberries
½ pint whipped cream,
  whipped stiffly

3 tablespoons grated orange
  rind
3 tablespoons grated lemon
  rind
1 cup juice from any canned
  fruit
  Dried macaroons, crushed

Puree raspberries. Combine with strawberries, peaches and Grand Mariner. Chill for six hours.

When ready to serve, divide the puree between 8 serving dishes, place a dollop of whipped cream in the center and place a long-stemmed strawberry in the center of this. Combine citrus peels with fruit juice and spoon over the top. Sprinkle macaroon crumbs over all.

Serves 8

LEMON ANGEL FOOD CAKE

1 package angel food cake mix
1 package lemon pudding pie filling
½ pint whipping cream
  Few drops of yellow food coloring
½ cup coconut

Prepare and bake cake mix according to package directions. Cool. Prepare pie filling according to package instructions. Cool. Whip cream until stiff, add food coloring. Fold into pie filling mixture. Split cake, making 2 layers. Spread pie filling between layers and on top and sides of cake. Sprinkle coconut over top and the sides of cake. Chill. Can also decorate with jelly beans.

FRESH FIG CHIFFON PIE

2 teaspoons plain unflavored
  gelatin
3 tablespoons cold water
¾ cup milk
2 eggs, separated

6 tablespoons sugar
½ teaspoon vanilla
1½ cups diced fresh figs
1 cup heavy cream, whipped
1 (9-inch) baked pie shell

Soften gelatin in cold water. Scald milk in double boiler. Beat egg yolks slightly, add 4 tablespoons sugar and the salt, stir in scalded milk. Return mixture to double boiler, cook over hot water, stirring constantly, until mixture coats metal spoon. Remove from heat and stir in softened gelatin and stir until dissolved. Add vanilla. Let mixture cool thoroughly, then fold in figs and whipped cream. Gradually heat remaining 2 tablespoons sugar into stiffly beaten egg whites fold into fig mixture. Turn into baked pie shell and chill until firm. Before serving dust top of pie lightly with nutmeg.

LEMON ZUCCHINI COOKIES

    1 cup grated unpeeled zucchini (1 to 2 medium)
    2 cups all-purpose flour
    ½ teaspoon salt
    1 teaspoon baking powder
    ¾ cup butter or margarine
    ¾ cup sugar
    1 egg, beaten
    1 teaspoon grated fresh lemon peel
    1 cup chopped walnuts
    Lemon Frost (optional)

Grate zucchini and sift flour with salt and baking powder. Cream together butter and sugar. Beat in egg and lemon peel. Stir in flour until dough is smooth; then blend in zucchini and nuts. Drop from rounded teaspoon onto greased cookie sheet in mounds about 1½-inches across and ½-inch thick. Bake at 375° 15 to 20 minutes. Cookies will brown only lightly. While hot, drizzle with Lemon Frost, if you wish. Cool on wire racks.

Yields 6 to 7 dozen

Lemon Frost
Blend together ¼ cup powdered sugar and about 1½ teaspoons fresh lemon juice.

SOUR CHERRY PUDDING PIE FROM NASHVILLE

    1 cup sugar
    ⅓ cup butter or margarine
    2 teaspoons baking powder
    1 cup milk
    ¼ teaspoon salt
    2 cups flour

Cream sugar and butter until light and fluffy. Add dry ingredients alternately with the milk. Pour batter evenly into a 9 × 13-inch greased baking pan.

    2 cups pitted sour cherries
    2 cups sugar
    ⅓ cup butter or margarine, melted
    2 cups hot water

Mix all ingredients together until the sugar is dissolved. Pour batter into the baking pan. Try to distribute the cherries evenly. Bake in a 350° oven for 45 minutes. Serve warm with vanilla ice cream over all.

Serves 8 to 10

ZUCCHINI CHOCOLATE CAKE

2½ cups unsifted flour
½ cup cocoa
2½ teaspoons baking powder
1½ teaspoons baking soda
1 teaspoon salt
1 teaspoon cinnamon
¾ cup soft butter or margarine
2 cups sugar
3 eggs
2 teaspoons vanilla
2 teaspoons grated orange peel
2 cups shredded zucchini
½ cup milk
1 cup chopped pecans or walnuts

Mix all dry ingredients and set aside.

Beat butter and sugar until blended. Add eggs one at a time. Mix in vanilla, orange peel and zucchini. Alternately stir in dry ingredients and milk. Add nuts.

Pour into greased and floured 10-inch tube or bundt pan. Bake in 350° oven for one hour. Cool in pan 15 minutes; turn out on wire rack to cool thoroughly. Drizzle glaze over cake. Cut in thin slices to serve.

Makes 10 to 12 servings.

Glaze
2 cups powdered sugar
3 tablespoons milk
1 teaspoon vanilla

Mix until smooth; drizzle on cake.

BANANA SPLIT DESSERT

Graham cracker crumbs
3 or 4 bananas
½ gallon Neapolitan ice cream
1 cup walnuts, chopped
1 cup chocolate chips
½ cup softened butter
2 cups powdered sugar
1½ cups evaporated milk
1 teaspoon vanilla
1 pint whipping cream

Cover an 11 × 15-inch pan with cracker crumbs. Slice bananas over crumbs. Slice ice cream ½ inch thick and place slices over bananas. Sprinkle with the nuts. Place in freezer until firm. Melt butter and chocolate chips over low heat. Add sugar and milk and cook until thick, stirring constantly. Cool and pour over crumb mixture. Chill. Whip cream. Add ¼ cup powdered sugar and the vanilla. Spoon over all. Freeze. Serve in slices or squares.

Makes 25

AMARETTO CHEESECAKE

  1 cup unsifted all-purpose flour
  ¼ cup sugar
    Grated rind of 1 lemon
  1 egg yolk
  ½ cup cold butter or margarine
  5 packages (8-ounces each) cream cheese
1½ cups sugar
  ¼ cup flour
  ¼ teaspoon salt
  6 eggs
  ⅓ cup Amaretto
  2 tablespoons instant coffee
    Sweetened whipped cream

In a bowl, mix flour, sugar and lemon rind. Add egg yolk and butter or margarine; mix with the fingers until a smooth ball of dough is formed. Wrap and chill dough for 1 hour.

With floured fingers, pat dough evenly into the bottom and sides of an ungreased 9-inch springform pan.

In a bowl, beat cream cheese until fluffy. Gradually beat in sugar, flour and salt. Beat in eggs one at a time, beating well after each addition.

Mix Amaretto and coffee until coffee is dissolved. Beat this mixture into cheesecake. Pour into dough-lined pan. Bake in a preheated slow oven (250°) for 1½ hours, or until firm when touched in the center. Cool cake and then chill.

When ready to serve, remove sides of pan and decorate top of cake with rosettes of sweetened whipped cream or topping. Dust rosettes with additional crushed instant coffee.

Cheesecake may be prepared without crust, if prefered.

Makes 1 (9-inch) cheesecake.

DESSERT FRUIT SAUCE

1 (10-ounce) package frozen strawberries
1 (10-ounce) package frozen raspberries
½ teaspoon corn starch
1 tablespoon water
¼ cup brandy
¼ cup kirsch
1 pint strawberries, washed hulled and sliced

Defrost strawberries and raspberries. Puree in blender. Strain to remove seeds. Heat to simmering in a saucepan. Mix cornstarch with water and add to puree. Cook, stirring for 1 minute. When serving stir in brandy, kirsch, and strawberries.

GLAZED SWISS CARROT CAKE

    Vegetable shortening
1 cup fine dry bread crumbs
3 to 4 medium carrots
1⅔ cups almonds or filberts, with skins on
½ teaspoon cinnamon
¼ teaspoon ground cloves
6 eggs, separated
1¼ cups sugar
    Grated rind and juice of 1 lemon

Preheat oven to 350° 15 minutes before baking cake.

Grease the bottom of a springform pan. Cut a circle of waxed paper to fit the bottom, then grease the paper and, at the same time, grease the sides of the pan. Add 3 spoonfuls of bread crumbs. Working over the sink, tip the pan back and forth so the crumbs coat the bottom and sides of the pan. Tap the pan to knock out any surplus.

Peel the carrots, then grate fine (you need ⅔ cup packed down tight). Grind the nuts in electric blender until fine. Mix carrots, nuts, remaining bread crumbs and spices in a large mixing bowl.

Combine egg yolks, sugar and lemon juice in a medium bowl and beat vigorously with rotary or electric beater until thick. Then stir into the carrot mixture along with the lemon rind.

Beat the whites until they stand in firm, shiny peaks. Using a whisk, whip about a third of the whites into the batter. Fold in remainder carefully with rubber spatula. Spoon into the prepared pan and bake in the preheated oven for 45 to 60 minutes, or until a toothpick inserted in the center comes out dry.

Cool on a bottom rack. When cold, release the sides of the pan, turn upside down to remove the bottom and pull off the waxed paper. Wrap in foil or plastic wrap and allow to mellow in refrigerator 2 or 3 days.

Glaze

Combine 2 cups sifted confectioners' sugar with 4½ tablespoons water and ¼ teaspoon lemon juice. Mix until smooth. Pour over top of cake, smoothing with a metal spatula.

Of all the things I have lost
I miss my mind the most

KICHLACH (PUFFY EGG COOKIES)

3 eggs
½ cup salad oil
2 tablespoons sugar
1 cup sifted flour

¼ teaspoon salt
4 tablespoons poppy
seeds (optional)

Beat the eggs until light, then beat in the oil, sugar, flour and salt. Beat until very smooth. Stir in the poppy seeds, if you like. Drop by the teaspoon onto a greased baking sheet, leaving about 3 inches between each. (They spread and puff in baking.) Bake in a 325° oven 15 minutes or until browned on the edges.

Yields approximately 36

STRAWBERRY CAKE

1 package white cake mix
1 (3-ounce) box strawberry
gelatin
3 tablespoons flour

½ cup water
½ cup oil
4 eggs
½ cup sliced strawberries

Mix together cake mix, gelatin, oil, flour and water. Beat 2 minutes with mixer at medium speed. Add eggs one at a time and beat well after each addition. Fold in strawberries. Pour batter into a greased 9 × 13-inch baking pan. Bake at 350° for 30 to 35 minutes, or until done. Frost with whipping cream and fresh sliced strawberries. Yummy.

STRAWBERRY SHORTCAKE

¼ pound butter
1 cup sugar
3 eggs

1½ cups all-purpose flour,
unsifted
2 teaspoons baking powder
¾ cup milk

Topping

¾ cup butter
1 cup sugar
3 cup strawberries, mashed
1 cup heavy cream, whipped
½ teaspoon vanilla extract

Preheat oven to 350°. Cream together the butter and sugar. Add eggs, one at a time, beating well after each addition. Mix flour and baking powder. Pour batter into a buttered 9 × 9-inch baking pan and bake for 25 to 30 minutes or until a toothpick inserted in the center comes out clean.

For the topping, melt butter and sugar together in a small saucepan, stirring until sugar is dissolved. Add mashed strawberries and cool or refrigerate. To assemble, pour chilled topping mixture over hot cake. Top with whipped cream, whipped with vanilla, and garnish with reserved strawberries.

Yield 8 to 10 servings

FAVORITE EASTER COFFEE CAKE

      1 cup butter (don't fudge)
    1¼ cups sugar
      2 eggs, beaten
      1 cup sour cream
      1 teaspoon vanilla
      2 cups sifted flour
      1 teaspoon baking powder
      ½ teaspoon baking soda

Cream butter and sugar. Add eggs, sour cream and vanilla. Beat well, gradually add flour, sifted with baking powder and soda. Place one half the mixture in a greased tube or bundt pan. Sprinkle with half the topping mixture. Add remaining batter and topping mixture. Bake in a 350° oven for 1 hour, or until a tester inserted in the center comes out clean. Sprinkle with powdered sugar while still hot. Make the children wait 15 to 20 minutes before you cut into it. Yummers.

Topping

      1 cup finely chopped nuts
      4 tablespoons sugar
      1 teaspoon cinnamon

BAKED BANANAS IN FRESH ORANGE JUICE

Peel whole bananas and place in a baking dish. Pour 2 tablespoons of fresh orange juice and 1 teaspoon fresh lemon juice over each banana. Bake in preheated hot oven (400°) for 10 to 15 minutes.

Serve as a meat accompaniment

BAKED BANANAS WITH HONEY

Peel bananas and cut into halves lengthwise. Arrange in a shallow baking dish. Sprinkle 1 tablespoon strained honey mixed with 1 teaspoon fresh lemon juice over each banana. Bake in preheated hot oven (400°) for 10 to 15 minutes.

Serve as a meat accompaniment or for dessert.

BAKED BANANAS IN CURRANT JELLY

Peel bananas and cut into halves lengthwise. Arrange in a shallow baking dish. For each banana, mix 1½ teaspoons currant jelly, ½ teaspoon butter or margarine and 1 teaspoon hot water. Pour over each banana. Bake in preheated hot oven (400°) for 10 to 15 minutes.

Serve as a meat accompaniment.
1 banana per serving

MAY

They say the hardest meal for Mom to get is one in bed. We have some great brunch ideas for that special lady and some fabulous graduation party ideas.

BACKYARD STRAWBERRY WINE

    7 pounds strawberries
    2 gallons boiling water
      Juice of 1 lemon
    5 pounds sugar

Mash strawberries in a crock. Add boiling water and lemon juice and stir with much vigor. Cover with a cheesecloth and let stand 1 week, giving it a good stir every day. Strain through a cheesecloth and discard the fruit. Return to a clean crock. Stir in the sugar, cover with a cloth, and let it stand one more week giving it a good stir every day. Funnel into glass jugs and cork loosely. Can rack after 3 months. Re-bottle when fermentation has ceased and wine is clear. Age for 1 year.

Makes about 2½ gallons wine.

FRESH LEMON STRAWBERRY PARTY PUNCH

    2 teaspoons fresh grated lemon peel
      Juice of 6 fresh lemons (1 cup)
    2 cups strawberries, cut in half
    1 quart lemon or orange sherbet, softened
    2 bottles (28-ounces each) lemon flavored soda, chilled
      Lemon cartwheels
    5 strawberry halves

In blender, combine lemon peel, juice and 2 cups strawberries; blend until smooth. In punch bowl, combine sherbet and strawberry mixture; stir well. Pour in soda, stirring to blend. Float lemon cartwheels and strawberry halves in punch. Makes about ten cups.

10 (8-ounce) servings

CHEESE WRAPPED GRAPES

    1 (8-ounce) package cream cheese, softened
    1 (8-ounce) package sharp Cheddar cheese, grated
    ½ cup butter, softened
    1 tablespoon prepared mustard
    ½ teaspoon Worcestershire sauce
      Fresh seedless grapes
      Paprika
      Walnuts or pecans, chopped

Beat together the cheeses, mustard and Worcestershire sauce. With damp hands, form mixture around individual grapes. Roll each ball in paprika and then chopped nuts. Chill.

Makes 50 appetizers

CHICKEN WINGS

    32 chicken wings
     6 to 8 tablespoons melted butter
    1½ cups bread crumbs
     ½ cup grated Parmesan cheese
     1 teaspoon salt or lemon-pepper
     1 teaspoon garlic powder

Discard tip of wing; cut remaining wing in 2 pieces. Dip chicken in melted butter. Combine bread crumbs, cheese, salt and garlic powder in a plastic bag. Shake wings in crumb mixture. Place chicken on greased 15 × 10-inch baking sheet and bake in a preheated 400° oven for 30 minutes. Serve hot.

Serves 10

HAWAIIAN CHICKEN WINGS

    36 chicken wings
     ½ cup soy sauce
     1 clove garlic (crushed)
     1 teaspoon Worcestershire sauce
     ¼ cup pineapple juice
     4 tablespoons brown sugar

Cut chicken wings in pieces, discarding bony tips. Combine remaining ingredients. Place wing pieces in baking dish. Pour marinade over all. Marinate for 2 hours in the refrigerator. Bake in the same pan for 1 hour at 375°. BASTE frequently while baking! Just keep warm until serving time.

Serves 10

STRAWBERRY SOUP

     1 cup fresh ripe strawberries, washed, hulled and sliced
     4 cups port
     1 cup water
     ¼ cup sugar
     3 tablespoons arrowroot
     ¼ cup hot water
       hot cream

In a saucepan, mix strawberries, wine and water. Bring to a boil. Stir in sugar and salt. Mix arrowroot with water, add a few spoonsful of hot soup, then stir into hot soup. Cook stirring frequently until soup thickens. Chill. Serve cold, topped with hot cream. Frozen raspberries can also be used, omitting the sugar.

Yield 8 servings

QUICK AND EASY CHILI

    1 large onion, chopped
    1 tablespoon oil
    1 pound ground sirloin
    1 medium sized can stewed tomatoes
    2 beef bouillon cubes
    1 can kidney beans, drained
    1 large can small red beans, drained
    1 large can chopped ortega chilies
    1 can chili without beans
    1 can beer (may need more)

Brown onions in oil. Add ground sirloin and when browned add remaining ingredients and simmer open kettle for 45 minutes. Can add hot sauce if you like.

Serves 6 to 8

Can serve with chopped onion, cheese and a little chopped cilantro.

CONSOMME POTATO SALAD

    2 (10½-ounce cans) beef consomme
    2 garlic cloves
    8 medium potatoes, peeled
    6 tablespoons tarragon vinegar
    4 tablespoons olive oil
      Salt and pepper to taste
    1 cup onion, chopped
    1 cup celery, chopped
  ¾ cup parsley, chopped
    6 hard cooked eggs, cut into quarters
      Green or black olives

Bring consomme and garlic to the boiling point. Add the potatoes and cook until tender, but still firm. Be careful not to overcook. Drain potatoes, throw away the garlic and save consomme you can use later for soup stock or gravies. Dice potatoes while still hot. Combine all the remaining ingredients except the eggs and olives. Blend well. Add potatoes while warm, if you don't they won't absorb the dressing. Toss carefully so as not to break the potatoes. Place into a serving dish and garnish with egg quarters and olives. If you find the potatoes are a little dry in the consomme add a little water while cooking.

Serves 6 to 8

SPRING LUNCHEON CHICKEN SALAD

        2 cups mayonnaise
        2 tablespoons lemon juice
    1½ tablespoons soy sauce
        1 heaping tablespoon curry powder
        1 tablespoon onion, grated
        1 tablespoon chutney
        3 cups cooked chicken or turkey, cubed
    1½ cups celery, chopped
        1 (6 ounce can) water chestnuts, sliced
        1 package (any size you like) slivered almonds, toasted
          Lichie nuts
          Chutney

Mix together the first 6 ingredients for your dressing. Combine with the remaining ingredients, except the nuts, and chill overnight to marry all the flavors.

Toss with the nuts just before serving. Serve on a bed of lettuce and garnish top of salad with 1 large can of lichee nuts, drained and stuffed with chutney.

Serves 6 to 8

AVOCADO, ASPARAGUS AND ARTICHOKE SALAD

        1 pound thin asparagus
        4 artichokes
        ½ lemon
        ½ teaspoon salt
        3 peppercorns
        2 avocados, cut in half
        ½ pound fresh ricotta cheese
        3 tablespoons olive oil
        1 tablespoon lemon juice
        ¼ teaspoon salt, or to taste
          White pepper

Break off and discard the root ends of the asparagus stalks, then boil the asparagus in a wide saucepan in salted water to cover for 5 minutes or until tender but still crisp. Drain thoroughly and spread on absorbent toweling. Prepare the artichokes and cut them into fourths. Boil until tender in water with the half lemon, salt, peppercorns and bay leaf. Drain thoroughly and spread on paper toweling. Cut the avocados in half, remove and discard the pit, and peel the halves. Fill the avocado halves with ricotta and put them in the center of a serving plate. Arrange the asparagus stalks and artichoke wedges around the avocado. Shake the olive oil with the lemon juice, salt, white pepper. Dribble dressing over the entire serving plate.

Serves 4

WONDERFUL HEAVENLY HASH

    1 cup mandarin oranges, drained
    1 cup crushed pineapple, drained
    1 cup miniature marshmallows
    1 cup shredded coconut
    1 cup sour cream

The day before combine all ingredients and chill overnight covered. Serve on a bed of lettuce.

Serves 10

CHICKEN BREASTS WITH YOGURT-NUT SAUCE

    6 to 8 chicken breasts

Sauce
    1 large egg yolk
    2 tablespoons lemon juice
    1 teaspoon salt
    ½ teaspoon ground cumin
    1 cup parsley leaves, firmly packed
    1 cup spinach leaves, firmly packed (may use frozen 10-ounce spinach, thawed)
    ½ cup walnut pieces
    ¼ cup olive oil
    ¾ cup plain yogurt

Poach chicken breasts for about 15 minutes in chicken stock. Remove bones and place in a serving dish, cover with sauce.

For Sauce
In a food processor-blender, blend egg yolk, lemon juice, salt and ground cumin. Add parsley and spinach, as well as walnut pieces. Blend. With motor running, add olive oil and plain yogurt. Blend until smooth.

Makes 1⅔ cups

The first thing you lose on a diet
Is your sense of humor

"BACK HOME AGAIN" CANTALOUPE SALAD

    1 medium cantaloupe
    ½ cup diced orange
    ½ cup diced banana
    1 tart apple, cored and diced
    ½ cup crushed pineapple
    ½ cup French dressing
    ½ cup mayonnaise
    Lettuce

Chill all fruits. Just before serving, cut cantaloupe in quarters. Pare off rind; scrape out seeds. Arrange on salad plates. Combine orange, banana, apple, pineapple and French dressing; mix lightly. Pile on cantaloupe, top with mayonnaise. Garnish with lettuce.

Makes 4 servings

SESAME SEED DRESSING

    ¾ cup sugar (or less)
    ¼ teaspoon dry mustard
    ½ teaspoon paprika
    ½ teaspoon salt
    ¼ teaspoon Tabasco sauce
    ¼ teaspoon Worcestershire sauce
    ¾ tablespoons minced onion
    1 cup salad oil
    ½ cup wine vinegar
    ¼ cup toasted sesame seeds

Combine all ingredients in blender container and blend thoroughly. May be stored in refrigerator. If dressing separates, blend briefly before serving on mixed greens or fruit salads.

PARSLEY BUTTER SAUCE

    ¾ cup butter or margarine
    2 tablespoons lemon juice
    2 tablespoons finely chopped parsley
    ½ teaspoon seasoned salt
    ¼ teaspoon pepper

Melt butter and stir in remaining ingredients. Serve hot.

Makes 6 large artichoke servings

WONDERFUL SCRAMBLED EGGS FOR MOM

   ½ pound cheese, grated
   4 tablespoons melted butter
   1 cup heavy cream
    Salt and pepper to taste
 1½ teaspoons dry mustard
  12 eggs, lightly beaten

Spread cheese in a greased 9 × 13-inch baking dish. Pour melted butter over all. Combine remaining ingredients and pour over cheese. Bake at 325° for about 35 minutes or until set.

Serves 6

Serve this with slices of fresh fruit and sliced quick bread of your choice or a croissant. Lovely.

EGGS PORTUGAL

   8 slices of white bread (without crusts)
   ¾ pound grated cheddar cheese
 1½ pounds skinless sausage links
   4 eggs
 2½ cups milk
   ¾ tablespoons prepared mustard
   1 can (10¾-ounce) cream of mushroom soup
   ¼ cup dry vermouth
   1 can (4 to 5-ounce) sliced mushrooms

Cut sausage links into thirds and brown. Cube bread and place in a 9 × 13-inch casserole. Top with cheese and cooked sausages. Mix together eggs, milk, mustard and a small dash of salt. Pour over casserole. Place casserole in refrigerator and let stand overnight.

Next morning blend together soup and mushrooms with dry vermouth. Pour over casserole. Bake 1½ hours at 300°. Serve with small danish and white champagne.

Count your age by friends not years
Count your life by smiles not tears

CRUSTLESS QUICHE

¼ pound butter
½ cup flour
6 large eggs
1 pound Monterey Jack cheese, cubed
1 (3-ounce) package cream cheese, softened
1 cup milk
2 cups cottage cheese
1 teaspoon baking powder
1 teaspoon salt
1 teaspoon sugar

Melt butter in small saucepan, add flour and cook until smooth. Beat eggs, add milk, cheeses, baking powder, salt, sugar and butter-flour mixture. Stir until well blended. Pour into well greased $9 \times 13 \times 2$-inch pan. Bake uncovered at 350° for 45 minutes.

Serves 6 to 8

Note
May be cut into small pieces and served as an hors d'oeuvres.

MUSHROOM CRUST QUICHE

½ cup finely crushed cracker crumbs
½ pound mushrooms, coarsely chopped
5 tablespoons butter or margarine
¾ cup finely chopped green onion
2 cups jack or Swiss cheese, grated
1 cup small curd cottage cheese
3 eggs
¼ teaspoon cayenne pepper
¼ teaspoon paprika

Saute mushrooms over medium heat in 3 tablespoons butter till limp. Stir in cracker crumbs and turn into a greased 9-inch pie pan. Press evenly over bottom and up sides. Melt remaining 2 tablespoons butter, add onions and saute til limp. Spread over crust. Sprinkle evenly with the cheese. In a blender or food processor combine cottage cheese, eggs and cayenne till smooth. Pour into crust and sprinkle with paprika.

Bake at 350° for 20 to 25 minutes. Let stand 10 minutes before cutting.

Serves 4

BAKED CUCUMBERS

  2 tablespoons wine vinegar
1½ teaspoons salt
  ⅛ teaspoon sugar
  3 tablespoons melted butter
  ½ teaspoon dill or basil
  3 green onions, minced
  ⅛ teaspoon pepper
    Minced fresh parsley

Use one cucumber per person. Peel and cut cucumbers in half lengthwise. Scoop out seeds. Cut in crosswise strips in 2 inches wide. Toss with vinegar, salt and sugar. Marinate at least 30 minutes. Drain and pat dry. Toss cucumbers with butter, dill, onion, pepper and parsley. Bake uncovered one hour at 350°, basting occasionally. This recipe will be adequate for 3 medium cucumbers. Increase ingredients as needed for larger amounts.

ASPARAGUS-MUSHROOM AND CHEESE SAUCE

  1 cup fresh mushrooms, sliced
  2 teaspoons butter
  1 teaspoon lemon juice
  1 egg, beaten
  1 cup milk
  1 teaspoon powdered mustard
  ½ teaspoon salt
  1 cup cheddar cheese, diced
2½ pounds asparagus, cooked
    Parsley
  6 mushroom caps, sauteed in butter

Saute mushrooms in butter and lemon juice until tender. In top of double boiler, combine egg, milk, mustard and salt. Stir and cook over hot water until hot and slightly thickened. DO NOT OVERCOOK. Blend in cheese. Heat until sauce has thickened. Add mushrooms and heat. Serve over hot cooked asparagus. Garnish with parsley and mushrooms caps.

Serves 6

EGGPLANT ROMA

1 medium eggplant, peeled
1 egg, beaten
  Salt to taste
6 tablespoons oil
4 tablespoons onion, minced
¼ pound Tillamook cheddar cheese, sliced
1 (8-ounce) can tomato sauce

Cut eggplant into slices about ¼-inch thick. Dip into beaten egg, seasoned with salt. Saute slowly in hot oil until browned on both sides but still crispy. Arrange slices in a shallow baking dish in stacks of three with slices of cheese in between and on top. Combine onion with tomato sauce that has been seasoned to taste with salt and pepper. Pour around the stacks. Bake at 350° for 25 minutes, or until the cheese is melted and the eggplant done and slightly browned on top.

Serves 4

TAMALE PIE CASSEROLE

1 small onion, chopped
  Oil
1 pound lean ground beef
8 ounces tomato sauce
  Salt to taste
1 teaspoon or more chili powder
12 tamales in husks
2 cups whole kernel corn, drained
¼ cup ripe olives, chopped
1 cup grated jack cheese

Brown onion in oil and add beef and saute until lightly browned. Pour off fat. Add tomato sauce and seasonings and simmer slowly. While beef is cooking remove the husks from the tamales and mash. Mix in the corn and the olives. Place half the mixture in a greased 2-quart casserole as the bottom layer of the pie. Taste beef and adjust seasonings to taste. Add meat as the next layer. Top with remaining tamale mixture and sprinkle cheese over all. Bake at 350° for 1 hour.

Serves 4 at my house and six at yours.

CHINESE RED PORK

    4 to 5 pound picnic shoulder (fresh)
    6 dry chinese mushrooms (available at Chinese grocer)
    ½ cup soy sauce
    1 whole star anise (available at Chinese grocer) (can substitute a
       few drops anise flavoring)
    2 tablespoons rock candy (can use 2 tablespoons granulated sugar)
    ¼ cup Chinese rice wine (can use pale dry sherry)
    2 scallions (including green ends) cut in 2 or 3 inch pieces
       lots of water

Put the chinese mushrooms in small bowl and soak for a few minutes. Put in pan with ½ cup water and cook for 30 minutes. Drain and discard stems keeping caps whole and save. Put the fresh pork in a large pot, fitting on the snug side. Cover 2 inches higher than the meat with water. Bring to boil and boil for 5 minutes. Transfer meat to a colander and run hot tap water over it. This blanches the meat. Discard the cooking water. Put meat back into pot, add rest of ingredients except the mushrooms and use 2 cups of cold water. Bring to a boil and cover pot. Cook on a simmer for 3 hours, turning meat 3 to 4 times during cooking. Add mushrooms and cook with cover for 5 minutes. Now remove cover and reduce liquid to about 1 cup. Remove meat and serve sliced on platter using sauce to pour over.

Serves 6

HAWAIIAN SPARERIBS

    8 pounds lean spareribs
    ½ to 1 cup olive oil
    1 cup honey
    1½ cups crushed pineapple, drained
    1½ cups brown sugar
    3 tablespoons dry mustard
       Juice of 1 lemon
       Salt and pepper to taste
    2 garlic cloves, crushed

Let ribs stand at room temperature about 1 hour before rubbing with olive oil. Cook over medium coals for 1 hours, turning often until meat shrinks ¼-inch from end of bone.

   Remove ribs to a flat dish and season with salt and pepper. Cut between bones to separate ribs. Mix remaining ingredients and pour over ribs, coating well. Cover with foil and return to grill for 10 minutes, allowing sauce to penetrate ribs.

Serves 6 to 8

...SY HAM AND CHEESE STRATA FOR MOTHER'S DAY

       16 slices white bread, without crusts and cubed
        1 pound ham, cut into cubes
        1 pound sharp cheddar cheese, grated
     1½ cups Swiss cheese, grated
        6 eggs
        3 cups milk
        4 green onions, chopped
        1 teaspoon Dijon mustard
        3 cup cornflakes, crushed
       ½ cup butter or margarine, melted

Grease a 9 × 13-inch baking dish. Spread half the bread cubes in dish. Add the ham and both cheeses. Cover with remaining bread cubes. Mix eggs, milk, onions, and mustard. Pour evenly over the bread cubes and refrigerate overnight. Combine cornflakes and butter. Top casserole with this mixture and bake at 375° for 40 minutes.

Serves 8 to 10

HAM ROLLS WITH CHEESE SAUCE

       24 slices boiled ham
        2 packages (10-ounces each) frozen chopped spinach, thawed and
          completely drained
        2 cups packaged corn bread stuffing mix
        2 cups sour cream

Cheese Sauce

        8 tablespoons butter or margarine
        8 tablespoons flour
        4 cups milk
       ½ cup grated cheddar cheese
          Paprika
          Parmesan cheese

Combine spinach, cornbread stuffing mix and sour cream together. Spread on ham and roll up each piece and place seam side down in a 9 × 13-inch baking dish. Melt butter in a large skillet, add flour and blend well. Add milk and continue stirring over medium heat until thick. Add cheese and remove from heat. Stir until cheese is melted. Pour over ham. Sprinkle with paprika and Parmesan cheese. Bake at 350° for 15 minutes covered and then 15 minutes uncovered.

Serves 8 to 10

PORK CHOPS FLORENTINE

   6 loin pork chops (½ to ¾-inch thick)
1½ pounds fresh spinach, chopped and lightly steamed
   2 tablespoons grated onion
   6 tablespoons butter
   6 tablespoons flour
1¼ cups strong chicken stock
1¾ cups milk
      Salt and white pepper to taste
      Dash of nutmeg
   2 egg yolks, lightly beaten
   1 cup Swiss cheese, grated
   3 tablespoons Parmesan cheese

Brown chops; lower heat on skillet and cook, covered, until tender. Keep warm. Combine the cooked spinach with the grated onion and set aside.

In a medium saucepan, melt butter; stir in flour and cook for 3 minutes. Slowly stir in chicken stock and milk and continue to stir until thickened. Add salt and pepper and nutmeg. Stir a little of this sauce into egg yolks and then return the yolk mixture to the sauce; stir until smooth and thick.

Mix 1 cup sauce with spinach mixture and spread it onto the bottom of a large greased shallow casserole. Arrange pork chops on top of the spinach. Meanwhile, stir the Swiss cheese into the sauce and stir over low heat until melted. Pour sauce over pork chops, sprinkle with Parmesan cheese and bake, uncovered, at 400° for 15 minutes or until bubbling and the cheese is lightly browned.

Serves 6

STUFFED ARTICHOKES

   2 cups bread crumbs
½ cup chopped parsley
½ cup Parmesan cheese,
      grated
   1 tablespoon minced onion
   1 clove garlic, minced
¾ teaspoon salt
   4 large artichokes
   4 tablespoons olive or
      salad oil

Mix bread crumbs, parsley, cheese, onion, garlic and salt in small bowl. Cut stem from artichokes to make base flat; trim leaf tips with scissors. Wash artichokes under running cold water; drain well. Spread petals slightly with fingers. Spoon stuffing into center and about 1 teaspoon stuffing into spaces between leaves.

Tie each artichoke tightly with clean string; stand in a large, deep saucepan. Drizzle 1 tablespoon oil over each. Pour in boiling water to a depth of about 1 inch; cover. Cook for 50 minutes or until tender when pierced with a fork. Remove string and serve hot.

Serves 4

NEW YORK STYLE BARBECUED CHICKEN

3 cloves garlic, minced
½ teaspoon oregano
½ teaspoon paprika
1 tablespoon lemon juice
8 pieces of chicken of
your choice

3 tablespoons oil
1 teaspoon oregano
⅓ cup catsup
⅓ cup vinegar
1 small onion, minced

Combine garlic, oregano, paprika and lemon juice. Combine with 1 table-spoon oil and rub over chicken. Place on grill and keep turning to brown evenly and to prevent charring. Meanwhile in a small saucepan add re-maining oil and saute onion at edge of grill, stir in oregano, catsup and vinegar and let simmer 15 minutes. When chicken is done brush liberally with sauce and grill 5 minutes longer. Place on platter and may use re-maining sauce as a table sauce.

Serves 4

CHICKEN CROQUETTES

2 tablespoons butter
¼ cup flour
Salt and pepper to taste
1 cup milk
1 teaspoon parsley, minced
1 teaspoon onion, minced

2 cups cooked, ground
poultry
Pinch of ground sage
Fine dry bread crumbs
1 egg mixed with
1 tablespoon water
Fat for deep frying

Melt butter, and flour and seasonings. Mix well. Gradually add milk stirring constantly, until thick. Combine with parsley, onion, poultry and sage. Chill. Now shape into 8 croquettes. Roll each croquette in crumbs, egg mixture and then crumbs again. Fry in fat at 375° for about 5 minutes, or until golden.

Serves 4

SESAME CHICKEN BREASTS AND MUSHROOMS

4 whole chicken breasts
3 tablespoons unsalted
butter or margarine
¼ cup flour
½ teaspoon paprika

2 tablespoons sesame seeds
½ pound sliced fresh
mushrooms
½ cup dry sherry

Remove the bones from the chicken breasts; split in half and then split each half into two thin cutlets.

Melt butter in a large skillet. Combine flour, paprika and sesame seeds; lightly dust the chicken pieces and fry in the melted butter. Brown on both sides. Cover the chicken with the sliced mushrooms. Pour sherry over the chicken and mushrooms, cover the skillet, and cook over very low heat for 20 minutes.

Makes 6 to 8 servings

SHRIMP VERACRUZANA (Microwave)

1 pound jumbo fresh shrimp, shelled and deveined
1 large onion, coarsely chopped
1 green pepper, coarsely chopped
2 cloves garlic, crushed
3 tablespoons cooking oil
1 can (8-ounces) tomato sauce
½ teaspoon oregano
¼ teaspoon cumin
½ teaspoon salt
⅛ cup dry white wine
⅛ teaspoon hot sauce
2 tablespoons parsley, chopped

In a glass roasting platter, stir together onion, green pepper, garlic and oil. Cook on HIGH 3 minutes. Add tomato sauce, oregano, cumin, salt and wine. Cook on HIGH 5 minutes, stirring once. Season to taste with hot sauce and add shrimp, spooning sauce over to cover shrimp. Cook on HIGH 5 minutes or just until shrimps are pink. Garnish with parsley and serve with hot rice or noodles.

Serves 4

EASY ZUCCHINI SPICE BREAD FOR MOTHERS DAY

3 eggs
1 cup dark brown sugar
1 cup sugar
¾ cup vegetable oil
1 tablespoon vanilla
2 cups flour, sifted
1 tablespoon cinnamon
2 teaspoons baking soda
1 teaspoon salt
¼ teaspoon baking powder
2 cups grated zucchini
1 cup nuts, chopped
¼ cup cream sherry

Beat together the first 5 ingredients. Fold in remaining ingredients and pour into 2 greased loaf pans. Bake in a preheated 350° oven for 50 to 60 minutes, or until done. Let cool on racks.

FRESH PEACH SABAYON

2 large peaches
1 cup sugar
¼ cup brandy
3 cups water
1 cinnamon stick
4 egg yolks
1 cup sherry
4 tablespoons superfine sugar

Peel peaches and cut into half. Remove pit. In a saucepan add 1 cup sugar, brandy, water and cinnamon stick. Bring to a boil and boil 5 minutes. Then add peaches and poach gently for 10 minutes and set aside. In a double boiler add egg yolks, sherry and superfine sugar. Set in boiling water and whisk briskly with wire whip until consistency of custard. Place one peach half in champagne glass and cover with sauce. Serve warm. Elegant. . . .

Serves 4

STRAWBERRY PIE

1 (9-inch) baked pie shell, of your choice
2 pints fresh strawberries
1 cup sugar
2 tablespoons cornstarch
1 cup water
2 tablespoons strawberry Jello powder
1 pint heavy cream, stiffly whipped
1 teaspoon vanilla

Wash, stem and drain berries. Taking a few berries mash enough to make ⅓ cupful. Now set aside. Combine sugar, cornstarch, and water. Cook over medium heat until thick and clear. Remove from heat and add Jello powder. Mix well then cool slightly. Now add mashed berries. Fill pie shell with whole berries. Pour mixture evenly over them. Chill 4 hours. Just before serving, top with flavored whipped cream. Delicious.

Serves 6 to 8

STRAWBERRY DESSERT SAUCE

2 cups strawberries
3 tablespoons water
3 tablespoons strawberry preserves
2 tablespoons sugar
½ teaspoon lemon juice
2 teaspoons kirsch

Wash, hull, drain berries and set aside. Place the water, preserves, and sugar in a small saucepan over low heat. Bring to a boil, give a stir now and then. Place berries in your food processor and puree. Add the warm strawberry preserve mixture and process once more. Place a wide but fine strainer over a wide bowl. Pour the puree into the strainer. Push puree through the strainer with a spoon to remove all the seeds. Stir in the lemon juice and the kirsch. Place in a covered container and chill.

Perfect sauce over anything wonderful or just for dipping fresh fruit.

Makes 1½ cups

STRAWBERRY PIZZA

1 cup flour
½ cup powdered sugar
1 stick margarine
8 ounces cream cheese
½ cup sugar
3 (10-ounce) boxes frozen strawberries or 2 pints whole berries
4 tablespoons sugar
4 teaspoons cornstarch

Cut together the first three ingredients as for a pie crust. Sprinkle evenly over a 12 or 13-inch pizza pan. Press firmly and bake at 325° for 15 to 20 minutes, or until light brown. Cool.

Combine cream cheese and ½ cup sugar and spread over cooled crust. Chill.

Thaw and drain berries if using frozen. For fresh, wash and slice. You will need 1 cup berry juice or 1 cup of apricot nectar. Combine with sugar and cornstarch, cook until thick. Cool. Spread over cheese filling and chill.

Serves 12

LUSCIOUS LEMON COCONUT CAKE

½ cup shortening
1½ cups sugar
2½ cups flour
1 teaspoon salt

1 cup milk
1 tablespoon baking powder
3 eggs
1 teaspoon vanilla

Cream shortening; add sugar and cream until light and fluffy. Sift flour and salt together; blend into creamed mixture. Add ¾ cup milk; beat 2 minutes. Stir in baking powder. Blend in eggs and remaining milk; beat 1 minute. Add vanilla. Pour into three 9-inch cake pans. Bake at 350° for 18 to 20 minutes. Cool; spread with filling; frost with favorite seven-minute frosting. Sprinkle with coconut.

Luscious Lemon Filling

¾ cup sugar
3 tablespoons cornstarch
¼ teaspoon salt
¾ cup water
1 teaspoon grated lemon peel
1 tablespoon butter
⅓ cup lemon juice
4 drops yellow food coloring

Mix sugar, cornstarch and salt in saucepan. Gradually stir in water. Cook, stirring constantly, until mixture thickens and boils. Boil 1 minute. Remove from heat; add lemon peel and butter. Gradually stir in lemon juice and food coloring. Cool thoroughly.

Note
Double recipe if top of cake is to be frosted with the filling.

FRESH PEACH SHERBET

5 large peaches, make sure there nice and ripe
1 tablespoon plus ¼ cup fresh lemon juice
1 cup powdered sugar
1 can sweetened condensed milk
4 eggs, separated

Dip the peaches into boiling water for about 30 seconds. Peel, pit and dice. Mix with 1 tablespoon of the lemon juice and the powdered sugar. In a bowl combine the remaining lemon juice, the sweetened condensed milk and the egg yolks and blend well. Stir in the peaches. Beat the egg whites until stiff but not dry and fold into the peach mixture. Pour into a 9 × 13 × 2-inch baking pan. Cover and freeze for about 2 hours, or until mixture is solid around the edges. Turn into a chilled bowl and beat until all the ice crystals are broken up, don't let it melt completely. Return to pan and freeze until firm, about 2 hours. Makes about 2 quarts.

STRAWBERRY RIBBON CAKE

1 cup butter
2 cups sugar
4 eggs
1 teaspoon vanilla
½ teaspoon almond extract
3 cups cake flour, sifted

2½ teaspoons baking powder
½ teaspoon salt
⅔ cup milk
⅛ teaspoon red food coloring

Cream butter; gradually add sugar, beating until light and fluffy. Add eggs, one at a time, beating until very light. Add flavorings. Sift dry ingredients together. Add to creamed mixture alternately with milk, mixing only until blended. Spoon half the batter into greased and floured 8-inch cake pans. Add food coloring to remaining batter; spoon into cake pans. Bake at 350° for 35 minutes or until done. Cool. Split each layer. Assemble cake with Strawberry Buttercream Frosting, alternating pink and yellow layers. Frost sides and top of cake.

STRAWBERRY BUTTERCREAM FROSTING

1 (3-ounce) package cream cheese
¼ cup butter
⅓ cup mashed fresh strawberries
1 package powdered sugar

Cream cream cheese and butter until light. Add strawberries, beat until smooth. Blend in 2 cups powdered sugar. Measure 1½ cups frosting to use as filling. Beat remaining sugar into reserved frosting; frost sides and top of cake.

FROZEN PEANUT BUTTER PIE FOR MOM

4 ounces cream cheese
1 cup powdered sugar
½ cup crunchy peanut butter
1 cup milk
1 large carton frozen whipped topping
   Hot fudge topping
   Graham cracker crust
   Peanuts

Beat cream cheese and powdered sugar together until light and fluffy. Add peanut butter and blend. Pour in milk slowly and blend. Fold in whipped topping. Set aside. Spread fudge topping over prepared graham cracker crust. Add peanut butter mixture. Sprinkle peanuts over all and freeze.

Serves 6—8

JUNE

Father's day is here and we salute Dad with special menus just for that great guy in your life. Also this is the month for June brides and we have a Wedding Calculator chart along with some great recipes for doing your own wedding reception.

WEDDINGS
Party Calculator for 50

	Serving	*Needed*
Champagne Punch	4-ounce cup	1½ gallons
Fruit Drink	6-ounce cup	2 gallons
Coffee	1½ cups	2½ gallons (1 pound)
Rolls	1½ to 2	6 to 8 dozen
Bread for sandwiches	2 slices each	6 loaves
Sandwich filling		2 quarts
Canned ham/cold meat	3 ounces	15 pounds
Cold cuts	2 ounces	10 pounds
Olives or pickles		2 gallons
Shrimp for cocktail	3 to 4 ounces	12 pounds
Lettuce salad		8 heads
Relish vegetables (carrots and celery sticks)		12 pounds
Fresh fruit (grapes or cut up)	½ cup	10 pounds
Cake (18-inch × 26-inch sheet)	3-inch square	1 cake
Ice Cream	½ cup	2 gallons
Cream for coffee		1 quart
Butter (for bread or rolls)		1½ pounds
Salad dressing (for greens)		1 quart
Potato or Macaroni Salad	½ cup	15 pounds

EASY SPINACH PIE (SPANAKOPITA)

      3 boxes frozen chopped spinach, thawed and drained
      1 onion, chopped finely
      2 cloves garlic, minced
      2 cups feta cheese, crumbled
      3 tablespoons butter or margarine, melted
      7 eggs, beaten
        White pepper, and nutmeg to taste
    ½ cup olive oil
    10 phyllo pastry sheets

Press excess water out of spinach. Saute onion and garlic in butter or margarine. Add spinach and cook to eliminate any moisture. Remove from heat, let cool and add cheese, eggs and seasonings. Combine butter and oil and brush the bottom of a 9 × 13-inch baking pan. Place 1 phyllo sheet in pan, brush with butter, top with another, and repeat process until 5 sheets are used. Spread spinach mixture over phyllo. Top with remaining 5 sheets, buttering each sheet as before. With sharp knife cut through the top pastry in 5 places. Bake at 375° for 50 minutes or until nice and browned.

This is a delightful party entree that will serve 16 or cut it into smaller pieces and can be used as an appetizer. The neat thing about this terrific dish is that it can be made a day ahead and then just re-heat it. This also could be used for a bridal brunch.

EGGPLANT CAVIAR

      4 small eggplants
      2 large onions, chopped finely
      2 cloves garlic, crushed
    ¼ teaspoon oregano
      5 to 6 tablespoons chopped parsley
      6 tablespoons olive oil
      2 (14-ounce) cans tomatoes, drained and chopped
        Salt and freshly ground pepper
        Generous pinch of sugar
      6 small black olives, pitted and halved

Preheat oven to 350°. Bake eggplants for about 20 minutes. In a skillet, saute onion, garlic, oregano and 4 tablespoons of the parsley in olive oil until onions are soft and golden. Add tomatoes and simmer for about 5 minutes longer until ingredients have blended into a sauce. When eggplants are soft, peel off skins; drain pulp thoroughly and chop finely. Stir eggplant pulp into tomato-onion mixture; season with salt, pepper and sugar and simmer for about 10 minutes longer, stirring until well blended. Turn mixture into shallow serving dish and allow to cool. Serve cold, garnished with remaining parsley and olives.

BEAN DIP FOR DAD'S DAY

1 large and 1 medium sized cans refried beans
1 pound lean ground beef
1 large onion chopped
6 medium tomatoes, chopped
¼ cup sliced black olives
    Diced jalapeno peppers to taste
½ pound jack cheese, grated
½ pound cheddar cheese, grated

Fry hamburger and onion, drain off grease. Add all the ingredients to a crock pot. Cook for 30 minutes on High. Turn to low to serve with chips.

Serves the gang . . . . . . Great if you have any of the family who loves Mexican type foods.

HOT RYES

1 cup finely grated Swiss cheese
¼ cup cooked and crumbled bacon
1 (4½-ounce) can chopped ripe olives
¼ cup minced green onions or chives
1 teaspoon Worcestershire sauce
¼ cup mayonnaise
    Party rye bread

Mix together all ingredients except bread. Spread on party rye or pumpernickel and bake at 375° for 10 to 15 minutes or until browned.

Note
These may be frozen after baking and reheated.

Makes 36 hors d'oeuvres

WEDDING HYMN BOOK PUNCH

1 pint bottle Hawaiian Punch concentrate
1 small can frozen lemonade concentrate
1 small can frozen orange juice concentrate
1 #5 can pineapple juice
2 quarts sparkling water (club soda)
1 quart 7-Up (can use Fresca)

Put orange juice and lemonade concentrate in punchbowl; add enough sparkling water to dissolve it. Place large chunk of ice in bowl and add rest of ingredients. Stir well. Garnish with orange slices or strawberries.

Makes about 32 (4-ounce) punch cup servings

PINK CHAMPAGNE WEDDING PUNCH

      2 fifths pink champagne, well chilled
      2 fifths sauterne, well chilled
      1 cup Mai Tai mix (non-alcoholic)
      1 cup brandy or vodka
      2 quarts lemon-lime soda
      1 (3-pound) block of ice
        Fresh fruit such as strawberries, orange slices or cherries for
        garnish

Place ice block into punch bowl. Pour on sauterne, Mai Tai and brandy.
Stir. Add lemon-lime soda. Stir. Add champagne last and stir gently.

A 3-pound block of ice is about the size of a half-gallon milk container.
You may also freeze orange blossoms, etc., in the ice block. If making your
own, be sure to use distilled water so that you will have clear ice.

Makes 50 (3-ounce) servings

JACKIE'S WEDDING PUNCH

        Juice of 7 lemons
        Juice of 2 oranges
      ½ pound confectioners sugar
      1 quart bourbon
      ¼ pint Triple Sec or Cointreau
      3 ounces Grenadine
      1 ounce Orange Bitters
      ½ pint cold strong tea
      1 quart carbonated water
        Red food coloring

Put all ingredients except carbonated water in punch bowl. Add red food
coloring to shade desired and large block of ice. Just before serving, add
carbonated water and stir well.

Makes 25 (3-ounce) servings

WEDDING CHAMPAGNE PUNCH

½ cup lemon juice	3 ounces Curacao
½ cup water	3 ounces Maraschino
1 cup sugar	1 bottle sparkling water
3 ounces brandy	3 bottles champagne

In a punch bowl, dissolve sugar in water and lemon. Add brandy, Curacao
and Maraschino. Mix well. Just before serving, pour in chilled sparkling
water and champagne. Stir gently. Garnish with fresh strawberries or pineapple.

Makes 35 (4-ounce) servings

WEDDING BUFFET SHRIMP
(Gorgeous for a large cocktail party!)

    2 pounds medium to large raw shrimp
    1 lemon, thinly sliced
    1 medium red onion, thinly sliced
    1 cup pitted black olives, well drained
    2 tablespoons chopped pimiento
    ¼ cup vegetable oil
    2 cloves garlic, minced
    1 tablespoon dry mustard
    1 tablespoon salt
    ½ cup lemon juice
    1 tablespoon red wine vinegar
    1 bay leaf, crumbled
      Dash of cayenne
      Chopped parsley

Shell and devein shrimp. Bring 1 quart salted water to a boil, add shrimp and cook for a scant 3 minutes. Drain at once. Rinse in cold water. Drain and set aside. In a bowl, combine lemon slices, onion, black olives and pimiento and toss well. Combine oil, garlic, dry mustard, salt, lemon juice, wine vinegar, bay leaf, cayenne and parsley and add to bowl with lemon mixture. Arrange shrimp on a serving dish and pour marinade over them. Cover and chill no longer than 3 hours. Serve with toothpicks.

This is absolutely wonderful!

Serves 10

GRADUATION FOOTBALL PIZZA

    1 pound ground beef
    1 small jar green stuffed olives, sliced
    1 green pepper, chopped
    1 medium sized can mushrooms, sliced with liquid
    1 (8-ounce) can tomato sauce
    1 pound American cheese, grated
      Italian seasonings to taste

Cook ground beef til browned. Drain off fat. Add remaining ingredients. Cook over low heat till well blended. Store in refrigerator. Next day hollow out 8 french rolls, cut in half. Fill hollows out with the meat mixture. Put halves together, roll in foil and freeze. Heat in a 350° oven till hot.

CELEBRATION SANDWICH LOAF
Fillings
1½ cups ground, cooked ham
⅓ cup chopped pickle
1 tablespoon prepared mustard
½ cup mayonnaise

Combine all of above ingredients

7¾ ounces canned salmon, drained and flaked
⅓ cup sliced ripe olives
Salt and pepper
¼ cup mayonnaise

Combine all of above ingredients

1½ cups ground cooked chicken
⅔ cup drained, crushed pineapple
¼ cup chopped green pepper
⅓ cup mayonnaise
Salt and pepper

Combine all of above ingredients

Sandwich Loaf
3 (8-ounce) packages cream cheese
½ cup mayonnaise
1 (16-inch) long loaf unsliced white bread

Remove crusts from 16-inch long loaf unsliced white bread, cut in five lengthwise slices. Spread with margarine and a filling. Stack layers. Chill. Combine cream cheese, mayonnaise; mix well. Frost sandwich loaf, reserving ¾ cup mixture for decorating. Garnish. Chill.

Makes 12 servings.

TERIYAKI HAMBURGERS FOR DAD

1 pound ground round
2 green onions, chopped
¼ cup green pepper, chopped
⅓ cup water chestnuts, chopped
1 tablespoon soy sauce

1 tablespoon lemon juice.
2 tablespoons wine or beef broth
1 tablespoon brown sugar
½ teaspoon ginger
1 tablespoon vegetable oil

Mix together the first 7 ingredients. Form into patties. Combine with the remaining 3 ingredients in a small bowl. Set aside. Barbecue the hamburgers to the desired doneness of your choice and just before the meat is fully cooked brush on the sauce ingredients over all. If Dad is a teriyaki freak he will really love this great recipe.

Serves 4 or whatever depending on how big the eaters are at your house.

JACKIE'S CHICKEN SALAD

    3 cups cooked chicken or turkey, cut into bit-size pieces
    1 cup diced celery
    2 tablespoons grated onion
    3 tablespoons capers, drained
    ⅔ cup browned, slivered almonds
    3 tablespoons tarragon vinegar(or more if you like)
    6 stuffed olives, sliced
    1 can water chestnuts, sliced
      Salt, pepper and paprika, to taste
    1 cup mayonnaise
    ⅓ cup sour cream

Mix all ingredients except mayonnaise and sour cream. Sprinkle with vinegar and seasonings. Let stand at least ½ hour longer.

Serves 10

"I turn this out on a lettuce-lined platter and surround the salad with strawberries, melon slices, pineapple, grapes, etc. Just delicious!"

SPECTACULAR FRUIT SALAD

    Mango, peeled and cut into thin strips
    Orange, peeled and sliced crosswise
    Pineapple, peeled and cut into small chucks
    Seedless grapes, cut into halves
    Bibb lettuce
    Watercress

Dressing
    ⅓ cup sugar
    1 teaspoon toasted sesame seeds
    1 teaspoon salt
    1 teaspoon dry mustard
    4 tablespoons vinegar
    1 cup salad oil
    1 teaspoon paprika
    1 teaspoon grated onion

Use any proportion of the fruits mentioned, or make substitutions. Mix ingredients for dressing in a jar. Cover, shake well and refrigerate. Place fruit, watercress and lettuce in a bowl; refrigerate. When ready to serve, shake dressing and pour over salad. Carefully toss, and serve.

STRAWBERRY SOUFFLE SALAD

    1 box strawberries, sliced
    1 package lemon jello (small size)
    ½ cup strawberry juice
    2 tablespoons lemon juice
    ½ cup mayonnaise
    ¼ cup walnuts, chopped

Dissolve the jello in 1 cup boiling water. Add juices, mayonnaise and blend well with a rotary beater. Pour into a refrigerator tray. Quick freeze 15 to 20 minutes or until firm 1 inch from edge but soft in the center. Turn mixture into bowl and whip with rotary beater until fluffy. Fold in berries and nuts. Pour into one large or individual molds and chill until firm. Unmold onto salad greens. Delightful spring salad for any occasion.

Serves 4 to 6

SWEET AND SOUR CHICKEN SALAD

    6 chicken breasts
    4 green onions
    1 package slivered almonds
    1 package wonton skins
    8 tablespoons sesame seeds
    1 head iceberg lettuce
    1 large can mandarin oranges
       Chopped cilantro

Season and bake chicken breasts in 350° oven til done. Shred into bite size pieces. Chop green onions, toast almonds in oven until brown, slice wonton skins in ½-inch pieces and deep fry until brown. Toast sesame seeds in oven, shred lettuce, drain oranges and reserve juice. Combine and serve with sweet and sour sauce.

Sauce
    ½ cup vinegar
    ½ cup catsup
    ½ cup water
    8 tablespoons sugar
    2 teaspoons soy sauce
    2 tablespoons cornstarch
    4 tablespoons water

Mix cornstarch with water, heat and add remaining ingredients. Stir until thickened. Let cool, add juice from oranges and pour over salad.

Serves 10 to 12. Approximate preparation time 1 hour. A delicious party dish.

LOVE BOAT SALAD

1 fresh pineapple
1 fresh papaya (or 1 can), cubed
1 orange, peeled and sectioned
1 banana, sliced
1 cup cooked ham, cubed (optional)
Chablis Fruit Salad Dressing (see recipe)
Poppy seeds
Maraschino cherries

Slice pineapple in half from top to bottom, leaving top on. Cut center from shell and discard core. Dice pineapple and combine with papaya, orange, banana, and ham. Dress with ½ cup Chablis Fruit Salad Dressing and spoon mixture back into pineapple shells. Garnish with poppy seeds and cherries. Chill and serve as summer salad or luau specialty.

Chablis Fruit Salad Dressing

½ cup Chablis or dry white wine or dry sherry
1 tablespoon sugar
1 teaspoon salt
2 tablespoons lemon juice
½ cup oil

Combine ingredients in a jar and shake until well blended. Refrigerate overnight to improve flavor. Shake again before serving over any fresh fruit or fruit-and-greens salad.

Variations: Substitute honey for sugar. Add ¼ teaspoon fresh onion juice. Add a little crushed fresh mint.

ANTICUCHO SAUCE

1 cup tarragon vinegar
1 cup bouillon, consomme or water
1½ teaspoons salt
¼ teaspoon saffron (this is the whole secret)
3 cloves garlic, minced
¼ cup olive oil
6 peppercorns
½ teaspoon chili powder

Marinate beef, shrimp or chicken (or a combination) overnight in all ingredients except oil. Thread on skewers, brush with oil, and grill, basting with marinade and oil.

THAI PEANUT SAUCE

  8 tablespoons crunchy peanut butter
  1 onion, finely chopped
  1 cup thick coconut milk
  1 tablespoon brown sugar
  1 teaspoon cayenne
  1 stalk lemon grass, finely chopped
  1 tablespoon fish sauce (Nam Pla)
  1 tablespoon dark sweet soy sauce

Combine all ingredients in a saucepan. Heat stirring constantly until boiling. Stir until smooth.

Serve as an accompaniment to your favorite Thai dishes.

WEDDING BRUNCH EGGS WITH SHRIMP AND DILL SAUCE

  16 hard-cooked eggs
  1½ pounds shrimp, cooked and cleaned (add 1 bunch dill to cooking water)
  ¼ cup butter
  1 bunch scallions, sliced thin, with 1-inch of green tops
  5 tablespoons flour
  2½ cups chicken broth (use 3 bouillon cubes and boiling water)
  ½ cup clam juice
  ½ cup dry white wine
  1 cup heavy cream
  4 tablespoons chopped fresh dill or 2 tablespoons dry dill weed
  1½ cups shredded Parmesan cheese

Melt butter in heavy saucepan, add onions and ½ cup cold water. Bring to a boil, then reduce heat to moderate and cook until all water has boiled away. Stir in flour and cook 3 minutes—do not brown. Add broth, wine, clam juice, cream and dill. Cook, whipping constantly with wire whisk until sauce comes to a boil. Stir in ½ of cheese. Take off heat. Set aside. Halve hard-cooked eggs lengthwise and place yolk side up in a flat 3-quart pyrex baking dish. Cover with layer of shrimp. Pour sauce on top of eggs and shrimp. Top with remaining cheese. Garnish with more dill. Refrigerate. Let stand at room temperature about 30 minutes, then bake uncovered at 400° for 20 minutes until hot and bubbly. Serve with rice.

Serves 12

BOURBON BAKED BEANS

4 (1-pound) cans baked beans
1 teaspoon dry mustard
½ cup chili sauce
1 tablespoon molasses
½ cup bourbon
½ cup strong coffee
Sliced canned pineapple
Brown sugar

Place all ingredients except pineapple and brown sugar in a buttered baking dish; cover and let stand at room temperature at least 3 hours. Place in a pre-heated 375° oven for 40 minutes, covered. Arrange pineapple on top and sprinkle with brown sugar and bake uncovered for another 40 minutes.

Serves 12 to 16

SQUASH CASSEROLE

3 pounds yellow squash, sliced
2 onions, chopped
2 carrots, sliced
2 cans cream of mushrooms soup
1 pint sour cream
1 small jar pimiento, chopped
1 stick butter
1 package bread dressing mix

Cook squash until al dente, with onions and carrots. Add soup, sour cream and pimientos. Melt butter, stir in dressing mix. Spread half the dressing mix in a greased casserole. Pour in squash mixture. Cover with remaining dressing mixture. Bake at 350° 45 to 50 minutes, or until hot and browned.

Serves 12

VEGETABLE LINGUINI

½ pound pasta
2 tablespoons butter or margarine
2 garlic cloves, crushed
3 green onions, chopped
2 small zucchini, sliced
¼ pound mushrooms, sliced
1 tomato, peeled and sliced
1 tablespoon chopped fresh basil (or 1 teaspoon dried)
Salt and pepper to taste
1 cup provolone cheese, grated
Parsley
Parmesan

In a large saucepan bring water to a boil. Cook pasta until al dente, about 11 minutes. Drain. Return to pan. Melt butter in a skillet. Saute garlic, onions, zucchini and mushrooms for 2 minutes. Add tomato, basil, salt and pepper. Cover and simmer 4 minutes. Add vegetable mixture and cheeses to the pasta and toss until the cheese is melted. Sprinkle with parsley. Bon Appetit

Serves 2 big eaters or 4 little ones-----yummers!

ARKANSAS CAMPERS' STEW

    2 large onions, chopped
    1 green pepper, chopped
    1 garlic clove, minced
      Oil
    2 pounds ground meat of your choice
    1 cup raw elbow macaroni
    2 (15-ounce) cans red beans
    2 (1-pound) cans stewed tomatoes
      Salt and pepper to taste

Saute onions, pepper and garlic in oil in your camp pot. Add meat and brown. Add remaining ingredients and simmer until macaroni is tender.

Serves 8

FATHER'S DAY BRISKET WITH BARBECUE SAUCE

    1½ teaspoons salt
    1½ teaspoons pepper
    2 tablespoons chili powder
    1 teaspoon crushed bay leaves
    2 tablespoons liquid smoke
    4 pounds beef brisket

Combine first 4 ingredients. Rub meat completely with liquid smoke. Place meat, fat side up, in large roasting pan. Sprinkle dry seasoning mixture on top. Cover tightly and bake 4 hours at 275° or until tender. Scrape seasoning off and cut meat in very thin slices across the grain. Serve with Barbecue Sauce.

Barbecue Sauce

    3 tablespoons brown sugar
    1 (14-ounce) bottle catsup
    ½ cup water
    2 tablespoons liquid smoke
      Salt and pepper to taste
    4 tablespoons Worcestershire sauce
    3 teaspoons dry mustard
    2 teaspoons celery seed
    6 tablespoons butter
    ¼ teaspoon cayenne pepper

Combine all ingredients. Bring to a boil, stirring occasionally. Cook for 10 minutes. Serve with sliced brisket.

Serves 6. This is absolutely dynamite served on onion rolls.

BARBECUED BONELESS CHICKEN BREAST WITH CILANTRO-YOGURT SAUCE

8 boneless chicken breast
  halves, skinned
½ cup olive oil
2 tablespoons lemon juice

3 teaspoons chopped
  tarragon or 1 teaspoon
  dried
Salt and pepper to taste
8 lime wedges

Cilantro-Yogurt Sauce

1 cup plain yogurt
3 tablespoons cilantro,
  minced

3 tablespoons mint, chopped
½ teaspoon ground cumin

Prepare Cilantro-Yogurt Sauce and set aside. Rinse chicken, pat dry with paper towels. Place chicken breasts one at a time between 2 pieces of plastic wrap. Pound with a mallet until meat is ¼ inch throughout. Arrange breasts, in a single layer, in a large flat baking dish. In a medium sized bowl, whisk remaining ingredients except the lime wedges. Pour over chicken. Turn chicken over to coat both sides, cover. Refrigerate 2 hours at least. Overnight is much better. Take from fridge about 30 minutes before barbecuing. Reserve marinade.

Grill about 6 minutes turning chicken and brushing with reserved marinade every 2 minutes. Don't overcook. Place chicken on a serving platter, place a spoonful of Cilantro-yogurt sauce on each piece. Arrange lime wedges around edge of platter. Pour remaining sauce into a serving bowl. Serve separately. Serves 4 to 8 depending on your family. . . . .

CHICKEN BREASTS ARROWHEAD

6 chicken breasts, boned,
  skinned and flattened
6 slices sugar cured ham
6 slices Monterey Jack
  cheese
6 pats butter
  Beaten egg
  Oil
1 pinch thyme
1 teaspoon dry mustard

Salt and cayenne pepper
  to taste
Sauterne wine to taste
¼ cup chopped celery
¼ cup chopped mushrooms,
  sauteed
¼ cup chopped
  onions, sauteed
  sauteed
2 cups prepared white sauce

Lay out flattened chicken breasts on a flat surface. Place 1 slice ham on each, place 1 slice cheese on the ham, and place 1 pat butter on the cheese. Fold up sides and secure with toothpick inserted through the chicken breast. Dip chicken rolls in egg and submerge in 350° oil until brown and crisp. Place all fried chicken rolls on a baking sheet and bake in a 350° oven for 15 to 20 minutes, or until done. To prepare sauce, add thyme, dry mustard, salt, papper, wine, celery, mushrooms and onions to white sauce. Serve over chicken rolls. Lovely served with pilaf or whole red potatoes.

Yield 4 to 6 servings

BLACKENED REDFISH

  *6 (8 to 10-ounce) fish fillets, cut about ½-inch thick
  ¾ pound (3 sticks) unsalted butter, melted in a skillet
  1 tablespoon sweet paprika
  2½ teaspoons salt
  1 teaspoon garlic powder
  1 teaspoon ground red pepper (preferably cayenne)
  ¾ teaspoon white & black pepper
  1 teaspoon onion powder
  ½ teaspoon dried thyme leaves
  ½ teaspoon dried oregano leaves

*Note: Redfish and pompano are ideal for this method of cooking. If tilefish is used, you may have to split the fillets in half horizontally to have the proper thickness. If you can't get any of these fish, salmon steaks or red snapper fillets can be substituted. In any case, the fillets or steaks must not be more than ¾-inch thick.

Heat a large cast-iron skillet over very high heat until it is beyond the smoking stage and you see white ash in the skillet bottom (at least 10 minutes). Meanwhile, pour 2 tablespoons of melted butter in each of 6 small ramekins; set aside and keep warm. Reserve the remaining butter in its skillet. Heat the serving plates in a 250° oven.

Thoroughly combine the remaining ingredients in a small bowl. Dip each fillet in the reserved melted butter, so that both sides are well coated; sprinkle seasoning mix generously and evenly on both sides of the fillets, patting it in by hand. Place in the hot skillet and pour 1 teaspoon melted butter on top of each fillet (be careful, as butter may flame up). Cook, uncovered, over the same high heat until the underside looks charred, about 2 minutes (the time will vary according to the fillets' thickness and the heat of the skillet). Turn the fish over and again pour 1 teaspoon butter on top; cook until fish is done, about 2 minutes more. Repeat with remaining fillets. Serve each fillet while piping hot. To serve, place one fillet and a ramekin of butter on each heated serving plate.
Serves 6

BARBECUED CHICKEN LEGS

  8 chicken legs
  1 tablespoon sugar
  1 teaspoon dry mustard
  1 teaspoon powdered ginger
  ½ cup apple juice

  ⅓ cup soy sauce
  ¼ cup lemon juice
  3 cloves garlic, chopped
  ½ cup cooking oil

Combine the seasoning ingredients. Pour over chicken legs and marinate overnight in the refrigerator. Place chicken in a spit basket. Cook at LOW about 35 minutes with the lid in the 1-inch position. Baste with marinade during cooking to brown. Heat any remaining marinade as a sauce, if desired.

Serves 4

ZUCCHINI NUT BREAD

   3 eggs
   1 cup vegetable oil
   2 cups sugar
   3 cups flour
   1 teaspoon salt
   1 teaspoon baking soda
  ¼ teaspoon baking powder
   1 teaspoon cinnamon
   2 cups zucchini, grated
   2 teaspoons vanilla
   1 cup nuts

Beat eggs, oil and sugar together. Add the flour, salt, soda, baking powder and cinnamon. Add the zucchini, vanilla and mix well. Fold in chopped nuts. Pour in 3 or 4 small pans $7 \times 3 \times 2\frac{1}{4}$ inches (well greased). Bake at 325° for 1 hour or until center tests done. Cool in pans 10 minutes then remove and cool on racks.

Freezes well.

PEACH SHORTCAKE

   4 cups sliced peaches, sprinkled with lemon juice and ⅓ cup sugar
  ¼ cup sugar
 1¾ cups all purpose flour
  ½ cup shortening
  ⅓ cup milk
   1 egg
   1 tablespoon baking powder
   1 teaspoon grated lemon peel
     Dash of salt
   1 cup heavy cream, whipped

Preheat oven to 450°. Grease a 9-inch round cake pan. Into a bowl, place sugar, flour, shortening, milk, egg, baking powder, lemon peel and salt. With mixer at medium speed, beat mixture until well combined and a soft dough forms. Pat dough evenly into pan. Bake 15 minutes, or until golden. Invert onto a platter. With a long sharp knife, split hot shortcake horizontally. Spread cut surfaces with butter. Place bottom half onto a serving platter, and cover with half the peaches, top with other cake half. Spoon remaining peaches over top. Refrigerate. When ready to serve, spread whipped cream over peaches and garnish with a few peach slices.

It should serve 8 but never does. . . . .

PEACH PECAN PIE

    4 cups peaches, peeled and sliced
    ½ cup sugar
    2 tablespoons tapioca
    1 teaspoon lemon juice
    ¼ teaspoon vanilla
    ¼ cup brown sugar
    ¼ cup flour
    ½ cup pecans, chopped
    ¼ cup butter
    1 (9-inch) unbaked pastry shell

Combine the first 5 ingredients and let stand 30 minutes. Combine brown sugar, flour, nuts and butter. Place ½ the nut mixture over the bottom of the crust. Add peach mixture. Sprinkle remaining nut mixture over the peaches. Bake at 425° for 10 minutes, lower your heat to 325° and bake 20 minutes more.

Serves 8

DAD'S DAY PIE

Crust

    2 squares baking chocolate
    2 tablespoons butter
    2 tablespoons hot milk or water
    ⅔ cup powdered sugar, sifted
    1½ cups coconut, plain or toasted

Melt chocolate and butter, stir until well blended. Combine milk or water and sugar. Add to chocolate mixture, add coconut. Spread on bottom and sides of a greased 9-inch pie pan. Chill until firm.

Filling

    1½ cups cream, whipped
    ¼ cup brandy
    ¼ cup Kahlua
    1 pint or more rich chocolate ice cream
    Prepared crust

Fold brandy and Kahlua into the whipped cream. Combine with softened ice cream. Pour into prepared crust. Top with a few extra crumbs for garnish. Freeze overnight.

Serves 10 unless you have any football players in the crowd.

CHAMPAGNE CAKE

2¾ cups sifted flour
3 teaspoons baking powder
1½ cups sugar
6 egg whites
   Fondant frosting

6 large marshmallows, quartered
1 teaspoon salt
⅔ cups shortening
¾ cup champagne
   Coconut filling

Resift flour with baking powder and salt. Cream shortening with 1 cup sugar until light and fluffy. Blend in flour mixture and Champagne alternately, mixing to a smooth batter. Beat egg whites until stiff. Gradually beat in remaining ½ cup sugar, continuing to beat to a stiff meringue. Fold about half the meringue into batter, mixing thoroughly with wire whip. Gently fold in remaining meringue. Turn into 2 greased and floured 9-inch layer cake pans. Bake at 350° 25 to 30 minutes, just until cake tests done. Let stand 10 minutes, then turn out onto wire racks to cool.

When layers are cold, put together with Coconut Filling between layers. Remove ⅔ cup Fondant Frosting and spread a thin layer smoothly over top and sides. This seals any crumbs. Pour about ½ cup additional frosting over top of cake and spread quickly to a smooth layer. Cover sides of cake with a second layer of frosting. Dip slices of marshmallow in remaining frosting to coat both sides and set them at random over top and sides of cake.

Coconut Filling

¼ cup butter or margarine
16 large marshmallows, quartered
1 tablespoon white wine
1 cup flaked coconut

Combine butter, marshmallows and wine in top of double boiler. Set over boiling water and stir occasionally until marshmallows are melted. Remove from heat and stir in coconut. Cool until thick enough to spread.

Fondant Frosting

1 pound powdered sugar
¼ cup water
   Dash salt
2–3 drops red food color, optional
¼ cup light corn syrup
1½ teaspoons vanilla
   Few drops almond flavoring

Sift sugar into top of double boiler. Add corn syrup and water. Stir over boiling water until smooth. Blend in vanilla, salt and almond flavoring. Stir in food color if desired. Keep frosting warm while using so it spreads smoothly. For a 3-tiered cake, use a fruitcake for the top layer. This will combine in one cake the tradition of the brides' white cake and the bridegroom's dark cake. The fruit cake must, of course, be smaller than the layer on which it rests. It is frosted exactly the same as the other layers.

WHITE SANDTORTE

    2 cups butter
    3 cups sugar
    6 eggs
    1 cup sour cream
    3 cups flour
    ½ teaspoon baking powder
 1½ teaspoons vanilla
    Confectioners sugar

Cream butter and sugar; add eggs and sour cream, beating until very light and fluffy. Sift flour and baking powder together; stir into creamed mixture. Blend in vanilla. Pour into well-buttered 2½-quart mold or 9-inch tube pan. Bake at 350° for 1 hour 25 minutes or until done. Cool. Wrap for 24 hours. Sprinkle with confectioners sugar before serving.

GINGERBREAD MUFFINS

    1 cup rolled oats
    1 cup walnuts, chopped
    2 tablespoons brown sugar
    1 cup raisins
    1 cup plus 2 tablespoons water
    1 (14-ounce) package gingerbread cake mix

In a small bowl, combine 2 tablespoons each of the oats, and walnuts and sugar. Set aside. In a large bowl, combine the remaining oats, the raisins and water, mix to blend. Stir in the gingerbread mix and the remaining walnuts. Mix to blend. Spoon into 12, greased or paper-lined muffin tins. Sprinkle tops with sugar mixture. Bake in center of oven at 400° 15 to 20 minutes, or until done. Serve warm.

Makes 1 dozen muffins for the cherubs in your family.

RECEPTION MINTS

    1 (1-pound) box confections' sugar minus ¼ cup
    ¼ cup margarine, melted
    7 drops red food coloring
    7 drops oil of peppermint
    3 tablespoons evaporated milk

Combine sugar, margarine, coloring and oil of peppermint. Mix with fork until sugar is moistened. Add 2½ to 3 tablespoons milk, working in with hands until candy is smooth and of proper consistency for molding. Do not get too moist. Pinch off small amounts; press into rubber molds, remove immediately.

TRADITIONAL WEDDING CAKE WITH ORNAMENTAL FROSTING

5¼ cups sifted cake flour
6 teaspoons baking powder
2 teaspoons salt
8 egg whites
1½ teaspoons orange extract
1 cup shortening at room temperature
1 teaspoon almond extract
3 cups sugar
2 cups milk
Ornamental Forsting

Mix flour, baking powder, salt and 2 cups sugar. Beat egg whites in a large bowl until frothy. Gradually add remaining sugar, beating until meringue holds soft peaks. Stir shortening in mixing bowl just to soften. Sift in dry ingredients. Add 1½ cups of the milk and the flavorings. Mix until all the flour is dampened. Then beat for 2 minutes at low speed in electric mixer. Add remaining milk and egg whites and beat for 1 minute more.

Line bottoms of 1 square (10 × 10 × 2 inches) and 2 squares (8 × 8 × 2 inches each) pans with paper. Pour batter into pans to equal depths. Bake in preheated oven at 325° for 45 minutes or until done. Cool on racks. When cold, brush cakes to remove any loose crumbs. Trim one of the 8-inch cakes to make a 5-inch square. Put 10-inch cake on a large flat tray or ornamental plate. Spread top and sides with a thin layer of ornamental frosting. Cover top of cake smoothly with more frosting. Center 8-inch cake on top of 10-inch cake and frost. Center 5-inch cake on 8-inch cake and frost. Spread frosting over entire cake to give a flat, even base for decoration. Force remaining frosting through a pastry tube to make flowers, garlands, etc.

Serves 50

ORNAMENTAL FROSTING

½ cup soft butter or margarine
½ teaspoon salt
12 cups sifted confectioners sugar (3 pounds)
¼ cup light cream
5 egg whites (unbeaten)
2 teaspoons vanilla extract

Cream butter. Add salt and half of the sugar gradually, blending after each addition. Add remaining sugar, alternately with the egg whites first, then with the cream until you reach the right consistency for spreading. Beat after each addition until smooth. Add vanilla and blend. While frosting cake, keep bowl of frosting covered with a damp dish cloth to help prevent evaporation. Will frost one 10 × 10 × 2-inch cake and two 8 × 8 × 2-inch cakes; enough remainder for decoration.

GROOM'S CAKE

    4 cups sifted all purpose flour
    1 teaspoon baking powder
    ½ teaspoon cinnamon
    ½ teaspoon ground cloves
    ½ teaspoon mace
    2 cups butter or margarine
    1 pound brown sugar, firmly packed (2¼ cups)
   10 eggs, well beaten
    ½ pound candied cherries
    2 cups nuts, chopped
    1 cup honey
    1 cup molasses
    ½ pound candied pineapple
    1 pound dates, seeded and sliced
    1 pound seedless raisins
    1 pound seedless currants
    ½ pound citron, thinly sliced
    ¼ pound candied orange peel
    ¼ pound candied lemon peel
    ½ cup cider or sweet sherry

Sift dry ingredients together 3 times. Cream butter or margarine. Gradually add sugar, cream until light and fluffy. Add eggs, fruits, peels, nuts, honey, molasses, and cider or wine.

Gradually add sifted dry ingredients, beating after each addition until well blended. Spoon into 3 loaf pans, 10×5×3 inches that have been greased, lined with heavy paper and greased again.

Bake in a preheated oven at 250° for 3½ to 4 hours, or until done. Many of my brides put a little piece of Groom's cake in a little gift box to be taken home as a memento of the wedding. Beautiful spice cake!

Serves 80 or more depending on the size of the slices.

FRESH FRUIT RUMPOT

Thoroughly wash a large crock or glass container. Fill ¼ full of fresh strawberries and enough rum to cover. (They will probably float for a day or to before sinking.) Add washed cherries, raspberries, plums, apricots, peaches or pears to three-fourths full. Cover with sugar to almost full and top with enough rum to fill. Cover jar air-tight and allow six weeks for mixture to mature. Stir well before serving. Serve as a dessert, fruit cocktail, with fruit salad or with ice cream and cake.

Variations: Use brandy instead of rum, honey instead of sugar.

Note
Fresh fruit may be added after each serving. Be sure to add equal parts of fruit, sugar and enough rum to cover. Do **not** use apples, black currants, bananas or blackberries.

RED RASPBERRY JAM

    2 quarts red raspberries
 6½ cups sugar
    2 scant teaspoons lemon juice
  ½ bottle liquid pectin

Select berries that are ripe, but not too ripe, for a better flavored jam. Grind or crush the berries. Put half the berries through a sieve to remove seeds. Combine 4 cups ground raspberries, sugar and lemon juice in a 6-quart kettle. Mix thoroughly. Place on high heat and bring to a full rolling boil. Boil hard for 1 minute, stirring constantly. Remove from heat. Immediately stir in pectin. Skim off foam with a round of waxed paper. Then use a metal spoon to remove the skim particles that are left. Stir for 5 minutes to prevent floating fruit. Seal half-pint jars or jelly glasses with paraffin.

INSTANT MICRO BERRY JAM

 1½ cups whole berries
  ¾ cup sugar
    2 teaspoons lemon juice
  ¼ teaspoon butter or margarine

Wash berries, hull and crush in a bowl. You should have 1 cup crushed berries. In a 3-quart casserole, stir together the berries, sugar, lemon juice and butter. Cook, uncovered, in the microwave on High for 8 minutes, stirring every 2 minutes until it reaches its desired thickness. Store in covered jar in the refrigerator.

Makes 1 cup

MULTI FRUIT JAM

    4 cups fresh fruit or berries (your choice peaches, nectarines,
      cherries, strawberries, raspberries or blackberries) crushed
    1 box (1¾-ounce) powdered pectin
    2 cups mild flavored honey
    2 tablespoons lemon juice

In a large saucepan combine crushed fruit and pectin. Bring to a full rolling boil. Boil hard 1 minutes, stirring constantly. Add honey and lemon juice. Return to a full rolling boil. Boil hard for 5 minutes, stirring constantly. Remove from heat. Skim off foam. Ladle into 5 (½-pint) jars that have been sterilized.

Terrific recipe when the fresh fruit hits the markets.

JULY

The Fourth of July is here. Happy Birthday, America and
of course there is nothing more American than the family
cookout or picnic. This is one of my favorite chapters because
we have enjoyed each of these recipes on so many occasions.
Enjoy!

DELICIOUS VEGETABLE DIP

½ pint sour cream
½ cup mayonnaise
1 teaspoon sugar
1 teaspoon seasoned salt
Pepper to taste
1 clove minced garlic
¼ cup green onion minced
¼ cup minced radishes
¼ cup minced and drained cucumbers
¼ cup minced green pepper

Mix all ingredients thoroughly, except vegetables. When well blended, stir in remaining ingredients. Serve in dish surrounded by your favorite fresh vegetables. (Celery, radishes, bell peppers, cucumbers, etc.)

SMOKED SALMON SPREAD

½ pound smoked salmon
1 medium onion, finely minced
1 tablespoon capers
2 teaspoons chopped fresh dill, or 1 teaspoon dried dill
½ cup sour cream
½ cup mayonnaise
freshly ground black pepper
chopped parsley

Chop the salmon and mix with the minced onion, capers, dill, sour cream, and mayonnaise. Blend well and spoon into a serving bowl. Top with pepper and chopped parsley. Cover and chill. Serve with thin slices of rye or pumpernickel.

Serves 8

SOUR CREAM HAM DIP

½ cup firmly packed ground cooked ham
1¼ teaspoons prepared mustard
1 tablespoon green onion (chopped)
1 cup dairy sour cream
1¼ teaspoons dry sherry

Mix all ingredients and chill until ready to use.

Serves 8

BACON DIP

> 1 package (8-ounce) cream cheese
> 3 tablespoons finely chopped chives or green onions
> 1 cup dairy sour cream
> 1 teaspoon fresh horseradish
>   Dash of garlic salt
>   Cayenne to taste
> 6 bacon strips, cooked crisp and crumbled

Soften cheese at room temperature. Blend with remaining ingredients and chill until ready to serve.

Makes about 3 cups

PAPAYA MILK SHAKE

> 2 large ripe papayas
> ⅔ cup sugar
> ¼ cup lemon or lime juice
> 3 cups milk
> 1 teaspoon nutmeg
> 1 cup cracked ice

Peel papayas cut in half remove the seeds and mash. Combine all the ingredients but the nutmeg in a blender. Give it a good whirl and serve it in a chilled glass topped with nutmeg.

Serves 4

PARTY BEEF STICK

> 5 pounds hamburger
> 5 teaspoons Morton Quick Cure Salt (rounded teaspoon)
> 3 teaspoons mustard seed
> 3 teaspoons coarse ground pepper
> 3 teaspoons garlic powder
> 1 teaspoon onion powder (optional)
> 1½ teaspoons hickory liquid smoke

Combine all ingredients and mix well in a glass bowl. Refrigerate for 4 days. Mix well each day. Knead and roll into 4 rolls. Bake on a foil covered cookie sheet at 140° for 8 hours, turning occasionally with your hands. Drain on paper towels and rub with additional liquid smoke.

Be sure you use a meat thermometer to make sure the inside temperature is 140°.

GREAT FOR ALL HOLIDAY PARTIES

COLD BRISKET OF BEEF SANDWICHES

    5 pounds beef brisket
1½ teaspoons salt
    2 tablespoons Worcestershire sauce
    2 tablespoons Tamari (natural soy sauce)
    ½ cup dry white wine
    1 tablespoon honey
    ½ cup water
    ¼ teaspoon cinnamon
    1 bay leaf
    1 large onion, peeled and cut
 10 onion buns or hard rolls

Trim excess fat and rub salt on meat. Place in heavy duty foil. Combine Worcestershire sauce, honey, cinnamon and Tamari. Brush over meat. Pour wine and water over meat. Add bay leaf and onion. Wrap and seal in foil. Bake at 350° for 3 to 4 hours. Cool.

Sour Cream Horseradish Sauce

    ½ cup sour cream
    2 tablespoons horseradish
    1 tablespoon chopped parsley
    1 teaspoon grated onion
    ½ teaspoon lemon juice
      Salt to taste

Combine and spread on onion buns or hard rolls. Fill with cold brisket. Wrap and take to picnic site.

Makes 10 Sandwiches

HOME SALAD BAR

Lettuce—Iceberg and
  Romaine
Spinach
Cherry Tomatoes
Sliced Red Onions
Sliced Cucumbers
Pickled Beets
Garbanzo Beans
Kidney Beans
Pickled 3-Bean Salad
Sliced Carrots
Radishes
Mushrooms
Bean Sprouts

Salad Dressings
Oil and Vinegar
Bleu/Roquefort
Thousand Island

Toppings
Croutons
Bacon Bits
Chopped Egg
Fresh-ground Pepper
Parmesan Cheese
Baby Shrimp or Flaked
  Crab

KIWI CHICKEN SALAD

 2 cups cubed cooked chicken or turkey
 1 (4-ounce) jar pimientos, sliced
 ½ cup thinly sliced celery
 2 or 3 kiwis, peeled, sliced and quartered

Chill all ingredients before assembling. Combine all ingredients in a lettuce lined bowl. Pour over KIWI DRESSING to moisten well.

Kiwi Dressing

 ½ cup white wine vinegar
 ¼ cup sugar
 1 teaspoon Dijon mustard
 1 kiwi peeled and cubed
 Salt to taste
 Dash of pepper
 1 cup oil

Place all ingredients but oil in a blender. Blend on high speed, gradually adding oil with blender on.

Chill before using.

Makes about 2¼ cups   Serves 4

COLE SLAW FOR THE CROWD

 3 pounds cabbage, sliced thinly
 2 yellow onions, sliced thinly
 1 carrot, shredded
 1½ cups sugar
 2 teaspoons celery seed

Layer cabbage, onions and carrot in a large bowl. Sprinkle over sugar and celery seeds.

Marinade

 1 cup oil
 1 cup cider vinegar
 Salt to taste

Bring the marinade to a boil. Boil for 2 minutes. Pour over cabbage. Cover bowl tightly and chill. Will last 9 days in the fridge and serve 12 amply.

This is a must for any family get together in the summer. Cole slaw was always a staple in Nebraska at any picnic, and this salad travels well.

FRESH FRUIT SALAD

          2 cups boiling water
          2 (3-ounce) packages apple jello
          1 envelope unflavored gelatin
        ¼ cup water
        ¾ cup sugar
          5 or 6 peaches, sliced and sweetened
      1½ cups sliced green grapes
          4 oranges, sectioned
          3 pears, diced
          3 bananas, diced
          1 cantaloupe, cut into balls
          1 basket blueberries
             Juice from the fresh fruits
        ½ pint whipping cream, whipped and sweetened
             Mayonnaise to taste

Pour boiling water over packages of the apple jello. Add unflavored gelatin which has been softened in ¼ cup water.

Add sugar and fruit to gelatin. Add enough water to fruit juices to make 2 cups and stir into gelatin mixture. Pour into favorite molds and chill until set.

Combine the whipped cream and mayonnaise for dressing. When ready to serve, unmold salad and top with the dressing.

Serves 30

This is fabulous for your 4th of July picnic. It serves the whole family and is wonderful with any type of barbecue.

BAKED PAPAYA SALAD

          3 ripe papayas, halved, peeled and seeded
        ¾ cup cottage cheese
        ¾ cup cream cheese
          1 teaspoon curry
          4 tablespoons mango chutney
          2 tablespoons raisins
        ½ cup water chestnuts, thinly sliced
             Butter
             Cinnamon or cinnamon sugar
             Butter lettuce leaves

Blend together the cheeses. Stir in seasonings, raisins and water chestnuts. Fill the papayas with this mixture. Place on baking sheet and dot with butter. Sprinkle with cinnamon. Bake at 450° for 15 to 20 minutes. Serve on butter lettuce.

Serves 6

EASTERN POTATO SALAD

¼ cup olive oil
2 tablespoons vinegar
1½ teaspoons salt
¼ teaspoon pepper
4 cups hot sliced cooked potatoes
1 cup ripe olives, cut into large pieces
2 eggs, hard-cooked and diced
1 cup sliced celery
¼ cup chopped dill pickle
¼ cup diced pimientos
1 small onion, minced
½ cup mayonnaise

Combine oil, vinegar, salt and pepper. Pour over potatoes; set aside to cool. When cool, add remaining ingredients; toss. Chill until serving time.

Serves 8

OLD FASHIONED COLE SLAW FOR 100

1 gallon prepared salad dressing
1 cup prepared mustard
1 cup shredded carrot
15 heads green cabbage, shredded
1 head red cabbage, shredded
Paprika
Parsley

Mix salad dressing and mustard. Combine with shredded cabbage and toss until well coated. Refrigerate at least one hour. Toss again at serving time and garnish with paprika and parsley.

Makes 100 3-ounce servings

FRESH MUSHROOM SALAD

2 pounds mushrooms, sliced
½ cup celery, diced
½ cup green pepper, diced
1 tablespoon onion, grated
1 clove garlic, crushed
Salt and pepper to taste
3 tablespoons lemon juice
3 tablespoons olive oil
1 tablespoon white vinegar
Lettuce

Toss mushrooms with all the ingredients and chill. Drain the marinade before serving on a bed of lettuce. Can decorate with crumbled egg yolk.

Serves 6

RELLENO CASSEROLE

    2 to 4 cans (4-ounces each) green chiles
    1 pound cheddar cheese
    1 pound jack cheese
    1 (16-ounce) can tomato sauce
    4 eggs, separated
    1 large can evaporated milk
    3 tablespoons flour
      Salt and pepper to taste

Beat egg yolks, add milk, flour, salt and pepper. Add stiffly beaten egg whites.

Remove seeds and flatten chiles. Slice cheese very thick. Layer in a casserole, chiles, cheddar slices, chiles, jack slices. Pour egg-milk mixture over all.

Bake covered in 325° oven for 1 hour. Pour tomato sauce to cover casserole. Bake another half hour, uncovered. Spoon out or cut in wedges to serve.

This is a good side dish with ham or beef. For a complete dinner, add a bottom layer of refried beans.

Serves 6 to 8

PICKLED RED BEET EGGS

    1 (1-pound, 4-ounce) can beets
    1 cup vinegar
  ½ cup sugar
    1 teaspoon salt
    4 cloves
      2-inch stick cinnamon
    6 hard-cooked eggs in their shells

Drain the beets and measure the juice. Add enough water to make 1 cup. To this liquid add the vinegar, sugar, salt and spices. Bring to a boil. Pour the hot liquid over the beets. Let stand 24 hours. After the beets have been pickled, remove them, and replace them with the eggs that have not been shelled. Let the eggs stand in the juice for 8 hours so that the flavor penetrates the whole egg.

Serves 6

This is just down home good.

SUMMER VEGETABLES

ΒΌ cup sour cream or yogurt
1 tablespoon green onion, chopped
2 medium zucchini, cut into 3-inch fingers
2 crookneck squash cut into ΒΌ-inch slices
2 medium ears of corn cut into 2-inch cobettes
1 cup broccoli flowerettes
ΒΌ cup water
3 tablespoons margarine
12 cherry tomatoes, cut into half
Salt and Pepper to taste
Parmesan cheese

Combine sour cream and green onions and set aside. Place zucchini and crookneck squash, corn and broccoli in a skillet. Add water and margarine, cover and simmer 5 minutes. Add tomatoes, salt and pepper. Cover and simmer 1 minute more, shaking the pan now and then during the cooking time. Sprinkle with Parmesan cheese and serve with sour cream mixture.

Serves 4

BARBECUED BEANS FOR THE GANG

1 (1-pound) can pinto beans
1 (1-pound) can French style green beans, drained
1 (1-pound) can kidney beans, drained
1 (1-pound) can pork and beans, drained
1 bell pepper, chopped
1 onion, chopped
1 tablespoon brown sugar
Β½ pound bacon, chopped
1 (12-ounce) bottle hot catsup

Mix everything together in a casserole and bake in a 300° oven for 3 to 4 hours.

Serves the whole family

There's no place like home
Except Grandma's

CHEESE AND BEAN CASSEROLE

    4 slices bacon
    1 medium onion, minced
    1 (1-pound) can baked beans
    1 (1-pound) can kidney beans, drained
    1 (1-pound) can lima beans, drained
    ½ pound cheddar cheese, cubed
    ½ cup brown sugar, packed
    ⅓ cup catsup
    2 teaspoons Worcestershire
    Parmesan for garnish

Cook the bacon until crisp, drain and crumble. Cook the onion in the bacon fat until golden. Remove from the heat and stir in beans, cheese, sugar, catsup and Worcestershire. Mix gently and spoon into a buttered casserole. Sprinkle with Parmesan. Bake at 350° for 30 minutes.

Serves 10

FLANK STEAK FOR THE FOURTH

    1½ pounds flank steak
    3 tablespoons sesame seed
    3 tablespoons oil
    ¼ cup soy sauce
    ½ cup green onions, chopped with green tops
    2 cloves garlic, crushed
    ½ teaspoon ground ginger
    1 tablespoon brown sugar

Score the steak and leave whole. Combine remaining ingredients and marinate steak in this mixture for at least 1 hour. Barbecue or broil 4 minutes then turn and cook 3 minutes on the other side. Slice on the diagonal.

Serves 4

LEMON MAYONNAISE

This is a way to spiff up commercial mayonnaise to make it taste more like homemade.

    1 cup mayonnaise
    1 tablespoon capers or more if you like
    ⅓ cup lemon juice
    ½ teaspoon dry mustard
    1 teaspoon salt or to taste
    ½ teaspoon white pepper

Combine all the ingredients thoroughly. Store in a jar with a tight fitting lid and refrigerate. Simply super.

Makes 1 large cup

TERIYAKI OF YOUR CHOICE

    1 cup soy sauce (may use regular or mild)
    ¾ cup mild flavored honey
    1 tablespoon fresh ginger, grated or 1 teaspoon ground
    1 to 2 cloves garlic, crushed
    2 pounds cubed meat of your choice
      Whole water chestnuts
      Green pepper
      Pineapple chunks

Combine the first 4 ingredients and pour over meat and let marinate 4 to 8 hours. Alternate meat on bamboo or metal skewers with water chestnuts, green pepper and pineapple chunks. Broil or barbecue to desired doneness.

Serves 6

Serve with rice and a fresh steamed vegetable and a small piece of fresh fruit.

PINEAPPLE-BEEF TERIYAKI KEBOBS

    1½ pounds sirloin cut into 1-inch pieces
     2 cups fresh pineapple cut into 1-inch cubes
    ½ cup soy sauce
    ¼ cup brown sugar
     2 tablespoons lemon juice
     1 teaspoon grated fresh ginger (if using dry ¼ teaspoon)
     2 cloves garlic, minced
     1 tablespoon oil

Cut meat into 1-inch cubes. Mix remaining ingredients and pour over meat and pineapple. Marinate at least 1 hour. Give it a stir now and then. Thread meat and pineapple on skewers alternately. Barbecue 2 to 4 inches from the coals 5 to 7 minutes. Baste with marinade during cooking process. Decorate the end of the skewer with a flower.

Serves 4 to 6

Having someplace to go is home
Having someone to love is family
Having both is a blessing

TANGY BEEF AND CUCUMBER SALAD

    1 pound beef sirloin steak, boneless (cut 1½ inches thick)
    1 medium sized cucumber, peeled
    ¼ cup thinly sliced red onion
    ¼ cup lime juice
    2 tablespoons soy sauce or fish sauce
    ½ teaspoon sesame oil
    ¼ to ½ teaspoon cayenne pepper
    1 head butter lettuce, leaves separated, washed and chilled
    1 teaspoon sesame seeds
      Mint or cilantro sprigs (garnish)
      Salt and pepper to taste

Slash fat on edge of steak at 2-inch intervals. Place steak on grill over medium-hot Kingsford charcoal briquets. Cook 6 to 8 minutes on each side or until done. Cut meat across the grain into thin slices. Cut cucumber in half lengthwise, scoop out seeds and slice thinly. Mix steak, cucumber, onion, lime juice, soy sauce, sesame and cayenne pepper in a large bowl and cover. Refrigerate at least 1 hour, no longer than 6 hours. Arrange lettuce leaves on a platter. Arrange beef mixture on leaves; garnish with sesame seed and mint. Serve as a salad or roll beef mixture in lettuce leaves to eat.

Makes 4 servings

PEPPER LAMB CHOPS

    4 sweet red peppers
    4 lamb chops, 1-inch thick
    1 teaspoon Worcestershire sauce
    1 teaspoon vinegar
    1 tablespoon oil
    2 cloves garlic, crushed
    3 tablespoons olive oil

Spear each pepper on a fork and hold over a hot grill or gas flame, or place peppers in a greased shallow baking dish and bake in a 450° oven, until skins wrinkle. Place peppers in cold water and peel off skins. Cut out stems and remove seeds and ribs, keeping peppers whole. Have peppers at room temperature before cooking. Rub lamb chops on both sides with Worcestershire sauce, vinegar and oil. Let stand at room temperature for 30 minutes. Place a skillet at the edge of the grill pop in olive oil and garlic. Add prepared peppers and saute slowly while barbecueing the chops. Place chops on the grill and barbecue 8 minutes on each side for rare and 12 minutes on each side for well. Serve a pepper on each chop. Yummers.

Serves 4

PARTY KEBOBS

   4 pounds sirloin or top round steak ¾ to 1 inch thick, cut into
     cubes
  16 to 20 mushrooms
  16 to 20 prunes, pitted
   3 ounces Bleu cheese
   2 tablespoons sour cream
   6 to 7 pieces of bacon, cut into thirds
   ½ cup beer
   ½ cup cooking oil

Mix Bleu cheese and sour cream together. Stuff each prune with cheese mixture and wrap a piece of bacon around prune, securing with a small wooden pick. Skewer beef chunks, mushrooms and prunes alternately. Place in shallow glass baking dish. Mix together beer and oil. Pour over kebobs. Let marinate 1 hour before cooking, turning occasionally. Preheat electric griddle with heat control set at 350°. Grease the griddle surface with oil. Place on grill and cook about 10 minutes, turning frequently, or until meat is browned and cooked to desired doneness. Also barbecue or broil!

Serves 8 to 10

BOURBON BARBECUED BEEF ROAST

   ½ cup oil
   ½ cup bourbon
   1 onion, chopped
   2 cloves garlic, crushed
   1 teaspoon pepper
   1 teaspoon dry mustard
   ¼ cup red wine vinegar
   1 (5 to 6 pound) rolled roast

Combine marinade ingredients in a plastic bag or dish. Pour over meat and let marinate at least 1 hour at room temperature. Be sure and turn meat at least 2 to 3 times. Drain meat and reserve marinade. Place meat on spit and be sure roast is balanced. Barbecue over medium coals for 1½ hours for rare or 2½ hours for well. Brush with reserved marinade the last 30 minutes of cooking. Can serve the marinade as a table sauce. Great for leftover sandwiches.

Serves 8 to 10

NEW YORK STYLE BARBECUED CHICKEN

    3 cloves garlic, minced
    ½ teaspoon oregano
    ½ teaspoon paprika
    1 tablespoon lemon juice
    8 pieces of chicken of your choice
    3 tablespoons oil
    1 teaspoon oregano
    ⅓ cup catsup
    ⅓ cup vinegar
    1 small onion, minced

Combine garlic, oregano, paprika and lemon juice. Combine with 1 table-spoon oil and rub over chicken. Place on grill and keep turning to brown evenly and to prevent charring. Meanwhile in a small saucepan add remaining oil and saute onion at edge of grill stir in oregano, catsup and vinegar and let simmer 15 minutes. When chicken is done brush liberally with sauce and grill 5 minutes longer. Place on platter and may use remaining sauce as a table sauce.

Serves 4

This is so easy and if you like garlic this is wonderful. . . . .

BARBECUE CHICKEN FOR 50

A do-ahead recipe!

    25 pounds chicken, cut up
     3 quarts cold water
    ¼ cup salt
     2 cups oil
     1 gallon prepared barbecue sauce
     6 onions, sliced

Trim off any excess skin or fat from chicken and place in a large container. Dissolve salt in water and pour over chicken. Toss chicken so that each piece is moistened. Let soak overnight or for serveral hours.

Drain chicken and dry with paper towels. Pour oil over chicken and toss to coat each piece. Preheat barbecue to MEDIUM heat and quickly char-brown chicken pieces on all sides. Remove chicken to one or more large baking pans and pour the barbecue sauce over it. Sprinkle the onions on top and stir to mix well and coat each piece.

Cover pans with foil and bake 1 hour at 350°, or until chicken is tender and sauce has baked onto chicken surfaces. Serve hot or chill for picnic chicken.

Chicken may be prepared ahead and barbecued, frozen, then baked with sauce for convenience.

BARBECUED FISH FILLETS IN ORANGE SAUCE

  2 pounds fish fillets of your choice
  ¾ cup orange juice
  1 teaspoon grated orange peel
  ¼ cup oil
  ¼ cup dry vermouth
    Fresh ground pepper to taste
  2 cloves garlic, crushed

    Orange wedges, lemon wedges and chopped cilantro for garnish

Place fish in a shallow baking dish. Combine remaining ingredients and pour over fish. Marinate at least 30 minutes. Be sure you grease the grill liberally. Barbecue over hot coals just until fish turns opaque. Garnish and serve easy and soo good.

Serves 4

GAMBAS CON QUESO

(Shrimp with Cheese)

  1½ pounds fresh jumbo shrimp
  2 packages (3-ounces each) cream cheese
  2 packages (3-ounces each) blue cheese
  2 pimientos, chopped fine
  8 thin slices lemon
  ½ cup Chablis or dry white wine

Shell and devein shrimp. Cream the cheese with pimientos. Form 4 (14-inch square) sheets of double-thick aluminum foil. Spoon equal portions of cheese on foil. Top cheese with equal amounts of shrimp. Place two lemon slices on each and fold foil to form a packet. Pour two tablespoons wine in each and twist top to close. Place packets on grill and cook at LOW, with lid closed, for 20 to 25 minutes or until shrimp is done.

Serve with toasted French bread.

Serves 4

A husband is the only labor-saving device you can cuddle

MAPLE-SUGAR CINNAMON ROLLS

    2 packages dry yeast
    1 cup lukewarm water
    ¼ cup sugar
    1 cup milk, scalded
    ½ cup sugar
    1 teaspoon salt
    7 cups flour
    4 eggs, beaten
    4 tablespoons butter
    1 cup brown sugar
    4 teaspoons cinnamon
    ⅔ cup raisins

Glaze

    2 cups powdered sugar
    1½ teaspoons maple flavoring

Dissolve yeast in lukewarm water and ¼ cup sugar; set aside. Scald milk; add shortening, ½ cup sugar, salt; cool to lukewarm. Add 2 cups flour, or enough flour to make a soft batter. Add yeast and beaten eggs; beat well. Add remaining flour, or enough to make a soft dough. Knead lightly and place in greased bowl. Cover and set in a warm place. Let rise until double in bulk, about 2 hours.

Divide dough into 2 parts. Roll out half the dough to ¼-inch thickness into a rectangular shape. Spread with 2 tablespoons of the butter and sprinkle generously with approximately ½ cup brown sugar and 2 teaspoons cinnamon. Soak raisins in warm water for a few minutes; squeeze out excess water before sprinkling on dough. Roll up tightly, beginning at wide side. Seal well by pinching edges of roll together. Slice ¾-inch thick and place on greased cookie sheet. Repeat with remaining dough.

Let rise 30 minutes. Bake 15 to 20 minutes at 375°. Glaze while still warm.

Glaze: Mix powdered sugar with enough warm water to make a thin but not watery icing. Add maple flavoring.

Frogs are smart
They eat the things that bug them

REFRIGERATOR ROLLS

    2 packages dry yeast
    ½ cup lukewarm water
    ¾ cup butter
    1 cup boiling water
    1 cup cold water
    ¾ cup sugar
    2 teaspoons salt
    2 eggs lightly beaten
    7 to 8 cups flours

Dissolve yeast in the warm water for 5 minutes. Set aside. Combine butter with boiling water and stir until butter is melted. Cool and place in very large bowl. Add cold water, sugar, salt, eggs and yeast. Mix well. Add enough flour (between 7 to 8 cups) to make a soft dough that when beaten does not stick to the sides of the bowl. Cover and refrigerate immediately for at least 6 hours or preferably overnight. (Dough may be kept in the refrigerator for 7 to 10 days). When ready to use, remove any amount needed, place on a floured board, roll out about 1 inch thick, and cut into any size desired. Place rolls on ungreased cookie sheet and let rise for 1 to 2 hours. Bake in a preheated 375° oven 12 to 15 minutes, depending on size of rolls.

Terrific! This dough can be used for just about anything even pizza.

5 dozen

CHOCOLATE SWIRL CAKE

    ¾ cup butter
    2 cups sugar
    1 teaspoon vanilla
    2½ cups cake flour
    2½ teaspoons baking powder
    1 cup milk
    5 egg whites, stiffly beaten
    2 squares Hersheys baking chocolate, melted

Cream the butter and sugar. Add the vanilla and mix. Sift together the dry ingredients and add to the creamed mixture alternately with the milk. Fold in egg whites. Remove 1 cup of the batter to a small bowl. Add the melted chocolate and blend. Arrange the white batter into a greased and floured 9 × 13-inch baking pan. Spoon over the chocolate batter. With a fork swirl back and forth to produce a marble effect. Bake in a 350° oven for 35 to 40 minutes, or until done. Ice with favorite icing.

Super for the whole family.

RHUBARB PIE

  3 cups rhubarb, diced
1¼ cups sugar
  ¼ teaspoon salt
  2 tablespoons water
  3 tablespoons flour
  1 tablespoon lemon juice
  2 eggs
  1 unbaked 9-inch pie shell

Crumb Mixture

  3 tablespoons sugar
  3 tablespoons flour
  2 tablespoons butter

Mix together

Place the rhubard in the unbaked pie shell. Combine remaining ingredients and stir to form a smooth paste. Pour over rhubarb. Sprinkle with crumb mixture. Bake in a 425° oven for 10 minutes, then at 325° for 30 minutes longer.

Makes 1 (9-inch) pie

This is for the purists who love rhubarb. My family has always been divided on rhubarb, the nice thing is there is no in-between you either love it or not.

APRICOT CRUMB PIE

  2 tablespoons quick-cooking tapioca
  ¾ cup granulated sugar
  ⅛ teaspoon salt
  2 pounds fresh apricots, halved and pitted
    Juice of ½ lemon
    Pastry for 1-crust 9-inch pie, unbaked
  ⅓ cup firmly packed light brown sugar
  ¼ cup all-purpose flour
  ½ teaspoon ground cinnamon
  3 tablespoons butter or margarine

Mix tapioca, granulated sugar and salt. Combine with apricots and lemon juice. Pack into 9-inch pie pan lined with pastry.

  Mix brown sugar, flour and cinnamon; cut in butter to form crumbs. Sprinkle over apricots.

  Bake in preheated hot oven (425°) for 15 minutes; reduce heat to moderate (375°) and bake for 30 to 35 minutes longer, or until apricots are tender.

FRESH BERRY PIE

1 cup sugar
4 cups fresh berries
2 tablespoons cornstarch
2 tablespoons lemon juice
1 (3-ounce) package cream cheese, softened
1 (9-inch) baked pie shell
Whipped cream

Mix 2 cups of the berries with the sugar and cornstarch. Mash slightly and cook until thickened. Add lemon juice and cool. Put remaining berries in baked pie shell which has been cooled and spread with the softened cream cheese. Pour cooked berries over this and top with whipped cream. Refrigerate and serve chilled.

Serves 6 to 8

PEACHES AND CREAM PIE

¾ cup sugar
¼ cup flour
1 cup heavy cream
¼ teaspoon vanilla
8 peaches, peeled and sliced
Dash of salt
1 tablespoon lemon juice
2 tablespoons butter
2 teaspoons cinnamon
1 (9-inch) unbaked pastry shell

Mix together the first 7 ingredients and place in the unbaked pie shell. Dot with butter and sprinkle over cinnamon. Bake at 425° for 15 minutes, lower temperature to 300° and bake 40 to 45 minutes longer.

Serves 8

Sooo easy and soo good

BILL DEMING COOKIES

¾ cup shortening
1 cup brown sugar
½ cup sugar
1 egg
¼ cup water
2 teaspoons almond flavoring
1 cup flour
1 teaspoon salt
1 teaspoon cinnamon
½ teaspoon cloves
½ teaspoon all spice
½ teaspoon ginger
1 cup raisins
1 cup nuts, chopped
3 cups quick cooking oatmeal, raw

Cream together the first 6 ingredients. Stir in remaining ingredients and mix well. Drop by rounded spoonsful onto a cookie sheet. Bake at 350° for 10 to 15 minutes. These are Bill's favorites and he wants to share them with the Food News Family. He said they make about 60 great cookies.

CARROT CAKE

    3 cups grated carrots
1½ cups oil
    2 cups sugar
    4 eggs
    2 cups flour
    3 teaspoons cinnamon
    2 teaspoons soda
    1 teaspoon salt
    ½ cup chopped nuts

Mix carrots, oil, sugar and eggs in large bowl. Set aside. In another bowl mix flour, cinnamon, soda, salt and nuts. Combine the two mixtures, mixing well. Turn into greased and floured pan. Bake at 350° for 45 minutes. 9 × 13-inch pan. Cool then frost.

Cream Cheese Icing

    3 ounces cream cheese (room temperature)
    3 tablespoons cream or milk
    ½ teaspoon salt
2½ cups powdered sugar

Soften cream cheese with cream or milk, add salt. Gradually add enough powdered sugar to give it a good spreading consistency. Beat until creamy.

RASPBERRY FALDERAH

1½ cups flour
    2 tablespoons sugar
    ½ pound butter, softened
    2 (3-ounce) packages cream cheese, softened
    1 stick butter
    2 cups powdered sugar
    ½ cup pecans, chopped
    1 (3-ounce) package raspberry jello
    1 cup boiling water
    2 packages frozen raspberries
       Sweetened whipped cream or whipped topping

Blend flour butter and sugar with a mixer. Spread in a 9 × 13-inch pan and bake at 325° for 25 minutes. Let cool. Mix cream cheese, butter and powdered sugar with mixer until creamy, fold in chopped nuts. Spread over crust. Dissolve jello in boiling water. Stir in raspberries. Let cool until syrupy. Pour over cream cheese mixture. Chill overnight. Next day when ready to serve top with whipping cream or whipped topping.

This serves 8 to 10

Delightful and easy for the busy person who likes to entertain at home.

APRICOT PICKLES

3 to 4 pounds fresh apricots, peeled
7 pounds sugar
1 pint cider vinegar
1 teaspoon chili powder
¼ teaspoon cayenne pepper
10 whole cloves

Mix all the ingredients except the apricots in a saucepan. Bring to a boil. Drop the whole apricots with the pits into the boiling syrup. Bring back to a boil and then reduce the heat and simmer until apricots are tender. Ladle into jars and pour over boiling syrup. Seal with lids.

Makes 18 pints

PICKLED OKRA

3¼ pounds okra
1 quart white vinegar
2 tablespoons salt
2 tablespoons pepper
1 tablespoon dry parsley
    flakes
1 tablespoon dill weed

1 clove garlic, crushed
1 tablespoon Worcestershire
    sauce
1 teaspoon Tabasco
3 cloves
1 medium onion, chopped

Wash okra; soak in cold water for 1 hour. Place in hot sterilized jars. Put other ingredients in pan; bring to a boil. Pour over okra in hot jars. Seal.

Note

Okra is better if refrigerated a day before using, to insure crispiness.

Yield 4 pints

GRANDMA'S PEACH CHUTNEY

4 pounds ripe peaches, peeled
1½ pounds sugar
1 tablespoon chili powder
½ pound seedless raisins
1 tablespoon salt
1 cup crystalized ginger
2 tablespoons mustard seed
¼ cup onion
3 cups tarragon vinegar

Put fruit, onion, ginger and raisins through a grinder. Add other ingredients and simmer 2 to 3 hours, uncovered. Ladle into 6 pint jars that have been sterilized. Seal.

Wonderful holiday hostess gift.

DAVID FENWICK'S VERMONT OIL PICKLES

    8 pounds finger-size cucumbers
    4 ounces whole white mustard seed
    1 pint olive oil
    1 bottle malt vinegar
        Salt

Wash the small cucumbers thoroughly in cold water and slice in thin rounds into porcelain bowl or other non-metal container (stainless steel is okay). As you slice cukes into bowl, pause now and again to douse them thoroughly with salt. Allow salted cukes to stay in bowl overnight. The following morning drain off all liquid off the cukes and add the mustard seed, distributing the seed thoroughly throughout all the cukes so that they will be even in the jars. Then add the pint of olive oil and stir thoroughly so that olive oil covers all of the cukes and the mustard seed sticks to the little slices. You then pack the oiled and seeded cukes into pint jars, packing them firmly to the top. Then pour the malt vinegar to cover. You will find that if you pack the pickles firmly into the jar you do not use much vinegar, so the vinegar does not have to be diluted. Seal the jars and keep in a cool place. Pickles should be ready to eat in six weeks.

Note
These small cukes are in season only in July and August.

PEACH PRESERVES

    3 pounds ripe peaches or 4 to 6 cups frozen peaches
  ¾ as much sugar as fruit
    1 tablespoon corn syrup
    2 ounces frozen pineapple juice concentrate
    1 tablespoon lemon juice

Dip peaches in boiling water for about 30 minutes. Slip off skins and peel. Coarsely chop fruit and spread sugar over fruit. Let sit 10 to 20 minutes to draw out juice. Place in a heavy 4-quart saucepan or Dutch oven. Add remaining ingredients and cook over medium heat until the fruit is transparent and the syrup thickened slightly. Remove from the heat. Cover. Let rest 1 to 2 hours for fruit to plump up. Return to heat, brint to a boil. Skim off any foam. Simmer till desired thickness. Ladle into hot sterilized half-pint jars. Seal or may use paraffin.

Makes 6 (½-pint) jars of great jelly

AUGUST

Back home in Nebraska we call this month the Dog Days
of the year. Hot, lazy summer days. In this chapter we are
featuring cool, easy summer entertaining. The last pool parties
before the kids go back to school and all the people are
home for vacations. Easy and good, hope you'll enjoy this
chapter for simple yet elegant entertaining.

PARTY FRANKS IN CUMBERLAND SAUCE

  1 cup red currant jelly
  1 cup port wine
    Juice of 1 lemon or ½ orange
  2 teaspoons grated lemon or orange rind
  2 teaspoons prepared mustard
  ¼ teaspoon salt
    Dash pepper
  ¼ teaspoon ground ginger
  2 pounds franks, cut into bite-size pieces.

Melt jelly and stir in wine and juice. Remove from heat and stir in remaining ingredients. Let sauce stand overnight to improve flavor. Serve hot or cold with ham, pork or poultry, or warm franks in sauce as an appetizer.

Serves 10

GREEN CHILI FRITTATA

  ½ cup flour
  1 teaspoon baking powder
 10 eggs lightly beaten
  ¼ pound butter, melted and cooled
  2 cups small curd cottage cheese
  1 pound Jack cheese, grated
  3 (4 ounce) cans diced green chilies
    Salt to taste

Preheat oven to 350°. Butter 9 × 13-inch baking dish. Mix flour and baking powder. Add eggs and butter, blend well. Blend in remaining ingredients. Put mixture in prepared dish and bake 35 to 45 minutes or until set. Cut into squares. Serve hot.

Serves 12

SOURCREAM HAM DIP

  1 cup dairy sour cream
  ½ cup firmly packed ground cooked ham
 1¼ teaspoons dry sherry
 1¼ teaspoons prepared mustard
  1 tablespoon green onion, chopped

Mix all ingredients and chill until ready to use.

Makes about 1½ cups

CALIFORNIA OREGANO SUMMER SALAD

1 head iceberg lettuce
1½ cups ripe olives
4 ounces jack cheese, cut
    into julienne strips
½ cup sliced cucumber
½ cup chopped green onion,
    be sure and use the tops
Oregano dressing

Combine all the salad ingredients in a bowl and chill thoroughly. Drizzle with dressing and toss just before serving.

Oregano dressing

½ cup oil
6 tablespoons vinegar
2 tablespoons sugar
2 teaspoons oregano
2 cloves garlic, crushed

Serves 6 to 8

MELON AND AVOCADO SALAD

5 cups melon balls (from
    melons of your choice)
1½ cups avocado balls
Dry wine
½ teaspoon salt
Fresh mint

Cover melon ball with wine and chill four hours, drain. Mix with avocado balls, salt and place in chilled large wine glasses. Garnish with mint.

Serves 4

DILLED VEGETABLE & CHEESE SALAD

Dill Dressing

6 tablespoons oil
2 tablespoons white wine vinegar
  Salt and pepper to taste
2 cloves garlic, minced
1 tablespoon dill, chopped or ½ teaspoon dill weed
1 teaspoon Dijon mustard

1 cup thinly sliced carrots
1 cup cauliflowerets
1 cup mushrooms, sliced
½ red or green pepper, diced
1 cup cherry tomatoes, cut into half
1 cup zucchini, sliced
⅓ cup green onions, sliced
3 tablespoons parsley, chopped
½ pound Swiss cheese, cut into julienne strips

Combine all the dressing ingredients in a jar and give it a good shake. Place vegies in a large bowl, pour dressing over all, toss and chill for several hours. At serving time give the salad another toss and top with cheese.

Simply super . . . Good to eat and good for your shape.

Serves 6

FOUR-BEAN SALAD

 1 can garbanzo beans, drained
 1 can green beans, drained
 1 can wax beans, drained
 1 can kidney beans, drained
 ½ cup chopped onions
 ½ cup chopped green pepper
 ½ cup sugar
 ½ cup vinegar
 ½ cup oil
 1 teaspoon salt

Combine all ingredients, refrigerate and let marinate for 24 hours before serving.

Serves 8

COLD RICE SALAD

 5 cups chicken stock
 2 cups uncooked long grain white rice
 3 (6-ounce) jars oil-marinated artichoke hearts
 5 green onions chopped
 1 (4-ounce) jar pimiento-stuffed olives, sliced (optional)
 1 large green pepper, diced
 3 large celery stalks, diced
 ¼ cup chopped fresh parsley
    Reserved artichoke marinade
 1 teaspoon curry powder
 2 cups mayonnaise
    Salt and freshly ground pepper to taste

Bring stock to boil, stir in rice and return to boil. Lower heat, cover and simmer for 20 minutes or until liquid is absorbed and rice is tender. Cool. Drain artichokes, reserving marinade, and chop. Add to rice with the onions, olives, green pepper, celery and parsley. Combine reserved marinade with the curry, mayonnaise, salt and pepper. Toss with rice and mix thoroughly. Refrigerate until ready to serve.

Serves 12 to 16

PARTY BUFFET SALSA

    6 tomatoes, chopped fine
    3 onions, chopped fine
    1 big can green chilies, chopped
    3 bunches fresh cilantro, chopped
        Salt to taste
    ¼ cup cider vinegar

Mix all ingredients and chill.

Tortilla Strips

    1 dozen flour tortillas
        Oil

Heat about ¼-inch oil in a large skillet. Cut tortillas in strips and fry until crisp. Drain on paper towels. May salt if desired. Store in airtight container.

Serves 14

Super-duper.

LINGUINE WITH ZUCCHINI AND TOMATOES

    ⅓ cup butter or margarine
    ⅓ cup onion, chopped
    1 green pepper, seeded and cut into strips
    4 ounces linguine, cooked and drained
    2 to 3 cups sliced zucchini
    4 medium tomatoes, peeled, seeded and cut into strips
    ¼ cup parsley, chopped
    ½ cup shredded Gruyere or other Swiss cheese
    ½ cup freshly grated Parmesan cheese

Melt butter in skillet and saute onion for about 5 minutes. Add green pepper and cook a few minutes more. Combine with remaining ingredients reserving a few tablespoons Parmesan cheese for top. Place in buttered 2-quart casserole and top with Parmesan. Bake covered at 350° for 30 to 40 minutes, or until cheese is bubbling. Do not covercook.

Serves 4 to 6

XTRA CREAMY CHEESE ENCHILADAS

  6 flour tortillas
  3 cups shredded Jack cheese
  6 tablespoons green onion, chopped
 ¼ cup butter or margarine
 ¼ cup flour
  2 cups chicken broth
  1 cup sour cream
  1 (4-ounce) can green chilies, chopped

Fill each tortilla with ½ cup cheese and 1 tablespoon green onion. Roll each individually and place in an 8-inch square shallow baking dish. Melt butter in a saucepan, add flour stirring constantly. Add chicken broth and stir to make a thick sauce. Remove from the heat and stir in sour cream and chilies, stir until smooth. Pour over tortillas. Bake at 350° for 20 minutes.

Serves 6

SUMMERTIME MAPLE BAKED BEANS

 20 cups of water
  5 pounds large white northern beans
  5 onions, cut into rings
1¼ cups brown sugar
  2 cups pure maple syrup (don't use pancake syrup)
    Salt to taste
  2 teaspoons dry mustard
  2 pounds salt pork cubed

Soak beans overnight in lots of water. Makes sure beans are covered. Next day bring beans to a boil and turn down to simmer, covered, until almost tender. Make sure they don't boil, just simmer. Make sure pot stays covered and you add water if needed.

Mix together brown sugar, maple syrup and dry mustard. Layer beans, onions, salt pork and maple syrup mixture. Bake at 300° for 3 to 4 hours, covered, uncover and bake 30 minutes. This recipe can be cut down but it will freeze very nicely.

Serves a ton of picnickers

SWEET & SOUR BEANS

  8 slices bacon
  4 large onions, coarsely chopped
½ cup brown sugar
  1 teaspoon dry mustard
    Salt to taste
½ teaspoon garlic powder
  2 cups cider vinegar
  2 cans (15-ounce each) butter lima beans, drained
  1 can (15-ounce) green lima beans, drained
  1 can (15-ounce) red kidney beans, drained
  1 (# 2½) can (3½ cups) New England baked beans

Fry bacon until crisp. Crumble and set aside. Saute onion in bacon fat until limp. Add sugar, mustard, salt, garlic powder and vinegar. Cook 20 minutes. In a 3-quart casserole mix the 4 types of beans. Pour onion mixture over all! Sprinkle crumbled bacon on top. Bake at 325° for 1 hour.

Serves 12 to 16

Terrific for your family get together. A different twist on an old standby.

VEGETABLE PITAS

  4 pita breads
    Margarine
¼ pound jack cheese, grated
¼ pound mushrooms, sliced
  1 avocado, sliced
12 cherry tomatoes, cut into half
  1 small red onion, chopped
  1 cup alfalfa sprouts
¼ cup plain yogurt
  3 tablespoons toasted sunflower seeds

Cut top of pita and spread margarine on the inside of the pocket. Wrap pita in aluminum foil and bake at 350° for 10 minutes. Fill each pocket with cheese, mushrooms, avocado, tomatoes, onions, sprouts, yogurt and sunflower seeds.

Serve immediately.

Fills 2 teenage boys or 4 adults

HAWAIIAN SPARERIBS

    2 pounds lean spareribs
    3 tablespoons flour
    3 tablespoons soy sauce
    3 tablespoons salad oil
    ⅔ cup sugar
    ⅔ cup wine vinegar
    ½ cup water
    ½ cup pineapple juice
    1 teaspoon fresh grated ginger (if using dry ¼ teaspoon)
    2 cups fresh pineapple chunks
    2 cups fresh papaya chunks

Cut spareribs into 2-inch pieces. Mix flour and soy sauce together to coat ribs. Let ribs stand 10 minutes after coating. Heat oil in skillet and brown ribs on all sides. Drain off excess fat, add sugar, vinegar, water, juice and ginger. Cover and simmer about 45 minutes. Stir in fruit and simmer 5 minutes longer. Serve garnished with chopped parsley and toasted sesame seeds.

Serves 4 to 6

COLD SLICED STEAK

    1 pound sirloin steak, around 3-inches thick
    ½ cup soy sauce
    ½ cup olive oil
    ⅔ cup brandy
    Dash Tabasco sauce
    Salt and pepper to taste

Combine the marinade ingredients and marinate the steak for at least 2 hours, turning several times. Broil the steak on the rare side and then season with the salt and pepper. Be sure to baste the steak with the marinade while it is broiling or barbecueing. Cool the meat but do not refrigerate. At serving time slice into thin diagonal strips and arrange on a platter lined with salad greens, garnished with olives, small pickles and pickled onions. I usually wrap steak and slice it at the picnic.

Serves 6 to 8

BARBECUED LAMB

Have your butcher bone and butterfly a 5 to 6 pound leg of lamb.

Marinade

  1¾ cups beef broth
  2½ tablespoons marmalade
   2 tablespoons wine vinegar
   1 tablespoon dried onion
   1 tablespoon rosemary
   1 tablespoon marjoram
   1 bay leaf, crumbled
   1 teaspoon seasoned salt or to taste
  ¼ teaspoon ginger

Place the sauce ingredients in a saucepan and simmer 20 minutes. Now marinate the lamb in the sauce for at least 4 hours. Barbecue over medium heat 10 to 15 minutes on each side. Wonderful.

Serves 8

COLD BUFFET MEATLOAF

   2 pounds lean ground beef (or 1½ pounds lean ground beef and ½ pound lean ground pork)
   1 cup tart apples, finely chopped, peeled and cored
   1 cup Bosc pears, finely chopped, peeled and cored
   1 onion, finely grated
   1 cup fine dry bread crumbs
   3 eggs, lightly beaten
  1½ teaspoons salt
  ¼ teaspoon freshly ground black pepper
  ½ teaspoon sage
  ¼ teaspoon grated nutmeg
  ½ teaspoon allspice

Preheat oven to 350°. Place all ingredients in a large bowl and mix gently, but thoroughly, with the hands. Pack into a 9×5×3-inch loaf pan and bake for 1¼ hours. Cool and chill.

Serves 6

HAMBURGER SURPRISES

    2 pounds lean ground beef
      Garlic salt and pepper to taste
      Dijon-style mustard
    4 dill pickle slices
    4 thin slices tomato
    4 thin slices onion
    4 thin slices Monterey Jack cheese
    ¼ cup chopped black olives
    ¼ cup diced green chilies
    4 large lettuce leaves
    4 large hamburger buns
    ¼ cup butter, melted
      Parsley (garnish)

Shape beef into 8 patties; spread with mustard, sprinkle each with garlic salt and pepper. On each of 4 patties, place 1 slice each pickle, tomato, onion and cheese. Sprinkle each patty with 1 tablespoon olives and chilies. Top each with another beef patty pinching edges together to enclose completely. In a covered grill, place patties on grill rack over medium-hot Kingsford charcoal briquets. Cover grill and open vents. Cook 10 to 15 minutes on each side or until done. Serve with lettuce and buttered grilled hamburger buns. Garnish platter with parsley.

Makes 4 servings

BELL'S BARBECUED BLEU CHEESE BEEF TENDERLOINS

    2 eight-ounce beef tenderloin steaks, cut 1-inch thick
    1 large clove garlic, cut in half
      Salt to taste
    1 tablespoon cream cheese
    2 teaspoons finely chopped onions
    2 teaspoons bleu cheese
    2 teaspoons unflavored yogurt
      Dash white pepper
      Chopped parsley (garnish)

Rub each steak on both sides with cut garlic; sprinkle with salt. Place on platter. Mix cream cheese, onions, bleu cheese, yogurt and pepper; reserve. Place steaks on grill rack over medium-hot Kingsford charcoal briquets. Cook 5 to 7 minutes on each side or until done. Top each steak with bleu cheese mixture. Garnish with parsley.

Makes 2 servings

PEPPERCORN BEEF STEAK BARBECUE

    2 pounds beef top sirloin steak (1½ inches thick)
    2 to 3 tablespoons cracked peppercorns
    ¼ cup brandy
    ¼ cup olive oil
    3 tablespoons Worcestershire sauce
    1 tablespoon instant beef bouillon
       Pinch rosemary
       Fresh rosemary (garnish)
       Cherry tomatoes (garnish)

Press peppercorns into steak; place in glass dish. Mix remaining ingredients; pour over steak. Let stand 20 minutes. Drain steak; reserve marinade. Place steak on grill rack over medium-hot Kingsford charcoal briquets. Cook a total of 10 to 14 minutes, turning steaks frequently. Brush with marinade each time steaks are turned. Serve sliced. Reserve juice and pour over slices. Garnish with rosemary and cherry tomatoes.

Makes 4 servings

BARBECUED CHICKEN WITH SWEET POTATOES

    ½ cup pineapple juice
    ½ cup catsup
    2 tablespoons cider vinegar
    1 tablespoon honey
    3 dashes Tabasco
    1 tablespoon Dijon mustard
    3 broilers, quartered
    3 tablespoons oil
    6 large sweet potatoes or yams

Combine pineapple juice, catsup, vinegar, honey, Tabasco and mustard. Mix well. Place chicken in a shallow dish. Pour sauce over all. Marinate at room temperature 2 hours. Drain well, reserve marinade. Brush chicken lightly with oil. Place chicken over hot coals and brown evenly.

Meanwhile peel sweet potatoes and cut lengthwise into slabs about ½-inch thick. Place sweet potatoes on grill around chicken. Brush chicken and sweet potatoes with reserved marinade. Grill, turning and basting until chicken and potatoes are tender, about 35 minutes. Serve with corn on the cob, coleslaw, and sliced beef steak tomatoes. Yummy! For dessert try a little chocolate cake and chilled watermelon.

Serves 12 medium-sized eaters or 6 at my house.

BARBECUED TURKEY

  1 (6 to 10 pound) turkey, thawed
    Salt and ground pepper to taste
  2 onions
  2 cloves garlic, crushed
  ¼ cup wine vinegar
  ½ cup dry vermouth
  ¼ cup light brown sugar
  2 teaspoons Dijon mustard
  ⅛ teaspoon cayenne pepper
  1 tablespoon lemon juice
  2 tablespoons oil
  ½ cup catsup
  2 tablespoons Worcestershire sauce

Wash and pat the bird dry inside and out. Sprinkle cavity with salt and pepper. Place 1 whole onion and 1 garlic clove in the cavity and truss the bird very tightly, tying the wings over the breast with butchers string. Insert rotisserie spit rod in front of tail, now run it diagonally through the breast bone. Fasten tightly with spit forks at both ends and tie legs together with butchers string. Test rod to see if it balances. Insert a meat thermometer in thickest part of thigh; be sure thermometer doesn't touch bone and clears coals as it turns. When coals are ash gray, place a drip pan of heavy duty aluminum foil directly under turkey in front of coals. Attach spit and start rotisserie.

A 6 to 8 pound bird takes 2½ to 3 hours, and 8 to 10 pound bird takes 3 to 4½ hours. Of course times may vary according to weather conditions. Meanwhile, chop the remaining onion and crushed garlic clove. Combine the onion, garlic and the remaining ingredients in a small saucepan. Simmer, uncovered, 20 minutes. Baste the turkey during the last 30 minutes of cooking time. Turkey is done when the thermometer registers 180 to 185°, or when the thickest part of the drumstick feels soft.

Serves 12 to 16

The world is full of beauty
When the heart is full of love

FISH JALAPENO

White fish fillets of your choice
1 can cream of mushroom soup
Chopped green onions to taste
Chopped cilantro to taste
Chopped and seeded jalapeno peppers to taste
Grated sharp cheddar cheese

Quickly brown fish fillets in a skillet. Layer in a casserole. Fish, soup, onion, cilantro, peppers and cheese. Bake in a 350° oven for 20 to 30 minutes or until bubbly and hot.

This is really one of those easy type things that taste wonderful, that anyone can do. Now if Jalapeno's aren't your bag try the Anaheim chiles, chopped for a milder version. Serve this with a little rice and a little fruit salad. Super.

One piece of fish per person

This recipe is from a listener.
It is easy and soo good for some who like it hot.

PICKLED FISH

3 pounds fish—Mackerel, Bonito, Salmon, Yellow Tail, Albacore
1 cup salt
1 large onion, sliced
2 or 3 garlic cloves
1½ cups vinegar
2 tablespoons sugar
1⅓ cups water
2 tablespoons salad oil (or olive oil)
3 tablespoons pickling spice

Remove fins and cut fish into serving pieces, about one-inch thick and three inches square (bite size). Put small amount of salt in a large bowl, then add a layer of fish, sprinkle with salt. Alternate layers of fish and salt until all are used. Set aside for six hours. Wash off salt and brine, soak fish in fresh water for an hour. Then place in colander or french fry basket and immerse in large pot of boiling water. When water reaches boiling point again, remove fish and let cool. At this point, it must be handled carefully or it will fall apart. Be sure fish is cooked. Place fish in jars. Add several slices of onion and garlic cloves to jar. Make a brine by combining remaining ingredients and bringing them to a boil. Pour over fish. It will be ready to eat in about eight hours. Jars don't have to be sealed, but should be kept in refrigerator after cooling.

SUGARLESS BRAN MUFFINS

This is a great recipe as it features no sugar, no milk and is terrific for those who have allergies.

    2 cups Kellogg's Bran Flakes
      12-ounce can Diet 7-Up
    ¼ cup oil
    2 large eggs
    1 tablespoon liquid artificial sweetener
    2 cups self-rising flour

In a medium-sized bowl, beat the first five ingredients together at medium speed for 1 minute. Stir in flour just until dry ingredients are moistened. Divide batter equally between 12 paper-lined muffin tins. Bake at 400° for 20 to 22 minutes, or until a pick inserted in the center comes out clean.

Makes 1 dozen

Easy and so-o-o-o good!

BLUEBERRY COFFEECAKE

    ½ cup butter
    1 cup sugar
    3 eggs, lightly beaten
    1 teaspoon baking powder
    ¼ teaspoon salt
    1 teaspoon soda
    2 cups unbleached white flour, unsifted
    1 cup sour cream
    2 cups fresh or frozen blueberries

Topping
    1 cup brown sugar
    ¼ cup butter
    ¼ cup flour

Preheat oven to 350°. Cream butter and sugar. Add eggs, baking powder, salt, and soda. Alternating, add flour and sour cream. Fold in blueberries. Pour into a well-buttered cake pan approximately 9 × 13 × 2-inch.

For the topping: Cream brown sugar and butter. Add flour to get a semi-dry, lumpy mixture. Spread on top of the batter. Bake for 30 minutes or until a toothpick inserted in the center comes out clean. The topping should melt and partially sink into the batter.

SUNSHINE SPONGE CAKE

 7 egg whites
 1 teaspoon cream of tartar
 ½ teaspoon salt
 ½ cup sugar
 7 egg yolks
 ¼ cup cold water
 1 teaspoon vanilla
 1 teaspoon lemon extract
 1¼ cups sifted cake flour
 1 cup sugar
 ½ teaspoon baking powder

In large mixing bowl, beat egg whites with cream of tartar and salt until soft mounds form. Add ½ cup sugar, a tablespoon at a time. Continue beating until very straight peaks form. Do not underbeat. In small mixing bowl, combine egg yolks, water and flavorings. Add flour, 1 cup sugar and baking powder to yolk mixture. Beat 1 minute at medium speed. Fold one-fourth of the batter at a time into beaten egg whites using wire whisk or spatula. Blend gently but thoroughly after each addition. Pour into ungreased 10-inch tube pan. Bake at 350° for 40 to 50 minutes. Invert pan immediately; cool in pan.

LEMON PUDDING CAKE

 2 eggs, separated
 1 teaspoon grated lemon peel
 ¼ cup lemon juice
 1 cup milk
 1 cup sugar
 ¼ cup all-purpose flour*
 ¼ teaspoon salt

Heat oven to 350°. Beat egg whites until stiff peaks form; set aside. Beat egg yolks. Blend in lemon peel, juice and milk. Add sugar, flour and salt; beat until smooth. Fold into whites. Pour into ungreased 1-quart casserole. Place casserole in pan of very hot water (1-inch deep). Bake 45 to 50 minutes. Serve warm or cool and, if desired, with sweetened whipped cream.

Variation: Lime Pudding Cake. Substitute 1½ teaspoons grated lime peel and ¼ cup line juice for the lemon peel and juice.

*If using self-rising flour, omit salt

Yield 6 servings

SLOVAKIAN NUT ROLL

1 yeast cake
½ cup milk
⅛ cup sugar
3 egg yolks
¾ cup sugar
3 tablespoons butter

1 cup sweet cream
4 cups flour
⅓ teaspoon salt
Rind of ½ lemon
Rind of ½ orange

Soften yeast cake in ½ cup of lukewarm milk and add ⅛ cup of sugar. Put aside in warm place to rise. Cream egg yolks with ¾ cup sugar. Put butter and sweet cream into pan and heat until lukewarm. Add creamed egg yolks and sugar. Add flour, salt, grated lemon and orange rinds. Fold in yeast and beat well, until it bubbles. Let this mixture stand in a warm place until doubled in bulk. Divide dough into two parts and roll on floured board. Roll ¼-inch thick and brush with melted butter. Spread with nut filling. Roll up into two loaves about the size of a rolling pin. Bake in moderate oven (375°) for one hour.

Filling

1 pound chopped walnuts
2 cups milk
1 tablespoon whiskey
1 cup honey
Grated lemon and orange rind

Scald walnut meats in hot milk. Add grated lemon and orange rind, whiskey and honey.

BURGUNDY ICE

2¾ cups cold water
1 cinnamon stick
1½ cups sugar
¼ teaspoon salt
¼ cup apple brandy
2 tablespoons unflavored gelatin (2 envelopes)
½ cup water

2 cups burgundy
½ cup lemon juice
1 tablespoon grated orange rind
1 tablespoon grated lemon rind
4 egg whites

Combine water, cinnamon, sugar, salt and brandy in a saucepan. Stir until the sugar dissolves, bring to a boil and boil about 10 minutes. Soften gelatin in ½ cup of water. Dissolve in hot mixture. Strain into a bowl and let cool. Add the burgundy, lemon juice and the grated fruit peel. Place in freezer until ice crystals start to form around the edges. Beat well until soft peaks form. Beat in the egg whites. Cover and return to freezer for at least 3 hours.

Makes 1½ quarts

PAVLOVA

Notes on baking

The problems with baking a Pavlova are in your oven. If your oven is excellent you'll have no problems. Basically your Pavlova should be either white or lightly tanned, not browned.

Baking technique is as follows:
Preheat your oven to 350°. You may either bake it in a springform pan (8-inch) or free-form. For a springform pan cut a circle of wax paper for the bottom to fit. Then cut a strip to extend about two inches above the pan and line sides. Generously butter all waxed paper and then dip your hand in cold water and sprinkle it. Set aside pan. If using free-form butter a sheet of waxed paper on a cookie sheet and sprinkle with water. Set aside.

PAVLOVA

    4 egg whites (room temperature)
1¼ cups sugar
    ¼ teaspoon salt
    3 tablespoons cold water
    1 tablespoon corn starch
    1 teaspoon vanilla
    1 teaspoon distilled white vinegar
       Whipped cream for Pavlova (see below)
       Kiwi fruit, strawberries, raspberries, bananas, etc.

In a large bowl of an electric mixer beat egg whites until soft peaks form. Add salt and sugar in stages and continue beating until sugar is incorporated. Add water and beat in well. Sprinkle with cornstarch and continue beating. Add vanilla and vinegar and beat until whites are glossy and stiff peaks form. Turn meringue into pan and spread evenly or if using free-form spread in about an eight inch circle.

Bake at 350° for 15 minutes. Check to see if Pavlova has started to puff. If it has turn off oven and let set for one hour. If your oven does not hold heat well, bake for one hour at 175°. Remove from oven and cool to room temperature. Remove waxed paper, place on serving plate. Cover top only with Whipped cream for Pavlova and cover top of cream with selected sliced fruit.

Whipped Cream for Pavlova
  1 cup whipping cream
  1 envelope whipping cream stabilizer
  2 tablespoons sugar
  1 tablespoon Cognac (optional)

Chill bowl and beaters. Mix stabilizer into whipping cream and beat until soft peaks form. Beat in sugar and cognac if used. Whip until stiff.

Additional note

If your Pavlova is not rising after the first 15 minutes (it usually is) continue baking at 350° for another 10 to 15 minutes, then continue as directed.

GRAPE JAM
  4 pounds ripe Concord grapes
  ½ cup water
  1 package pectin
  8 cups sugar

Wash grapes thoroughly and place in saucepan. Add water and simmer for 10 minutes. Put through a sieve; discard remaining pulp and seeds. Measure 6 cups grape liquid into kettle. Add pectin; stir well. Bring to a boil, stirring constantly. Add sugar. Continue stirring and bring to a hard boil. Reduce heat slightly and boil for 4 minutes. Remove from heat; skim if necessary. Ladle into hot sterilized jars. Seal with hot lids. Invert jars for 30 minutes, then shake gently. Turn right side up.

Yield 5 to 6 pints

HAWAIIAN BANANA PIE
  4 cups sliced bananas, ripe but firm
  ½ cup pineapple juice
  ½ cup sugar
  1 teaspoon cinnamon
  1 tablespoon butter or margarine
  Pastry for a 2 crust pie

Soak sliced bananas in pineapple juice for at least 20 minutes. Drain saving the juice. Place bananas in pastry lined pie shell, add sugar and cinnamon which has been mixed together. Add 2 tablespoons of the pineapple juice. Dot with butter and cover with the top crust. Bake at 400° for 30 to 45 minutes, or until the crust is browned.

Serves 6

SEPTEMBER

The kids are back in school. Hooray! Now this is the month that we feature casseroles and goodies for the kids lunch box. Fall is here and crispy apples are the forerunner for great ideas from pies to main dishes. Be sure you try our "Apple Pie Supreme". Absolutely to die for. This month we can begin some of our baking for the Christmas Holidays.

QUICK GRAPE JUICE

Wash 1 cup Concord grapes, put into a clean quart jar, add ½ cup sugar, fill to within ½-inch of jar top with boiling water. Put on cap, screw band on firmly. Give it a water bath for 10 minutes. If sugar settles to the bottom of the jar, shake before putting it in the water bath. Pour through strainer before serving.

Easy and great for those of you who have grape arbors in your back yard.

Makes 1 quart

LABOR DAY CHEESE ROUNDS

    ¾ pound sharp cheddar cheese, grated
    3 green onions, chopped
    3 to 4 teaspoons curry powder
    ½ cup mayonnaise, or as needed for spreading consistency
      Salt to taste
    1 loaf party size rye bread

Combine cheese, onions, curry powder, mayonnaise and salt. Chill for 1 hour. Toast the rye bread on one side. Spread the cheese mixture on untoasted side of bread and put on a cookie sheet. Place under broiler until cheese is melted. Serve immediately.

Makes 40 rounds

JACKIE'S CHILI DIP

    1 can chili without beans
    1 tablespoon chili powder
    1 package (8-ounce) cream cheese, softened
    1 can green chili salsa
    1 can (small) sliced black olives

Heat chili to boiling. Add remaining ingredients and cook and stir until well blended. Serve hot with fritos or tortilla chips.

Friendship is no plant of hasty growth

PAT'S PARTY PUNCH

   3 cups water
   3 cups sugar
   1 quart cranberry juice
   1 quart apricot nectar
   3 cups lemon juice
   2 cups orange juice
   2 cups pineapple juice
   2 quarts chilled ginger ale

Combine water and sugar in saucepan. Bring to boil over low heat, stirring until sugar is dissolved. Boil over medium heat for five minutes. Remove from heat, pour into large bowl. Add fruit juices, mix well, refrigerate until serving time. Just before serving, pour mixture into punch bowl, stir in ginger ale.

Serves 50

SWISS CHEESE FONDUE

   3 cups shredded natural Swiss cheese (12-ounces)
   1 cup shredded Gruyere cheese (4-ounces)
1½ teaspoons cornstarch
   1 clove garlic, halved
   1 cup sauterne
   1 tablespoon lemon juice
     Dash ground nutmeg
     Dash pepper
     French *or* Italian bread *or* hard rolls, cut in bite-size pieces, each with one crust

Combine cheeses and cornstarch. Rub inside of heavy saucepan with garlic; discard garlic. Pour in sauterne and lemon juice. Heat until bubbles cover the surface (do not cover or boil). *Stir vigorously and constantly from now on.* Add a handful of the cheese mixture, keeping heat medium. Do not boil. When cheese is melted, add more cheese and melt. After all the cheese is blended and bubbling, add nutmeg and pepper. Quickly transfer to fondue pot; keep warm over fondue burner. (If fondue becomes too thick, stir in a little warmed sauterne.) Spear bread cube with fondue fork; dip into fondue and swirl to coat. (Swirling is important to keep fondue in motion.)

Serves 4 to 6

JACKIE'S CROWD PLEASERS

  ½ pound butter, softened
  ½ cup prepared mustard
  25 hamburger buns, halved
  2½ pounds ready-to-eat, garlic-flavored corned beef brisket, thinly sliced
  25 (1-ounce) slices sharp, aged cheddar cheese
  75 slices dill pickle, cut lengthwise
  1½ quarts finely shredded green cabbage
  6 tablespoons mayonnaise-type salad dressing
  1 tablespoon caraway seeds

Beat butter and mustard until light and fluffy. Spread on cut surfaces of buns, 1½—2 teaspoons per sandwich. Arrange approximately 1½-ounces of thinly sliced corned beef on 25 bun halves. On remaining 25, place a slice of cheese and 3 slices of dill pickle. Blend cabbage, salad dressing and caraway seeds together and place approximately ¼ cup on each cheese half. Put bun halves together, place each on a piece of foil, wrap and refrigerate. These keep very well in the refrigerator for several days before baking. As needed, bake foil-wrapped sandwiches in preheated 400° oven for 15 to 20 minutes.

Yield 25 sandwiches

VERY DIFFERENT MACARONI SALAD

  2 to 3 cups seedless green grapes, halved
  1 (8-ounce) package shell macaroni
  1 (8-ounce) can pitted ripe olives, drained and halved
  ¾ cup chopped green onions
  2 to 3 ounces bleu cheese, crumbled
     Salt and pepper to taste
  ¼ teaspoon garlic powder
  3 tablespoons fresh lemon juice
  1 cup mayonnaise

Cook macaroni according to package directions. Drain. Combine hot macaroni with grapes, olives, onion, cheese, salt, pepper and garlic powder. Mix together lemon juice and mayonnaise until smooth. Combine macaroni and mayonnaise until evenly mixed. Refrigerate covered several hours or overnight. Add more mayonnaise if desired before serving.

8 to 12 servings

PEA-NUT SALAD

 2 boxes frozen peas, thawed but not cooked
 ½ pound bacon, fried crisp and broken into bits
 ½ cup sliced green onions
 ½ cup cashew nuts
 1 cup sour cream
   Season to taste

Serve on crisp lettuce cups.

Serves 8

SEAFOOD VERMICELLI SALAD

 5 hard-boiled eggs, chopped
 5 stalks celery, finely chopped
 6 sweet pickles, finely chopped
 ¼ cup chopped onions
 1½ cups mayonnaise
 ¼ cup juice from pickles
   Salt and seasoned salt to taste
 12 ounces vermicelli, broken, cooked and well drained
 1 pound raw shrimp, cooked, shelled, deveined, coarsely chopped
   Paprika
   Chopped parsley

Combine eggs, celery, pickles, onions, mayonnaise, pickle juice and salts. Add vermicelli, toss and chill overnight. Just before serving, add shrimp and toss. Garnish with paprika and chopped parsley. Chopped ham may be substituted for the shrimp. Makes a nice and easy luncheon dish that can be done ahead of time.

Makes 12 servings

MACARONI AND CHEESE SQUARES

 1¼ cups scalded milk
 ¾ cup soft bread crumbs
 3 tablespoons butter
 1½ cups cooked macaroni
 ½ teaspoon chopped onion
 1 teaspoon salt
 3 cups grated cheddar cheese
 2 eggs, well beaten

Pour milk over crumbs and butter. Add remaining ingredients in the order given. Mix thoroughly and place in buttered casserole, and set in pan of hot water. Bake in 375° oven for 45 minutes or until delicately browned and inserted knife comes out clean. When done, cut into squares and top each square with green pepper and a fluff of parsley.

FAVORITE SPANISH RICE

2 cups raw converted rice
2 tablespons oil
2 cups chicken broth
1 cup water
1 large onion, chopped

2 cloves garlic, crushed
Salt to taste
3 tablespoons tomato paste
1 small carrot grated

Preheat the oven to 350°. Place the rice into a large pot of boiling water, cover, turn off the heat, and let it stand for 15 minutes. Rinse in cold water to remove the starch. Drain rice well. In a large teflon pan, heat oil and add onion, garlic and rice. Saute until dry. Bring chicken broth, water, salt, tomato paste and carrot to a boil. Simmer for 10 minutes. Add rice mixture and stir. Pour all into a 3 quart casserole. Cover. Bake at 350° for 1 hour. Can remove rice from casserole and dump out onto a cookie sheet to dry out. Cover with a towel to keep warm in a turned off oven. The grains should be very plump and very dry, que sabroso.

Serves 6 to 8

PEROGI QUICHE

1 pint lo-cal cottage cheese
1 egg, lightly beaten
½ teaspoon pepper
1 large onion, chopped

4 tablespoons butter or margarine
4 large flour tortillas
2 tablespoons parsley, chopped for garnish

Moisten tortillas with water and place one in the bottom of a 9-inch glass pie plate which has been lightly greased. Mix together the cottage cheese, egg and pepper and set aside. Saute the onion in the butter and set aside. Place 4 tablespoons of the cottage cheese mixture over the tortilla. Top with another tortilla, alternating with the cottage cheese mixture until all tortillas are used with a tortilla on top. Pour sauteed onions over all. Cover with foil. Bake in a 300° oven for 20 minutes. Garnish with the parsley and serve with sliced tomatoes and a little green salad. Easy and soo good.

Serves 4

HAMBURGER PIE

1 pound ground chuck
1 can tomato soup
1 onion, chopped
1 can green beans, drained

Salt and pepper to taste
1 egg, beaten
Mashed potatoes

Brown ground meat and onion. Add can of soup and can of green beans. Season to taste. Place meat mixture into a casserole. Mix egg into mashed potatoes. Spread potatoes over meat mixture. Set dish under broiler and broil until potatoes are browned. Cheese strips can be also placed on top of mashed potatoes.

Serves 4

169

RATATOUILLE CREPES

  ¼ cup olive oil
  1 large green onion, sliced
  1 green pepper, cubed
  ½ teaspoon oregano leaves
  ½ teaspoon basil
  1 large clove garlic, crushed
    Salt and pepper to taste
  1 eggplant, peeled and cubed
  2 small zucchini, cut into ¼-inch slices
  1 can (1 pound 12-ounce) tomatoes plus liquid
  1 tablespoon chopped parsley
  6 cooked crepes
    Grated Parmesan cheese

Saute the onion slices in olive oil until they are transparent. Add the green pepper, oregano, basil, salt and pepper; cook over medium heat for 5 minutes. Next, add the zucchini and saute for 5 minutes. Add egg plant and tomatoes (with liquid) and chopped parsley. Simmer uncovered for 15 minutes on medium low heat.

Spoon mixture onto center of six crepes. Fold sides over center to enclose filling. Place on ovenproof dish and heat under broiler until crepes turn golden brown and edges start to curl. Sprinkle crepes with grated Parmesan cheese and serve.

Basic Crepe Recipe

  1 cup all-purpose flour
  1½ cups milk
  3 eggs
    Pinch of salt
  ½ cup oil or melted butter

Stir flour and salt together in a mixing bowl. Add milk and mix together thoroughly. Add eggs gradually and beat thoroughly until mixture is smooth. The batter will have the consistency of heavy cream. Let batter stand for half hour before using.

Brush a hot crepe pan with the butter or oil. Pour in approximately 1½ to 2 tablespoons of butter, depending on the size of the pan. Tip pan to coat it with a thin layer of batter. When the crepe is golden brown (about 1 minute), turn it and brown the other side. Continue cooking crepes, adding oil or butter to the pan when needed.

Makes 12 to 14 crepes

DOWN HOME PORK CHOP CASSEROLE

    4 pork chops
    4 slices tomato
    4 slices green pepper rings
    4 slices onion
      Salt and pepper to taste
    1 cup raw rice
    1 can consomme
      Marjoram
      Thyme

Brown pork chops in a skillet. Place chops on top of rice in the bottom of a fairly deep casserole. Put a slice of onion, a tomato ring and a ring of pepper on top of each chop. Salt and pepper to taste. Scrape the drippings from the pan, with enough water or wine to make 1 cup liquid. Pour over casserole with consomme. Sprinkle to taste with marjoram, thyme. Cover. Bake 1 hour at 350°.

Serves 4 very nicely. All you need is a little salad and you have a little time to sit down and relax before dinner is ready.

EASY BACK TO SCHOOL SPECIAL FOR THE GANG

    1 pound raw ground meat of our choice
    2 medium onions, chopped
    1 cup celery, sliced

Brown all ingredients together. Pour off fat.

In a large casserole put:

    1 cup cream of mushroom soup
    1 can cream of celery soup
  1½ cups water
  1½ cups minute rice
   ¼ cup soy sauce
      Dash pepper
      Chinese noodles for topping

Mix together all the ingredients, except the Chinese noodles. Add the meat mixture and stir. Bake covered at 350° for 30 minutes. Uncover and bake 30 minutes more. Top with Chinese noodles and bake 15 minutes more.

This will really serve the gang.

STUFFED TOMATO STEAK

   1 flank steak
  ½ pound Italian sausage
   2 (8-ounce) cans tomato sauce
   1 cup green onions, chopped be sure and use green tops as well
  ¼ cup parsley, chopped
   2 tablespoons flour
   3 tablespoons oil
  ½ cup beef bouillon
   1 bay leaf

Have steak tenderized. Remove sausage from casing and crumble into a bowl. Mix in ½ cup of the tomato sauce and the onions and parsley. Spread over the steak, roll up in a jelly roll fashion and tie with butchers string. Sprinkle with flour and brown in oil. Mix remaining tomato sauce, beef broth and bay leaf. Pour over steak. Bake covered 1½ hours or until tender, basting with the sauce often.

Serves 4 to 6

CHICKEN MACARONI BAKE

  ½ cup celery, chopped
  ¼ cup green onion tops, chopped
  ½ cup green pepper, chopped
   2 cloves garlic, minced
   2 cups cooked chicken, chopped (this is great for any leftover meat)
   4 tablespoons margarine
   2 (10¾-ounce cans) chicken broth
   4 tablespoons pimiento, chopped
    Salt and pepper to taste
   1 tablespoon chili powder
   1 (8-ounce) can tomato sauce
   1 (15-ounce) can stewed tomatoes
   2 cups cooked macaroni
  ½ cup parmesan cheese

In a large saucepan, saute celery, onions, pepper, garlic and chicken in margarine. Add remaining ingredients except macaroni and parmesan. Simmer for 10 minutes. Add macaroni and mix well. Pour in a 2 quart casserole and sprinkle with cheese. Bake in a 350° oven for 30 to 35 minutes or until golden brown.

Serves 6

Easy and soo good this you can make the night before. This is a great dish for a potluck or teenagers as it fills them up.

CHICKEN AND ARTICHOKE HEARTS

1 fryer, cut into pieces
White wine
2 packages frozen artichoke hearts
3 cups mushrooms, sliced
1 stick butter or margarine
2 cups wild rice, cooked

Remove chicken skin and saute in half the butter or margarine until browned. Remove chicken to a casserole. Add wine to pan to deglaze and pour over chicken in casserole. Should cover most of the chicken. Bake at 350° for 1 hour. Meanwhile, warm frozen artichoke hearts in butter or margarine. Remove and add mushrooms, may need more butter or margarine. Mix and pour over top of chicken and bake at 350° for 15 minutes. Serve over wild rice.

Serves 4

MOM'S TUNA NOODLE SLUMGULLION

8 ounces egg noodles
1 can albacore, drained
1 small jar pimientos, chopped
1 green onion, chopped
Garlic to taste
¾ cup mayonnaise
1 small can mushrooms, drained
1 can cream of mushroom soup
½ can milk
Cracker crumbs
Cheddar cheese

Cook noodles to al dente and drain, place in the bottom of a 2 quart casserole. In a bowl whisk together tuna, pimientos, onion, garlic, mayonnaise, mushrooms, soup, and milk. Pour over the noodles. Top with cracker crumbs and cheddar cheese. Bake at 350° for 30 minutes.

Serves 4

MALTED MULTI-GRAIN BREAD

This power-packed bread will energize your day.

  1 cup wheat flakes
  1 cup rye flakes
  ¼ cup butter, cut in 4 pieces
  ⅓ cup malt syrup or honey
  2 cups hot water (200°)
  2 (¼-ounce) packages active dry yeast (2 tablespoons)
  1 teaspoon malt syrup or honey
  ⅓ cup warm water (110°)
  1 cup nonfat-milk powder
  1 tablespoon salt
  ½ cup unprocessed bran flakes
  ½ cup wheat germ
  4¾ to 5¼ cups all-purpose or bread flour
  1½ cups whole-wheat flour
  1 egg white blended with 2 teaspoons water for glaze
    Wheat or rye flakes for garnish

In large bowl of elecric mixer, combine 1 cup wheat flakes, 1 cup rye flakes, butter, ⅓ cup malt syrup or honey and 2 cups water. Stir to combine; cool to room temperature. Dissolve yeast and 1 teaspoon malt syrup or honey in ⅓ cup water. Let it stand until foamy, 5 to 10 minutes. Stir into wheat-flakes mixture. Add milk powder, salt, bran flakes, wheat germ and 1—1½ cups all-purpose or bread flour. Beat at medium speed with electric mixer 2 minutes or, beat 200 vigorous strokes by hand. Stir in whole-wheat flour and enough remaining all-purpose or bread flour to make a soft dough. Turn out dough onto a lightly floured surface. Clean and grease bowl; set aside.

Knead dough 10 to 12 minutes or until smooth and elastic. Place dough in greased bowl, turning to coat all sides. Cover with a slightly damp towel. Let rise in a warm place, free from drafts, until doubled in bulk, about 1 hour. Grease 2 (9-inch × 5-inch) loaf pans or 2 (2-quart) casserole dishes; set aside. Punch down dough; knead 30 seconds. Divide dough in half; shape into loaves. Place in prepared pans. Cover with a dry towel. Let rise until doubled in bulk, about 45 minutes. Preheat oven to 375°. Brush tops of loaves with egg-white glaze; sprinkle with wheat or rye flakes. Slash tops as desired. Bake 30 to 35 minutes or until bread sounds hollow when tapped on bottom. Remove from pans. Cool on racks.

Makes 2 loaves

Variations

Substitute 2 cups regular rolled oats for wheat flakes and rye flakes.

Add 1½ cups raisins along with whole-wheat flour.

Note: Malt syrup is available in health-food stores.

HONEY BANANA CAKE

  2 tablespoons honey
  1 tablespoon instant coffee
  1 cup mashed bananas (about 2 or 3 large ones)
  ½ cup water
  1 package spice cake mix
  2 eggs

Mix together honey, coffee, bananas and water, add cake mix and eggs. Beat on medium speed of your mixer for 2 minutes. Spoon batter into 2 (9-inch) greased and floured cake pans. Bake at 350° for 30 to 35 minutes, or until cake tests done. Cool on wire racks. May frost with whipping cream sweetened with honey and instant coffee. If you like, it is good with any frosting of your choice.

Easy and super.

CHURROS

     1 cup water
     ¼ cup butter, cut into small pieces
     2 tablespoons sugar
       Dash of salt
  1¼ cups sifted flour
     3 large eggs
     1 teaspoon vanilla, lemon or rum extract
       Vegetable oil for frying (you will need about 3 quarts)
     ¾ cup powdered sugar

Place the first four ingredients in a saucepan and bring to a boil. Remove from the heat and mix in flour all at once, beating until smooth and glossy with a wire whisk. Add the eggs one at a time, beating well after each addition. You will notice that each egg will separate the dough into clumps and this is normal. Just keep beating until it is smooth again. When all the eggs have been added, continue beating until paste comes together in a ball, leaving the sides of the pan clean. Mix in the flavoring of your choice.

Spoon mixture into a pastry tube or bag fitted with a plain tip ¼-inch or ½-inch opening. Pour oil into pan and heat to 375° on a deep fat thermometer. Carefully press the paste through the bag into the hot fat, making fritters about 5 to 6-inches long and curling them round as you press them into the hot fat. Don't fry more than four at a time. Deep fry turning with a fork, until puffed and golden brown on all sides, about 5 minutes. Drain on paper toweling. Place fritters in a 200° oven and let dry out for 25 to 30 minutes. Dust with powdered sugar.

Makes about 1 dozen

DOWN SOUTH FRIED PIES

1½ cups sifted all purpose flour
½ teaspoon salt
⅓ cup shortening
4 to 5 tablespoons water
1½ cups drained cooked fruit sweetened to taste

In a large bowl, sift flour and salt together. Cut in shortening, mixing well. Add water, using just enough to hold pastry together. Press dough into a ball. Roll out onto a floured board to ⅓-inch thickness. Cut into rounds about 5-inches in diameter. on half of each round, place 2 to 3 tablespoons fruit mixture. Moisten edges of pastry with cold water, fold to make half circles and press together with a fork. Fry in deep shortening, heated to 375° for 5 to 6 minutes, or until golden brown. Drain on paper towels and dust with powdered sugar while warm.

Had these in Nashville and they are great fun.

RASPBERRY MOUSSE PIE

Crust

⅓ cup butter
2½ tablespoons sugar
Salt
1 egg yolk
1 cup flour, sifted
½ cup almonds, chopped

Cream butter, sugar and salt until fluffly. Add egg yolk, blend thoroughly. Mix in flour and almonds. Press into a greased 10 or 11-inch springform pan. Bake at 400° for 12 minutes. Cool.

Filling

1 (10-ounce) package frozen raspberries, partially thawed and drained
2 egg whites
1 cup sugar
1 tablespoon lemon juice
¼ teaspoon vanilla
¼ teaspoon almond extract
1 cup whipping cream

Combined all the ingredients except the cream into a large bowl. Beat 15 minutes until mixture thickens and becomes larger in volume. Whip cream in a separate bowl. Fold in raspberry mixture. Pour into crust. Freeze 8 hours before serving.

This is gorgeous on a buffet table and you can garnish the top with fresh raspberries and mind leaves. Super and so easy.

Serves 12

CREPES

Crepes may be made in advance, stacked with waxed paper between every 3 or 4, and refrigerated or frozen. Return crepes to room temperature before trying to separate. Handy to have around for desserts, hors d'oeuvres, first courses or luncheon.

    4 eggs
    2 cups milk
    6 tablespoons butter, melted
    ½ teaspoon salt
    1 cup sifted all-purpose flour

Combine ingredients in a blender and blend until smooth. Chill thoroughly before making crepes. Heat a 6 or 7-inch crepe pan and brush lightly with butter or oil. Ladle in about 2 tablespoons batter and quickly tilt pan to spread batter evenly; pour out any excess. Cook until lightly browned, about 1 minute, then turn and cook until browned on the other side.

Makes 24 crepes

CHEESE PALACINKE

    4 eggs, separated
    ¾ cup milk
    1 cup pastry flour
    2 tablespoons sugar
    ½ teaspoon baking powder
    ¼ teaspoon salt
      Cheese Filling or fruit preserves
      confectioners sugar or granulated sugar

Beat the egg yolks well. Beat in the flour, salt and baking powder. Add the milk gradually, beating constantly. Fold in the stiffly beaten egg whites. Melt a little butter to cover the bottom with a thin layer. Spread the batter by moving the pan from side to side. When the underside is golden turn the palacinke over and brown the other side. Spread with filling and roll the palacinke up into a cylinder. Place it in a shallow baking dish and place in a warm oven until the other palacinke are cooked. Continue making palacinke until all the batter is used up. Sprinkle with confectioners' sugar and, if desired, with ground walnuts. Serve hot or cold.

Cheese Filling
    1 pound cottage cheese
    3 tablespoons sugar
    1 egg
    ½ teaspoon vanilla

Beat the egg. Add the remaining ingredients and mix well. Fill the palacinke. If desired, cover the filled palacinke with sweetened sour cream and return to the oven for 8 to 10 minutes at 350° before serving.

Serves 4 to 6

DEEP SECRET CUPCAKES

 1 package chocolate cake mix
 1 (8-ounce) package cream cheese
 ½ cup sugar
 1 egg
 1 (6-ounce) package chocolate chips
   Dash of salt

Mix cake mix according to package instructions. Set aside. Cream cheese and sugar. Beat in egg and salt. Stir in chocolate chips. Fill cupcake paper ⅔ full with cake batter. Drop 1 tablespoon chocolate chip mixture into each batter filled paper. Bake in a preheated oven 350° for 25 minutes.

Yields 12 cupcakes

DREAM CAKE

  1 cup flour
 1¼ teaspoons baking powder
  ¼ teaspoon salt
  ½ cup butter, softened
  1 cup sugar
  3 eggs, separated
  1 teaspoon vanilla
  ¼ cup milk
  ¾ cup Macadamia nuts

Filling

 1 (8¾-ounce) can crushed pineapple in heavy syrup
   water
 1 tablespoon cornstarch
   whipped cream

To make cake grease and line 2 (8-inch) cake pans and set aside. Combine first three ingredients. Cream butter and ½ cup sugar. Beat in egg yolks and vanilla. Beat in ½ flour mixture with 2 tablespoons of the milk; repeat the procedure. Spread batter in pans. Sprinkle with all but 2 tablespoons of the nuts. In a large bowl, beat egg whites until soft peaks form; add ½ cup sugar and beat until stiff but not dry. Spread mixture evenly over batter. Bake at 350° for 30 to 35 minutes. Remove and cool on cake racks.

 To make filling, drain syrup from pineapple and add enough water to make ½ cup liquid. Place in a saucepan and add cornstarch. Cook and stir until thick. Add pineapple and chill in refrigerator. Place cake on serving plate. Place filling over one layer, place top layer over filling. Frost the top and sides of cake with whipped cream. Sprinkle additional Macadamia nuts on top.

CHEDDAR CHEESE COOKIES

2 cups grated sharp Cheddar cheese
½ cup butter
1 cup flour
1 teaspoon salt
¾ cup finely chopped nuts

Cream the cheese and butter together. Add flour, nuts and salt. Form long rolls (about size of silver dollar). Wrap in wax paper, chill in refrigerator until ready to use. Slice thin, bake at 375° for 10 minutes.

Yields 6 dozen

CORNFLAKE COOKIES

2 cups cornflakes
¾ cup chopped nuts
¾ cup sugar
¾ cups shredded coconut
2 egg whites, beaten stiff
½ pound raisins

Stir together cornflakes, nuts, sugar and coconut. Fold in beaten egg whites. Drop mixture, one teaspoonful at a time, onto a greased baking sheet. Press a raisin on the top of each cookie. Preheat oven to 325° and bake 10 minutes. Using a spatula, quickly remove cookies from the baking sheet to waxed paper to cool.

Variations
Use other "flake" cereals in place of cornflakes. Substitute brown sugar for white sugar for a darker, richer tasting cookie.

Yields 5 dozen

SOUR CREAM BANANA SPICE CAKE

2 eggs, separated
½ cup butter
1½ cups firmly packed brown sugar
2 cups flour, sifted
1 teaspoon soda
1 teaspoon cinnamon
½ teaspoon salt
½ teaspoon ground cloves
½ cup mashed bananas
½ cup sour cream
1 teaspoon vanilla
½ cup finely chopped nuts

Beat egg whites until stiff but not dry; set aside. Cream butter and sugar, beat in egg yolks.

Mix together bananas, sour cream and vanilla. Sift dry ingredients together; add alternately with banana mixture to sugar mixture. Fold in egg whites. Pour into greased 9-inch square cake pan. Sprinkle with nuts. Bake at 350° for 45 minutes. Cut in squares and serve warm.

HERB OLIVES

½ cup salad oil (part olive oil for flavor, if possible)
½ bay leaf
1 small hot chili pepper
1 tablespoon drained capers
1 small garlic clove
6 rosemary leaves
1 tablespoon finely chopped celery leaves

Purchase large black or green olives. Press each olive gently between a nutcracker or the fingers, being careful not to loosen the stone. This will make it easier for the flavor of the marinade to penetrate the olives. Place 1 cup of olives in a pint jar and add the above ingredients. Cover jar and shake well. Let stand in refrigerator for 3 or 4 days before using; shake several times. The oil will be flavored, too, and may be strained later to use in making French dressing. Remove garlic if olives are stored for any length of time.

ITALIAN STYLE OLIVE MARINADE

1 teaspoon salt
½ teaspoon cracked pepper
¼ teaspoon dry mustard
1 teaspoon Worcestershire sauce
¼ cup wine vinegar
1 tablespoon water
⅔ cup olive oil
1 clove garlic, mashed
1 tablespoon parsley, chopped
¼ teaspoon powdered thyme
¼ teaspoon powdered oregano
1 tablespoon capers
¼ cup chopped onion
2 tablespoons chopped pimento

When you have finished the pickled olives, and waited at least six weeks, drain the olives and marinate in the above dressing at least overnight. Mix well.

OCTOBER

This is the month for Octoberfest sausages, Pumpkins and just plain old good cooking. This is a great time for the family and some of my ethnic recipes are here. The Holidays are just a whisper away. . . . . .

CRAB DELIGHT

    1 envelope unflavored gelatin
    3 tablespoons cold water
    1 can cream of mushroom soup
    6 ounces cream cheese, softened
    ¾ cup mayonnaise
    1 cup chopped celery
    ½ pound crab meat, fresh if possible
    1 small onion, grated
      Parsley
      Soften gelatin in cold water

Warm soup to simmering, add softened gelatin and cream cheese, stir over medium heat until dissolved, about 3 minutes. Remove from heat, add mayonnaise, celery, crab meat and onion. Rinse a 4 cup mold with cold water. Pour mixture into mold, refrigerate overnight. Unmold, garnish with parsley. Serve with crackers.

Serves 12

FESTIVE PUNCH

    1 large can pineapple juice
    2 large cans apricot-orange juice
    1 quart apple juice
    2 quarts ginger ale
    1 quart orange sherbert

Combine fruit juices and ginger ale in punch bowl. Float sherbert in punch.

Serves 50

BURGUNDY APPLE PUNCH

    2 large bottles burgundy or other red dinner wine, chilled
    1 quart bottle apple juice
    2 tablespoons lemon juice
    1 cup sugar
    1 large bottle ginger ale chilled

Combine wine, apple juice, lemon juice and sugar in punch bowl; stir to dissolve sugar. Blend in ginger ale. Add block of ice or tray of ice cubes. Serve at once.

Makes 35 3-ounce servings

HOT BEEF DIP SANDWICHES

        5 pounds rump roast
    1½ tablespoons garlic salt or fresh garlic to taste
      ¼ teaspoon ground pepper
      ¼ teaspoon marjoram
      ¼ teaspoon thyme
      ¼ cup flour
        3 tablespoons oil
    2½ cups water
        1 onion, thinly sliced

Trim off excess fat. In a small mixing bowl, combine garlic salt, pepper, marjoram & thyme. Mix well. Rub mixture into the beef, then coat with flour. In a Dutch oven, brown meat on all sides in oil. Add water and onion slices. Cover and bake at 325° for 2½ to 3 hours. Pour off pan juices into a measuring cup, spoon off excess fat. Add water to measure 2 cups. Slice roast as thin as possible. Place sliced beef on warm French rolls. Serve with Hot Beef Dip.

Hot Beef Dip

        1 cup strong coffee
        1 can (10¾-ounce) beef broth
        2 cups pan juices
        3 tablespoons Worcestershire sauce
        1 tablespoon onion, minced

Place all ingredients in a medium sized saucepan and simmer 15 minutes. Easy and that extra goodie you need to make French Dip Sandwiches.

Feeds the whole family.

DOLLY MADISON'S BOUILLON

        1 pound beef stew meat
        1 beef knuckle
        1 cup carrot, chopped
      ½ cup onion, chopped
      ½ cup turnip, chopped
      ½ cup parsley, chopped
          Salt and cayenne to taste

Combine all the ingredients in a large Dutch oven with 12 cups water. Cover and simmer for 2 hours. Strain the broth. Season to taste.

Serves 10

ITALIAN ORANGE SALAD

6 seedless oranges, peeled
1 medium Bermuda onion
½ cup dry sherry wine
  Juice of 1 lemon
⅓ cup salad oil
3 tablespoons honey
¼ teaspoon pepper
3 tablespoons Pernod or Anisette liqueur
2 cups watercress (after trimming)

Slice onion very thin and separate into rings. Place in a strainer and hold under cold running water for 3 minutes; pat dry. Place rings in a bowl and pour over sherry. Cover and marinate two hours.

Meanwhile, blend the lemon juice, oil, honey, pepper and liqueur in a bowl. Add 2 tablespoons of the sherry from the onions and beat or whisk until blended; chill.

Before serving, place watercress in the bottom of a chilled glass salad bowl. Slice oranges very thin and arrange them on the watercress in over-lapping circles. Drain the onions and scatter them over the oranges. Beat the dressing again and pour over all. Mix at table.

Serves 6

HOT SWEET-SOUR KRAUT & CABBAGE SALAD

¼ head white cabbage sliced finely
¼ head red cabbage, sliced finely
2 cups sauerkraut
1 tablespoon Dijon mustard
2 cups salad dressing (may use mayonnaise if you prefer)
¼ cup sugar
1 tablespoon celery seeds
  Salt and pepper to taste

Place cabbages in a bowl. Heat sauerkraut with the remaining ingredients for about 10 minutes, stirring frequently. Do not allow to boil. Pour over cabbage and toss well. Serve hot.

Serves 6 to 8

One of the most unusual slaws you will ever eat, red and white cabbage teamed with sauerkraut. Terrific.

PEAR SALAD WITH CELERY DRESSING

    ½ cup sharp cheddar cheese, shredded
    1 cup ground ham
    2 tablespoons green onion, minced
    3 tablespoons mayonnaise
    1 tablespoon sweet pickle, chopped
    1 teaspoon Dijon mustard
    8 canned pear halves, chilled
      Lettuce
      Celery dressing

Combine cheese, ham, green onion, mayonnaise, sweet pickle and mustard. Using 2 pear halves for each serving, spread filling in centers and put halves together to form a whole pear. Chill on lettuce leafs and garnish top with piece of green onion and celery dressing.

Dressing

    ½ cup oil
    3 tablespoons vinegar
    1 tablespoon honey
    ½ teaspoon salt
    ¼ teaspoon paprika
    ½ teaspoon celery seeds

Combine all ingredients in a jar. Cover and shake to blend.

PARTY BUFFET PECANS

     6 cups shelled pecans
    10 shakes Tabasco, it couldn't hurt to use more
    ⅓ cup Worcestershire sauce
    ½ cup butter, melted

Preheat oven to 325°. In large bowl mix melted butter and seasonings. Stir in the pecans until all the nuts are well-coated. Spread on a cookie sheet. Bake 15 minutes. Stir again. Salt if you wish at this point. Return to oven 10 minutes. Remove pan. Place on slant to drain extra butter from nuts. When cooled store in covered container. Reheat in 300° oven for 5 minutes before serving.

Makes 6 cups

MEXICAN LASAGNA

 1½ pounds ground beef
  1 medium onion, chopped
  1 clove garlic, minced
  1 pound canned tomatoes
  1 (10-ounce) can red chili sauce
  1 (4-ounce) can chopped ripe olives
  1 teaspoon salt
  1 teaspoon pepper
  ½ pound Ricotta cheese
  1 egg
  ½ pound jack cheese, thinly sliced
  8 corn tortillas
    Fritos
  ½ cup shredded Cheddar cheese

Brown meat, onion and garlic in a large skillet. Add tomatoes, chili sauce, olives, salt and pepper stirring to blend. Simmer 20 minutes. Mix Ricotta cheese with egg. Spread ⅓ of meat mixture in 9 × 13-inch baking dish. Top with half of the Jack cheese and Ricotta mixture. Add layers of tortillas cut in half. Repeat layers saving ⅓ of meat mixture for top. Top with layer of fritos and sprinkle with grated Cheddar cheese. Bake at 350° for 20 minutes or until hot and bubbly.

Makes 6 servings

MACARONI AND CHEESE SUPREME

 3½ cups cooked elbow macaroni
    4-ounce can sliced mushrooms, drained
  ¼ cup chopped pimientos
 1¼ cups cubed American cheese
  ¾ cup evaporated milk
  3 tablespoons grated onion
  2 teaspoons dry mustard
  1 teaspoon salt
  ¼ teaspoon Worcestershire sauce
  4 slices American cheese
  1 large tomato, sliced

Preheat oven to 350°. Grease a 1½-quart casserole. Put macaroni, mushrooms, pimientos and cubed cheese in casserole; mix well. Combine milk, onion, mustard, salt and Worcestershire sauce. Pour over macaroni mixture. Top with cheese slices and tomato. Bake in a preheated oven for 30 minutes.

Makes 6 servings

PANSIT GISADO (Fried Stewed Noodles)

½ cup each of julienne cooked shrimp, chicken, ham and pork
1 onion, sliced
4 garlic cloves, sliced
¾ cup lard or cooking oil
2 tablespoons soy sauce
2 tablespoons patis (patis is a liquid fish sauce and is sold in oriental food stores)
2 cups shredded cabbage
1 pound fine egg noodles or rice noodles
2 limes sliced thin

Fry shrimp, chicken, ham and pork with onion and garlic in ¼ cup lard for 3 minutes. Drain and reserve half of mixture. Add soy sauce, patis, and cabbage to the remainder, cover and cook for 5 minutes, or until cabbage is tender. Cook noodles for 2 minutes in boiling unsalted water, drain. Fry all at once in remaining lard until light brown. Break up and add to cabbage mixture. Serve with lime slices and reserved meats and shrimp.

Serves 6

PAUL PRUDHOMME'S COOKED RICE

2 cups uncooked rice (preferably converted)
2½ cups stock
1½ tablespoons finely chopped onions
1½ tablespoons finely chopped celery
1½ tablespoons finely chopped green pepper
1½ tablespoons unsalted butter or margarine
½ teaspoon salt
⅛ teaspoon garlic powder
A pinch of white pepper, cayenne and black pepper

In a 5×9×2½-inch loaf pan, combine all ingredients, mix well. Seal pan tightly with aluminum foil. Bake at 350° until rice is tender, about 1 hour, 10 minutes. Serve immediately. However, you can count on the rice staying hot for about 45 minutes or warm for 2 hours. To reheat leftover rice, either use a double boiler or warm the rice in a skillet with unsalted butter.

Makes 6 cups

"KUO PA" RICE PATTIES

1½ cups long-grain rice
2 cups cold water
 Oil
 Fine salt to taste

Rinse rice with water. Put the rice and cold water on a 10 × 15-inch jelly-roll pan and spread the rice evenly to make a thin layer, with grains touching each other. If you must use a smaller pan, adjust quantities of rice and water accordingly. Let stand for 30 minutes. Cover pan with aluminum foil and bake in a preheated 350° oven for 30 minutes. Remove the foil, wet the back of a spatula and press the rice down firmly. Reduce the heat to 300° and continue baking the rice, uncovered, for about 1 hour. The rice will be dry at the sides of the pan, but the center will still be damp. Take the rice out of the oven and break it into 2 × 2-inch pieces. Leave them out overnight. Make sure the rice patties have thoroughly dried.

Fry the dried rice patties in very hot oil (about 400°) 2 pieces at a time for about 10 seconds on each side. Drain. The patties will be light brown and crispy. Sprinkle on some fine salt while the patties are still hot. Break into desired-size pieces for snacks or appetizers. Unsalted fried rice patties can be kept in tins and reheated just before serving in a very hot oven (475°) and used for Sizzling Rice Soup. Thoroughly dried rice patties can be kept in tins for a long time. Fry when needed.

DUCHESS POTATOES

3 tablespoons butter or margarine
1 beaten egg
 Salt
 Pepper
4 medium potatoes, cooked and mashed (about 4 cups)

Beat 1 tablespoon of the butter, egg, and salt and pepper to taste in the mashed potatoes. Using a pastry bag with a large star tip, pipe 2-inch rosettes onto a greased baking sheet. Drizzle remaining butter over top of rosettes.
Bake at 500° for 10 to 12 minutes.

Serves 6 to 8

MILLS HOUSE SAUTEED MUSHROOMS, BACON & ONIONS

    5 slices bacon, snipped crosswise with kitchen shears into julienne
      strips
    1 large onion, minced
 1½ pounds mushrooms, sliced
      Salt and pepper to taste

Brown the bacon in a large heavy skillet until crisp. Drain bacon on paper towels. Measure the drippings and return 3 tablespoons to the skillet. Add onion and saute 5 to 8 minutes until golden, add mushrooms and saute, stirring, for about 5 minutes, or until lightly browned. Season to taste with salt and pepper and serve.

This is terrific with roast pork, turkey or chicken.

Serves 4 to 6

STEAK & DUMPLING BAKE

    2 pounds round steak, cut into serving pieces
    2 medium onions, sliced
    1 bay leaf
    1 (10½-ounce) can cream of chicken soup
    1 (10½-ounce) can onion soup
    1 (4-ounce) can sliced mushrooms, drained
    1 tablespoon Worcestershire sauce
  ⅓ cup flour
    1 package frozen pea pods
    4 green pepper rings

Preheat oven to 350°. Place steak in a 3-quart casserole, cover with onion slices. Add bay leaf. Combine soups, mushrooms, Worcestershire and flour. Pour over steak and onions. Cover. Bake for 2 hours or until meat is tender. Remove from oven. Raise oven to 400°. Remove bay leaf. Place peas on top of casserole, place pepper rings in center. Drop dumplings by rounded teaspoonfuls around the pepper rings. Bake for 20 to 25 minutes.

Parsley Dumplings

1 egg	¼ teaspoon sage
⅓ cup milk	1 cup flour
2 tablespoons minced parsley	1½ teaspoons baking powder
2 tablespoons cooking oil	½ teaspoon salt

Combine in a small mixing bowl egg, milk, oil, parsley and sage. Add flour, baking powder and salt. Stir only until dry ingredients are moistened.

This is a recipe sent in by one of the Food News Family and can be soo good for those of us that are busy. Serve with a little salad, yeast roll and a chocolate something—you're in the ball park.

Serves 6

TEXAS HASH

Oil
2 onions, chopped
2 green peppers, chopped
1 pound ground meat
Salt and pepper to taste
1 teaspoon chili powder
2½ cups canned tomatoes
1 cup cooked rice or spaghetti

Brown onions and peppers in oil. Add meat and cook until meat looses pink color. Add remaining ingredients and blend. Place in a covered casserole and bake at 350° for 45 minutes.

Serves 4 to 6

HOMEMADE COUNTRY SAUSAGE

½ pound lean pork
½ pound pork fat
½ pound lean veal
1 cup bread crumbs
Grated rind of 1 lemon
¼ teaspoon sage
¼ teaspoon sweet marjoram
¼ teaspoon thyme
⅛ teaspoon summer savory
½ teaspoon freshly ground black pepper
2 teaspoons salt
A grating of fresh nutmeg

Grind pork, pork fat and veal very fine using finest grinder knives. Put through grinder twice. Mix all other ingredients in large bowl. Add the ground mixture to the bowl and form this into a 1½-inch layer. Store overnight refrigerated and covered to blend the seasonings. To cook fresh sausages, start the patties in a cold ungreased pan over moderate heat and cook until medium brown on both sides and done throughout.

Makes 6 medium patties

Please note, the seasonings are a matter of personal taste, but this is a good guide.

DOWN HOME WINTER CHICKEN AND NOODLES

    2 cans cream of chicken soup
  ½ can milk
    1 large chicken (4 pounds or more)
    1 (12-ounce) package of wide egg noodles
    1 can sweet peas, drained
    1 can sweet corn, drained
    1 package sliced American cheese
  ½ package bread crumbs
      Salt and pepper to taste

Cover chicken with water and simmer until tender. While the chicken is cooking combine the soup and milk. When the chicken is cooked de-bone the chicken, discarding bones and skin. Cut into bite size pieces. Cook noodles in the stock from the chicken. Drain. Combine noodles, soup mixture, peas, corn and the chicken. Mix well. Place half the mixture in a 9 × 13-inch pan. Cover with cheese, add second half of mixture and remainder of cheese. Bake at 350° for 25 minutes, after 15 minutes sprinkle with bread crumbs.

Serves 6 to 8

LEMON-CAPER-BUTTER CHICKEN

    4 whole chicken breasts, halved and skinned
  ½ cup butter
  ½ pound mushrooms, sliced
    2 tablespoons fresh lemon juice
  ½ teaspoon paprika
  ⅛ teaspoon white pepper
  1½ tablespoons capers
    1 tablespoon caper juice
    2 cloves garlic, minced
    1 cup parsley, chopped

In a large saute pan, place butter and melt over medium heat. Add mushrooms and saute 5 minutes. Add lemon juice, paprika, pepper, capers, juice and garlic. Heat to boiling. Place chicken in a single layer in the pan. Heat to boiling. Cover and simmer very gently about 20 minutes or until a fork can be inserted in the chicken with ease. Uncover and cook turning once until chicken is lightly browned. Serve with rice and a fruit salad. Easy and soooo good.

Serves 4

FABULOUS BAKED CHICKEN

2 cups celery, chopped
¼ cup onion, chopped
¼ cup green pepper, chopped
2 cups toasted bread crumbs
¼ cup margarine
½ cup milk
4 cups chopped, cooked chicken
Salt and pepper to taste
½ cup walnuts, chopped
1 cup Swiss cheese, grated
1 (10-ounce) package frozen sliced peaches
Paprika

Combine all the ingredients. Spoon into a 3-quart casserole. Sprinkle with paprika. Bake in a 350° oven for 45 minutes.

You say you've tried every chicken recipe and you need new ideas, well step right up and take a chance this is really a lot of fun.

Serves 6

CHICKEN CASHEW (Microwave Oven)

3 whole chicken breasts (6 halves)
½ pound edible pod peas (or 2 packages frozen)
1 cup sliced mushrooms
½ cup sliced green onion
1 can (about 6 ounces) bamboo shoots, drained
½ cup sliced water chestnuts
1 teaspoon chicken bouillon concentrate (or 1 cube)
¼ cup soy sauce
2 tablespoons cornstarch
½ teaspoon sugar
Dash of pepper
½ teaspoon salt
4 ounces cashew nuts

Skin, bone, and cut the chicken into small bite-size pieces. Break off the ends and remove any strings on the pea pods. Prepare the mushrooms, onions, bamboo shoots and water chestnuts.

Mix the chicken bouillon concentrate, soy sauce, cornstarch, sugar, pepper and salt. Most cashews on the market are toasted but if raw cashews are being used, put them in the microwave oven with 1 tablespoon butter and cook them, uncovered, until they are nicely toasted, stirring from time to time (about 5 minutes or so). Set aside.

Put the chicken in a casserole and cook, covered, until it is opaque and tender. Stir several times during the cooking period. Add the peas, onions and mushrooms. Stir. Cook, covered, 2 minutes. Add the bamboo shoots, water chestnuts and the soy sauce mixture. Stir. Cook, covered, in the microwave oven until the sauce has thickened and the food is well-heated throughout. Stir in the cashew nuts. Serve with rice.

Serves 6

TUNA CASHEW CASSEROLE

For 6 Servings:

1 can Chinese noodles
1 can cream of mushroom soup
¼ cup water
1 can chunk style tuna (7-ounces)
½ can cashew nuts (about ¼ pound)
1 cup finely diced celery
¼ cup minced onion
Salt and pepper

For 54 People:

9 cans Chinese noodles
9 cans cream of mushroom soup
2¼ cups water
9 cans chunk style tuna (7-ounce cans)
4½ cans cashew nuts
9 cups finely diced celery
2¼ cups minced onion
Salt and pepper

Set aside 6 cans noodles to top casserole. In a wide pan mix soup, water, tuna, nuts, celery, onion, salt and pepper. Sprinkle rest of noodles over top; bake at 350° for minutes.

DATE NUT BREAD

1 cup boiling water
1 cup dates, chopped
1 teaspoon baking soda
4 tablespoons shortening
¾ cup brown sugar
1 egg
1½ cups sifted flour
½ teaspoon salt
1 cup chopped walnuts

In a mixing bowl, pour water over dates. Stir in baking soda and let stand 5 minutes. Cream together shortening and sugar, then egg, beating well. Stir in flour, salt and nuts. Stir in dates, combining alternately. Line a 10-inch loaf pan with waxed paper and pour in batter. Bake in preheated oven 350° for 45 to 60 minutes, or until firm.

Grow where you are planted

OLD FASHIONED BREAD PUDDING

    4 cups milk
    ⅔ cup mild flavored honey
    4 cups dry bread crumbs (without crusts)
    6 eggs
    ½ teaspoon salt
    2 teaspoons grated lemon peel
    2 tablespoons lemon juice
      Nutmeg

Warm milk and honey together. Place bread cubes in a 2-quart buttered casserole. Beat eggs with salt. Add to bread cubes with honey mixture, peel and juice. Sprinkle nutmeg over top. Bake in a preheated 300° oven 50 to 60 minutes or until set in the center.

Serves 8

TYLER'S COCONUT PIE

    3 beaten eggs
    1 cup sugar
    ¼ cup butter, melted
    ⅔ cup freshly grated coconut, or flaked coconut
    ½ cup light cream or milk
    1 teaspoon vanilla
    1 unbaked 8-inch pie shell

Combine eggs, sugar and butter. Beat well. Stir in coconut, cream and vanilla. Pour into a unbaked pie shell and bake at 350° for 45 to 60 minutes or until a knife inserted in the center comes out clean.

HERSHEY BAR PIE

    1 vanilla wafer crust
    1 (8-ounce) Hershey bar (large one with almonds)
    1 big and 1 small container of whipped topping

Make your crust and set it aside. Melt the Hershey bar and let it cool. Fold in the whipped topping and then pour the whole thing into your pie crust. Chill 5 hours. Delicious and easy.

Serves 2 to 8

EASY FROZEN LEMON PIE

Crust

⅓ cup butter or margarine, melted

¼ cup sugar

1¼ cups graham cracker crumbs, reserve a few for the top

Filling

1 quart ice milk

3 tablespoons lemon juice

Grated rind of one lemon

1 small can frozen lemonade concentrate

Combine melted butter, sugar and crumbs. Press into a 9-inch pie plate and bake at 375° for 8 minutes. Cool. Combine the ice milk, lemon juice and rind. Mix and add the lemonade concentrate. Spoon into cooled crust. Dust with reserved crumbs on the top. Freeze.

Serves 6 to 8

MEXICAN BREAD PUDDING

1 pound panocha or brown sugar

3 whole cloves

2 sticks cinnamon

1 pinch nutmeg

1 pinch salt

½ loaf sourdough bread

½ pound Jack cheese, cubed

1 cup raisins

½ cup almonds, blanched and chopped

3 bananas, if desired

Make a syrup of the water, panocha or brown sugar, cloves, cinnamon, nutmeg and pinch of salt. Stir well, strain and set aside. Cut the sourdough bread into 1-inch pieces; fry to a nice brown in very little shortening so it will not absorb too much fat, then arrange in a buttered casserole in layers with Jack cheese, raisins, almonds and bananas. Repeat layers until all ingredients are used. Pour syrup over all and bake in a moderate oven for ½ hour at 350°. Serve piping hot.

JELLO CAKE

   2¼ cups cake flour
    3 teaspoons baking powder
    1 teaspoon salt
   1¼ cups sugar
    3 tablespoons any flavored gelatin
    ½ cup oil
    1 cup milk
    2 eggs
    2 teaspoons vanilla

Preheat oven to 350°. Grease and flour 2 (8 or 9-inch) cake pans. Mix dry ingredients in a bowl. Stir in the oil and milk and beat for 2 minutes. Add the eggs and vanilla. Pour into pans and bake 25 to 30 minutes. Cool in pan 5 minutes before turning out onto racks.

JELLO FROSTING

In the top of a double boiler combine:

    Remainder of gelatin
    2 egg whites
    1 cup sugar
    ⅛ teaspoon cream of tartar
    ¼ cup boiling water

Place over boiling water and beat until icing holds soft peaks, about 4 minutes. Remove from boiling water and beat until peaks stiffen.

FALDERAH VANILLA WAFER CAKE

    ½ pound butter or margarine
    2 cups sugar
    6 eggs
    1 (12-ounce) box vanilla wafers
    ½ cup milk
    1 (7-ounce) package flaked coconut
    1 cup finely chopped pecans

Cream butter and sugar together. Beat in the eggs, one at a time. Crush wafers and add to creamed mixture alternately with the milk. Fold in coconut and pecans. Turn into a greased tube pan. Bake at 300° for 1 hour and 15 minutes, until firm but still moist.

Super duper for any festive occasion.

Serves a big bunch because it is so very rich.

OATMEAL PEANUT BUTTER COOKIES FOR GOBLINS

1 egg
½ cup sugar
½ cup packed brown sugar
⅓ cup shortening
½ cup chunky peanut butter
½ cup chocolate chips

½ cup chopped nuts
½ teaspoon salt
½ teaspoon baking soda
½ teaspoon nutmeg
½ cup flour
1 cup oatmeal

Mix together the first 5 ingredients well.
Mix together the remaining ingredients and add to the creamed mixture.
Drop by spoonsful onto a cookie sheet and bake in a 350° oven for about
15 minutes. Makes about 5 dozen bite-sized cookies if you use a teaspoon
measure. They also freeze if you can keep the kids away from the cookie
plate.

HONEY TEA COOKIES

½ cup butter or margarine
2 tablespoons milk
1 cup all purpose flour
¾ cup honey
½ teaspoon salt
1 teaspoon vanilla
1 cup shredded coconut
2 cups rice crispys
   Coconut or chopped nuts

In a 2-quart saucepan, melt butter. Blend in milk, flour, honey and salt.
Cook over medium heat, stirring constantly, until dough leaves sides and
bottom of pan and forms a ball. Remove from heat. Stir in vanilla and
coconut. Cool. Add cereal. Form into 4 (1-inch) rolls. Roll in extra coconut
or chopped nuts. Wrap in plastic wrap. May chill or freeze. To serve just
slice into ¼-inch thick slices.

COOKIES FROM A CAKE MIX

1 package chocolate cake mix
½ cup oil
¼ cup water
1 egg
6 ounces chocolate chips

Mix all together and drop by teaspoonful onto an ungreased cookie sheet.
Bake at 350° for 10 to 12 minutes.

NOVEMBER

Over the meadows and through the woods to grandmother's house we go. Pumpkin pie, juicy browned turkey, spicey cranberry sauce and the smell of fresh baked bread. These are a few of my favorite things. Crispy air, orange leaves, smoldering embers and apple cheeked youngsters. Hooray for this time of the year.

FRIED FONDUE PARMESAN

¼ pound butter or margarine
¾ cup flour
¾ cup cornstarch
1½ cups milk, scalded
2 eggs
¼ cup milk
½ cup grated parmesan cheese
Salt, pepper and nutmeg to taste

Make a roux with the butter, flour and corn starch, being sure the flour and starch are cooked over low heat. Add the scalded milk, salt, pepper and nutmeg and stir well while it cooks three minutes. Remove from fire. Mix the eggs and other ¼ cup milk, pour over the paste and stir in quickly. Pour into buttered deep pan about an inch deep. Chill. Cut into squares. Dredge in flour, dip in beaten eggs and then coat with crumbs. Deep fry or saute in chafing dish.

NACHOS SUPREME

12 corn tortillas
Oil for deep frying
½ pound lean ground beef
½ pound chorizo sausage
1 large onion chopped
2 (16-ounce) cans refried beans
1 (4-ounce) can chopped green chiles
3 cups grated Monterey Jack cheese (12-ounces)
¾ cup bottled taco sauce
⅓ cup chopped green onion
1 avocado, peeled, seeded and mashed
1 cup sour cream (8-ounces)

Cut tortillas into sixths. Fry in deep hot oil until crisp. Drain on paper towels. Salt to taste. Remove casing from sausage and crumble into a skillet. Saute sausage, ground beef and onion until meat is lightly browned. Drain off grease and salt to taste.

Use a large oven-proof baking dish or platter about 10 × 15-inches or equivalent area. Spread refried beans on baking dish and top evenly with meat mixture. Cover with chiles, sprinkle with grated cheese. Drizzle taco sauce over cheese. This may be covered and refrigerated at this point for later use. Bake uncovered at 400° 20 to 25 minutes or until hot. Put a mound of avocado in the center. Put dollops of sour cream over all. Tuck fried tortilla pieces around edges of platter. This may be served as an appetizer when baked in a large oven-proof platter. Keep it warm over a warming tray while serving.

This recipe may be served as a casual main dish for 4 to 6 people.

PICKLED OYSTERS

   3 pints shucked oysters
  ¾ tablespoon salt
   8 cloves
   1 teaspoon mace
   1 teaspoon allspice
   1 teaspoon white peppercorns
 1½ cups white wine vinegar
     Lettuce leaves
     Lemon slices

Drain the oysters of their liquid, put the liquid in a saucepan with salt, and bring to a boil. Make a bouquet garni of the cloves, mace, allspice, and white peppercorns, add to the liquid. Then add the oysters. Bring to boil, remove from heat, and let sit until the oysters begin to curl around the edges and appear plump. Remove them from the liquid immediately with a slotted spoon, place in cold water to stop further cooking. Add the vinegar to the spiced oyster juices, bring to a boil once again, strain, and cool. Replace the oysters in the liquid and serve on individual plates garnished with a lettuce leaf and a lemon slice as an appetizer.

Serves 6 to 8

BANANA RUMAKI

 16 to 20 slices of bacon (cut in half)
   1 cup brown sugar
 10 bananas (slightly underripe)
   2 tablespoons curry powder

Blanch bacon in boiling water for 10 minutes. Drain and dry thoroughly. Cut bananas into 1½-inch chunks and wrap in bacon, securing it closed with a toothpick. Combine brown sugar and curry powder and sprinkle on wrapped bananas. Place on rack in baking pan for about 10 minutes at 350° until bacon is crisp and sugar is lightly caramelized.

Serves 16

This is a different type of Rumaki that is always a hit.

PARTY SHRIMP QUICHETTES
(This will be one of your favorites)
Pastry
½ cup butter
3 ounces cream cheese
1 cup flour

Beat together the butter and cream cheese till smooth, add flour and form into a ball. Wrap in waxed paper and chill for 30 minutes or longer. The pastry can be made a day ahead. Make miniature pie shells by shaping the dough into 1-inch balls and pressing it into the bottom and sides of small muffin cups 1½ to 2 inches in diameter.

Filling
4 ounces small shrimp
1 medium onion chopped and slightly sauteed
½ cup grated Swiss cheese
2 eggs lightly beaten
½ cup milk
⅛ teaspoon nutmeg
Freshly ground pepper to taste

Preheat oven to 450°. In each miniature pie shell place a few small shrimp, a little sauteed onion, then a little grated cheese. Combine the eggs, milk, nutmeg and ground pepper. Pour into cups. Bake for 10 minutes. Reduce heat to 350° and continue baking 15 minutes more. Serve immediately. These can be frozen after baking and reheated at 450° for 10 minutes directly from the freezer. Substitution for shrimp can be crab, canned clams, chopped cooked ham, sauteed chopped bacon.

Serves 8

NON-ALCOHOLIC GOLDEN PARTY PUNCH
1 gallon cold water tea (see below)
2 (1-pint, 2-ounces each) cans grapefruit juice
Juice of 12 oranges
Juice of 12 lemons
2 (1-pint, 2-ounces each) cans pineapple juice
6 cups sugar
3 cups water
2 quarts chilled ginger ale

To prepare cold water tea, pour 1 gallon cold water over 1½-ounces tea. Let stand 12 hours. Strain. Add juices to tea. Combine sugar and water in saucepan. Bring to a boil, boil for 5 minutes. Sweeten juice mixture with syrup to taste. Chill. Just before serving add chilled ginger ale.

Serves 50

WINE DRESSING FOR FRUITS

    1 cup dry white wine
    1 cup oil
    2 teaspoons lemon juice
    2 tablespoons sugar
    1 teaspoon salt

Shake ingredients together in a jar and chill. At serving time give the jar another shake and pour over fresh or canned fruit.

Keeps well refrigerated.

COLD BROCCOLI SALAD

    2 pounds broccoli
    1 cup mayonnaise
    ½ cup sour cream
    ½ onion, chopped
    1 teaspoon sugar
    1 clove garlic, crushed
      Salt and pepper to taste

Wash and trim broccoli. Cook al dente. Drain and plunge into cold water. Drain well. Dice and combine with remaining ingredients. Chill.

Serves 6

SHRIMP CURRY SALAD

    1 box Uncle Bens chicken rice (or any other brand you like)
    1 pound cooked shrimp
    6 green onions, chopped
    ½ green pepper, chopped
  16 green olives, chopped
    2 jars marinated artichoke hearts (reserve marinade)
    ⅓ cup mayonnaise
    ¾ teaspoon curry powder

Cook rice as directed on box omitting butter. Cool. Have all the ingredients chopped and chilled. Combine mayonnaise, curry and artichoke marinade. Mix together and chill. Combine all salad ingredients and toss with dressing. Super for any type get together.

Serves 8

CORN BREAD AND CITRUS STUFFING

1 (6-ounce) bag of corn bread stuffing mix
¾ cup grapefruit segments
½ cup orange segments
¼ cup walnuts, chopped
¼ cup celery, chopped
2 tablespoons parsley, chopped
½ cup butter or margarine, melted
¾ cup orange juice

Combine all the ingredients and place in a covered casserole. Bake at 325° for 20 to 25 minutes. Wonderful with ham or pork.

Serves 4

NORTHERN ITALIAN DRESSING

1 (6-ounce) bag Mrs. Cubbison's Corn Bread Stuffin'
¼ pound dry salami, cut into thin strips
1 (10-ounce) package frozen chopped spinach, thawed and well-drained
½ cup Parmesan cheese
1 small onion, chopped
¼ cup margarine, melted
¾ cup dry wine (white), dry vermouth or water

Combine dressing mix with salami, spinach, cheese and onion. Add margarine and wine and toss slightly. Place in greased casserole and bake, covered, at 350° for 40 to 50 minutes.

Makes 6 servings

Crock Cooker
Combine dressing as above and place in well greased crock cooker. Cover and cook on low 2½ to 3 hours.

SPINACH NOODLES A LA CREME

1½ tablespoons grated Parmesan cheese
2 tablespoons grated Romano cheese
5 tablespoons sour cream
1 teaspoon curry powder
1 (12-ounce) package spinach noodles

Mix first four ingredients together. Cook noodles as directed on package, but do not overcook. When noodles are ready, drain them and toss in first mixture as you would a salad, coating all noodles with the mixture. Garnish with hot hard boiled eggs if desired.

Serves 4

NEW WORLD FETTUCINE

 12 ounces green fettucine
  3 tablespoons olive oil or butter
  1 large onion, finely chopped
  1 large green pepper, chopped
  3 cloves garlic, chopped
  2 tablespoons oregano
  2 cups thinly sliced mushrooms
  8 large, very ripe tomatoes, chopped
  1 cup chopped parsley
  1 tablespoon sugar
  1 (8-ounce) can tomato puree
  1 cup red wine
    Grated Parmesan cheese

Place fettucine in 8-quart pot of boiling salted water and cook until it is al dente. Drain and set aside.

Heat 2 tablespoons of the oil or butter in large pot and in it saute the onion, pepper, garlic and oregano until onion is transparent. Add mushrooms and continue frying until mushrooms are tender. Add tomatoes and cook until very soft. Add parsley and sugar. Mix everything with a wooden spoon. Add tomato puree and wine. Mix everything together well. Bring to a boil, lower heat and simmer 1 hour, uncovered.

Place fettucine in clean pot with remaining oil or butter. Cook, stirring, until fettucine is heated through. Empty out onto serving plate, cover with sauce and sprinkle with grated Parmesan cheese.

Makes 6 to 8 servings

SWISS RICE BAKE

  2 cups Swiss cheese, grated
  ½ stick butter or margarine
  1 (4½-ounce) can mushrooms, sliced
  ¼ teaspoon dill weed
  3 eggs, beaten
  1 cup milk
  1 cup diced cooked meat
  ¼ teaspoon salt
  ¼ teaspoon marjoram
  1 cup raw rice

Cook rice according to package directions. Heat milk and butter in a saucepan or microwave. Combine all the ingredients and place in a shallow 1½-quart greased casserole. Bake in a 350° oven for 45 minutes, or until a knife inserted in the center comes out clean.

Serves 6

ONION SHORTCAKE

       1 large onion
   1½ cups corn muffin mix
       ⅓ cup milk
       2 drops Tabasco sauce
       ¼ teaspoon dill weed
       ¼ cup butter
       1 egg, beaten
       1 cup cream-style corn
       1 cup sour cream
       1 cup sharp cheddar cheese, grated

Slice onion and saute in butter very slowly. Combine muffin mix, egg, milk, corn and Tabasco. Pour into a buttered 8-inch square baking pan. Combine sour cream, dill weed and ½ cup of the cheese with the onions. Spoon over the batter and top with remaining cheese. Bake at 425° for 25 to 30 minutes. Cut into squares.

Serves 4 to 6

RUTABAGA CHIPS

       2 pounds rutabaga   1 teaspoon salt
       ⅓ cup butter   ⅛ teaspoon black pepper
       1 cup rich chicken broth   3½ tablespoons sugar

Pare rutabagas and cut into eighths. Then cut into strips 1/16-inch thick. Combine butter, chicken broth, salt, pepper, and 1½ tablespoons of the sugar. Heat to the boiling point. Add the rutabaga and cook for 10 minutes. Turn into a buttered 1-quart casserole. Sprinkle with the remaining sugar and bake in preheated 375° oven for 45 mintues. This dish is excellent with baked ham or pork chops. It is delectable reheated as a leftover, too— a characteristic of most recipes for this succulent root vegetable.

Yield 6 servings

GREEN PEPPER SAUTE

       4 large green peppers, seeded and cut into lengthwise strips
       2 to 3 tablespoons olive oil
       1 to 2 tablespoons garlic salt
       1 teaspoon freshly ground pepper

Saute green pepper strips in fairly hot olive oil until limp but still crunchy, about 5 to 10 minutes. Sprinkle with garlic salt and freshly ground pepper. May use some red peppers for color without changing taste. Excellent with beef, roast leg of lamb or spareribs; pretty with veal piccata.

Makes 6 servings

THANKSGIVING YAM CASSEROLE

        6 to 8 yams (okay to use canned)
        2 to 3 oranges
        5 to 6 cooking apples, peeled and sliced
            Maraschino cherries
        2 cups boiling water
        1 cup sugar
        4 tablespoons cornstarch
        1 teaspoon salt
        ¼ pound butter or margarine

Cook yams, peel and slice. Peel and core apples, slice. Peel and slice
oranges. Layer yams and apples in a buttered baking dish. Top with sliced
oranges. Arrange cherries on top to add color. Add boiling water to the
dry ingredients. Stir. Add butter or margarine and cook until sauce thickens.
Pour sauce over yams. Bake in a 325° oven for 35 to 45 minutes.

Serves 8 to 10

Lucious and easy. . . .

ROAST BEEF

Slow Cooking Method . . .
Rub tender roast with oil. Do not salt. Place on roasting rack, fat side up.
Roast at 275°, 23 minutes per pound for rare. Check for doneness with
meat thermometer (140° for rare, 150° for medium). For roasts larger than
15 pounds, reduce cooking time to 20 minutes per pound. Season roast
after cooking and use drippings for au jus. Let roast "rest" 20 to 30 minutes
before carving.

SHIMMERING MUSTARD RING

        4 eggs   1 envelope gelatin
        1 cup water   1½ tablespoons dry mustard
        ½ cup cider vinegar   ½ teaspoon turmeric
        ¾ cup sugar   1 cup sour cream

Beat eggs in top of double broiler. Stir in vinegar and water. Mix remaining
ingredients except sour cream and stir into eggs. Cook over boiling water,
stirring until mixture thickens. Continue to cook and stir until mixture becomes very thick. Remove from heat and cool. Fold sour cream into cooled
custard. Pour into favorite ring mold. Chill overnight. To serve, unmold,
and it is just terrific with any beef, ham, lamb or chicken entree for your
buffet table.

Serves 10

BUFFET MEAT LOAF

     3 pounds ground beef, pork and lamb, or just beef
       Salt to taste
    ¼ teaspoon thyme
    ¼ teaspoon oregano
     4 green onions, chopped with some of the green
     2 cups bread crumbs
    ¾ cup wine, broth or water
     2 eggs, lightly beaten
     1 (8-ounce) can mushrooms, sliced
    ⅓ cup parsley, chopped
    ½ teaspoon pepper
     2 cloves garlic, crushed
     1 bay leaf, crumbled
    ⅛ teaspoon marjoram

Sauce
    ½ cup brown sugar
     1 cup catsup
     2 teaspoons dry mustard

Mix meat and all other ingredients together, tossing lightly. Lightly pack in a 9 × 13-inch baking pan. Shape into a loaf. Cover top and sides with sauce ingredients. Bake at 350° for 1½ hours, covering with aluminum foil the last half hour, or when getting overly brown.

Serves 10

ROAST TURKEY BREAST

To bone a turkey breast, slip a knife between the bone and the meat and separate the two, using a sawing motion. Tie the two halves together to make a cylindrical roll.

     1 whole boned turkey breast
     4 tablespoons butter
       Salt
       Freshly ground pepper

Preheat the oven to 325°. Rub the turkey breast liberally with butter and sprinkle with salt and pepper. Place in a shallow pan and roast for 25 minutes per pound or until the meat thermometer registers 170°.

Turkey Breast With Red Currant Sauce
Mix ½ cup red currant jelly, 4 tablespoons port wine, 3 tablespoons butter, and 1½ teaspoons Worcestershire sauce in a small saucepan. Stir over low heat until melted and simmering, then brush on the roasting turkey breast every 15 minutes. Spoon some of the sauce over the sliced meat.

(1 pound serves 3)

CORNISH GAME HENS WITH APRICOT CHUTNEY (Microwave)

    2 (1-pound) Cornish game hens
    1 cup Apricot-Chutney Glaze
    1 quart Corn Bread Dressing
    8 canned apricot halves, drained
      Parsley or watercress

Split hens in halves. Rinse and dry. Place in a 9 × 12-inch baking dish, breast side down. Cover with waxed paper and cook 7 minutes. Turn pieces over and cook, covered, another 7 minutes. Remove halves from dish and spread dressing evenly over bottom. Replace halves, cut side down, and brush with sauce. Cover tightly with plastic wrap and cook 10 minutes. Remove wrap and rebrush with sauce. Garnish with apricot halves filled with a little of the chutney sauce. Recover and cook 2 minutes longer. Let stand 10 minutes before serving with sprigs of parsley or watercress.

Serves 4

APRICOT-CHUTNEY GLAZE

    1 cup apricot-pineapple preserves
    ½ cup mango chutney
    ¼ cup sherry
    1 tablespoon brown gravy sauce or molasses
    1 teaspoon Worcestershire sauce

Stir ingredients together and use to baste poultry, lamb or pork, brushing on during final 10 or 15 minutes of cooking.

Makes 4 servings

SLOW TURKEY COOKING METHOD

Rub turkey inside and out with butter. Sprinkle inside and out with salt and pepper. Place on roasting rack *breast side down*. Roast at 275° 23 minutes per pound . . . or until meat thermometer reaches 175°. Do not baste, tent or turn. Allow 30 minutes for turkey to set before carving.

Note
Time may change for very large or small turkeys . . . rely on thermometer for doneness.

BONED ROAST DUCKLING WITH SAVORY RICE

4 pound duckling
Onion salt
Pepper
Salt
½ bay leaf
1 small garlic clove
1 chicken bouillon cube
1 cup raw long grain rice
1 onion, chopped
¼ cup parsley, chopped
¼ cup celery tops, chopped
¼ cup butter or margarine
1 teaspoon sage
1 teaspoon marjoram
1 (3-ounce) can sliced mushrooms, undrained
1½ tablespoons all-purpose flour

Wash duckling and sprinkle generously inside and outside with onion salt and pepper. Put breast side up on a rack in a shallow pan. Roast uncovered in a preheated 325° oven for 2½ hours. Pour off fat after 1 hour of cooking. Cover neck, giblets and wing tips with water. Add ½ teaspoon salt, bay leaf and garlic. Cook covered 10 minutes; remove liver, and continue cooking for 50 minutes.

Chop giblets, including liver and neck meat. Add bouillon cube and enough water to broth to make 2 cups. Bring to a boil and stir in rice. Cover and simmer until rice is tender, about 20 minutes. Saute onion, celery and parsley in butter for 5 minutes. Add giblets, neck meat, herbs and mushrooms. Stir into rice with a fork. Season with salt and pepper. Cool duckling. Pour off fat and add 1½ cups water to pan. Cook over low heat, scraping brown bits from pan.

Blend in flour mixed with a little cold water. Cook until slightly thickened; season if necessary. Line shallow pan with foil. With sharp knife, split breast off duck into 2 long pieces, keeping skin in place. Slip larger pieces off wing, drumsticks and thighbones. Arrange in pile in pan and cover with 1 piece of breast, skin side up. Do the same with the other side. Cover with foil and reheat in 325° oven for 25 minutes before serving. Remove foil and put under broiler to crispen skin. To serve, lift each portion with spatula to plate. Arrange reheated rice beside duck and serve with gravy.

Yield 2 servings

CHERRY SAUCE FOR DUCK

Duck neck, heart, gizzard and trimmings
1 medium-sized sliced onion
Salt
Black pepper
1 tablespoon cooking oil
2 cups beef bouillon or chicken broth
2 teaspoons chopped parsley
Thyme
Sage or ½ bay leaf
Juice from roasted duck
⅔ cup kirsch
1½ cups Montmorency sour cherries

Slice duck giblets and trimmings into small pieces and brown in saucepan with onion, dash of salt, dash of pepper and oil. Pour out oil. Add beef bouillon or chicken broth, herbs and a little water so that duck pieces are covered. Simmer while duck is roasting (about 90 minutes).

Remove excess fat from surface of liquid with baster and strain. When duck is roasted, remove to heated flameproof platter. Skim off excess fat in roasting pan and deglaze with about ⅓ cup kirsch. Add kirsch and roasting pan juices to small saucepan with 1 cup duck stock. Bring to boil and reduce slightly. Add cherries and simmer until warmed through. Correct seasoning. Place remainder of kirsch in ladle, warm, ignite and pour blazing over duck. Pour hot sauce and cherries over duck.

Yield 4 servings

TURKEY SCALLOPS WITH VERMOUTH AND MUSHROOMS IN A SOUR CREAM SAUCE

1 cup mushrooms, sliced
¼ cup butter or margarine
½ cup black olives, sliced and pitted
¼ cup celery, finely chopped
6 turkey scallops
1½ cups dry vermouth
1 cup sour cream
¼ cup parsley, chopped

Saute mushrooms in butter until lightly browned. Add olives and celery; cook for 2 minutes. Remove vegetables, leaving butter in pan. Lightly season turkey. Saute a few moments on each side, leaving slightly undercooked. Remove turkey.

Add wine to butter and reduce to ¼ cup. Add sour cream and whisk until smooth. Return all ingredients to pan and slowly simmer 15 minutes.

Serves 2

GLAZED TURKEY WITH SOURDOUGH STUFFING

    1 (10 to 12-pound) turkey
      Salt and pepper
    2 tablespoons butter or margarine, melted
  ⅓ cup maple syrup
  ⅓ cup dark corn syrup

Mix margarine, maple syrup and dark corn syrup. Brush over turkey during last hour of cooking, basting several times.

Stuffing

    8 slices sourdough bread
  ¼ cup butter or margarine
    1 cup onion, chopped
  ½ cup celery, chopped
    1 large apple, peeled, cored
      and chopped

  ½ cup pecans, chopped
  ½ pound mushrooms, sliced
    1 cup stock
    1 egg
  ½ teaspoon sage
      Salt and pepper to taste

Tear bread into small pieces. Saute onion and celery in butter. Combine onion mixture with bread, apples, pecans and mushrooms. Beat together stock, egg, sage, pepper and salt. Slowly add to bread mixture, tossing lightly to mix. Add additional stock if more moist dressing is desired. Bake in a 325° oven for 50 minutes. Uncover the last 10 minutes of baking.

Serves 6

HOLIDAY SWEET POTATO BALLS

    2 cups sweet potatoes, cooked and mashed
      Salt to taste
  ¼ teaspoon nutmeg
  ½ cup walnuts, chopped
    3 tablespoons butter or margarine, melted
    6 slices pineapple
    6 large marshmallows
    6 walnut halves

Mix potatoes, salt, nutmeg and chopped nuts together. Form mixture into 6 balls. Place each ball on a drained pineapple ring in center. Brush each with butter or margarine. Press the ball down with your hand to flatten it a little to cover the pineapple ring all around. Place in a baking dish. Bake for 20 minutes at 350°. Press a marshmallow into the center of each and top with a plump walnut. Return to oven until marshmallows are golden about 5 minutes.

This is so much fun.   Happy Holidays

Serves 6

SALMON NUT ROLL

    1 (15½-ounce) can salmon
    ¼ teaspoon liquid smoke
    2 tablespoons catsup
    1 tablespoon grated onion
    1 (8-ounce) package cream cheese
    1 tablespoon lemon juice
    2 teaspoons horseradish
    ¼ teaspoon salt
    1 cup walnuts, chopped
    ¼ cup parsley, chopped

Combine all ingredients except nuts and parsley. Mix well. Chill 1½ hours. Combine nuts and parsley on waxed paper. Shape salmon mixture into a log. Roll in nut and parsley mixture. Refrigerate several hours.

Served on a lettuce leaf and some dill sauce would be a nice accompaniment.

Sour Cream Dill Sauce

    1 cup sour cream
    1 teaspoon dill weed
    1 tablespoon wine vinegar
    ¼ teaspoon sugar
    ½ teaspoon salt

Mix all ingredients and let blend several hours in the refrigerator.

Makes 1 cup

CARROT COCONUT BREAD

    2 eggs, beaten
    1 cup sugar
    ¾ cup oil
    1½ cups flour
    ½ teaspoon salt
    1 teaspoon soda
    1 teaspoon cinnamon
    2 cups finely grated raw carrot
    ½ cup fine coconut

Mix together eggs and sugar. Add oil and beat well. Add remaining ingredients, blending well. Bake at 325° for 45 minutes.

CARROT ORANGE MUFFINS

    2 cups whole wheat flour
    2 teaspoons baking powder
    1 teaspoon cinnamon
    ¼ teaspoon salt
    ½ cup nuts, chopped
    ½ cup raisins
    2 eggs
    ¼ cup orange juice
    ½ cup oil
    ½ cup honey
    1 teaspoon vanilla
    1 teaspoon grated orange peel
    1 cup shredded carrots

In a large mixing bowl combined the first 6 ingredients. Set aside. In a small bowl, blend together remaining ingredients and stir into dry ingredients until moistened. Fold in carrots. Spoon batter into paper lined or greased muffin tins. Bake at 375° 20 to 25 minutes, or microwave 6 muffins on High for 2½ minutes.

Simply super

GRAND MARNIER CREME ANGLAISE

    5 egg yolks (use extra large or jumbo eggs)
    ¼ cup sugar
    Pinch of salt
    1 cup milk
    1 cup heavy cream
    2 tablespoons Grand Marnier
    1 cup heavy cream, whipped

Combine the egg yolks, sugar and salt in the top of a double boiler. Beat with a whisk until pale and creamy. Put the milk and the 1 cup heavy cream in a saucepan. Bring to a boil. Slowly pour the milk and cream mixture into the egg mixture, stirring constantly. Put the top of the double boiler over simmering not boiling water. Cook, stirring constantly, with a wooden spatula, until thick as a light cream that coats the spatula. The mixture must not approach the simmering point or it will curdle. Remove from the heat. Cool. Stir in the Grand Marnier and the remaining whipped cream. Chill and serve over any fruit salad.

BROWN SUGAR POUND CAKE

    3 cups sifted all-purpose flour
    ½ teaspoon baking powder
    ¼ teaspoon salt
    ¾ cup butter, at room temperature
    ¾ cup vegetable shortening
    1 pound light brown sugar
    1 cup sugar
    5 large eggs
    1 cup milk
  1½ teaspoons vanilla
    1 cup pecans or walnuts, chopped

Sift together the flour, baking powder and salt, set aside. Cream the butter and shortening until light and fluffy, add brown sugar, mix now add the white sugar and cream until light. Beat in eggs, one at a time. Add the sifted dry ingredients alternately with the milk, beginning and ending with the dry ingredients and beating after each addition only enough to blend. Stir in vanilla and nuts.

Pour into a well greased and floured 10-inch tube pan and bake in a 325° oven for 1¾ to 2 hours or until the cake begins to pull from sides of pan and top springs back slowly when pressed with a finger. Cool cake upright in its pan on a wire rack for 10 minutes, then invert and turn out on the wire rack. Let cool to room temperature.

Serves the whole gang. This has the same firm moist texture as plain pound cake, and a rich caramel flavor with plenty of pecans or walnuts baked into the batter.

MOCK CHOCOLATE MOUSSE

    1 (3¼-ounce box) chocolate fudge pudding (NOT INSTANT)
  1⅔ cups milk
    1 (8-ounce) carton Cool Whip
    1 (1-ounce) bottle rum or brandy flavoring

Put both pudding powder and milk in your blender. On high speed process for 1 minute. Pour into a 1½-quart sauce-pan and cook, stirring constantly, over medium high heat, until thickened and smooth. As soon as it comes to a boil, remove at once from heat. Cover pan and chill pudding 1 hour or until completely cold. Fold in Cool Whip and flavoring. Divide between 4 wine glasses. Garnish with a dollop of Cool Whip, chopped nuts and a maraschino cherry. Its so easy and always so good. So easy for summer entertaining.

Serves 4

CHOCOLATE APPLESAUCE CAKE

½ cup shortening
½ cup sugar
½ cup honey
1 teaspoon vanilla
3 eggs
½ cup applesauce
¼ cup honey
1 (6-ounce) package
   chocolate chips

2¾ cups sifted cake flour
1 teaspoon salt
3 teaspoons baking powder
½ teaspoon soda
½ teaspoon cinnamon
¼ teaspoon nutmeg

Cream shortening with sugar until light and fluffy. Continue creaming while adding honey in a fine stream. Add vanilla. Add eggs one at a time, beating after each addition. In a saucepan, combine applesauce, ¼ cup honey and chocolate pieces. Heat slowly until chocolate is melted and mixture is smooth. Cool.

Sift together dry ingredients. Add alternately to creamed mixture with chocolate-applesauce mixture. Beat after each addition until smooth. Spoon into two 9-inch greased, lightly floured layer cake pans. Heat oven to 350° (moderate). Bake 25 to 30 minutes or until cake tests done in center. Cool on racks five minutes. Remove from pans. Finish cooling on racks before frosting as desired.

ORANGE BUNDT COFFEE CAKE

1 (8-ounce) carton sour cream
1 (6-ounce) can frozen orange juice concentrate
4 eggs
1 (18-ounce) box yellow cake mix

In a large mixing bowl, beat sour cream with orange juice concentrate on medium high speed, until smooth. Beat in eggs on high speed for 3 minutes. Dump in dry cake mix right from the box. Beat until completely smooth, be sure and scrape down the side of the bowl. Spread the batter evenly in a greased and floured bundt pan. Bake at 350° for 55 minutes, or until done. Frost with ORANGE ICING.

Orange Icing

⅓ cup orange marmalade
2 tablespoons margarine

1 teaspoon orange extract
1 cup powdered sugar

In a small mixing bowl, beat all ingredients on high for 2 minutes. Drizzle over cooled coffee cake.

Serves 8

PUMPKIN BARS

2 cups flour	Dash cloves
2 teaspoons baking powder	2 cups sugar
1 teaspoon baking soda	1 cup nuts, chopped
½ teaspoon salt	1 cup salad oil
2 teaspoons cinnamon	4 eggs
½ teaspoon ginger	1 (16-ounce) can pumpkin
½ teaspoon nutmeg	

Combine all the ingredients and mix until well blended. Bake in a lightly greased 10 × 15-inch baking pan for 20 to 25 minutes at 350°.

Frosting

1 (3-ounce) package cream cheese	1 teaspoon vanilla
	2 cups powdered sugar
6 tablespoons butter	1 tablespoon milk

Combine ingredients and beat until smooth, you may need a little more milk.

EASY PUMPKIN CRISP FOR THANKSGIVING

Crust
1 package yellow cake mix less 1 cup for the topping
½ cup butter or margarine melted
1 egg

Filling
1 (14-ounce) can pumpkin pie mix
2 eggs
⅔ cup milk

Topping

1 cup reserved cake mix	¼ cup butter or margarine
¼ cup sugar	1 teaspoon cinnamon

Grease the bottom of a 9 × 13-inch baking pan. Combine cake mix, butter and egg. Press into pan. Combine topping ingredients with a fork, it will be very crumbly. Sprinkle over the top. Bake at 350° for about 45 to 50 minutes or until the filling is set.

Serves 10 to 12

PUMPKIN ICE CREAM PIE

1 cup canned pumpkin	½ teaspoon cinnamon
½ teaspoon salt	½ teaspoon ginger
¼ cup brown sugar	1 quart vanilla ice cream
½ teaspoon nutmeg	1 graham cracker pie crust

Combine pumpkin, brown sugar, salt and spices. Stir ice cream to soften. Fold in pumpkin mixture. Turn into shell and freeze until firm.

LAST-MINUTE PUMPKIN CHIFFON PIE

    1 carton dessert whip
    1 can pumpkin
    ¾ teaspoon cinnamon
    ¼ teaspoon nutmeg
    ¼ teaspoon ginger
    ⅓ cup half and half
    1 package instant vanilla pudding
    1 graham cracker crust (8-inch shell)

Combine dessert whip, pumpkin, spices, and cream. Add pudding and blend. Pour into shell and refrigerate. Keeps several days. Garnish top with whipped cream (optional). Great for Thanksgiving after a big meal.

PUMPKIN CHEESE PIE

      Pastry for 9-inch one crust pie
    1 (8-ounce) package cream cheese softened
    ¾ cup sugar
    2 tablespoons flour
    1 teaspoon cinnamon
    ¼ teaspoon nutmeg
    ¼ teaspoon ginger
    1 teaspoon grated lemon peel
    1 teaspoon grated orange peel
    ¼ teaspoon vanilla
    3 eggs
    1 (1-pound) can pumpkin

Heat oven to 350°. Prepare pastry. In large mixer bowl, blend cream cheese, sugar and flour. Add remaining ingredients except topping; beat at medium speed until smooth. Pour into pastry lined pie pan. Cover edge with 2 to 3-inch strips of aluminum foil to prevent excessive browning. Remove foil last 15 minutes of baking. Bake 50 to 55 minutes or until knife inserted in center of pie comes out clean. Immediately spread top of pie with Sour Cream Topping. Cool. Refrigerate at least 4 hours. Serve well chilled.

Sour Cream Topping
Blend ¾ cup dairy sour cream, 1 tablespoon sugar and ¼ teaspoon vanilla.

SWEET POTATO PIE

    1 (9-inch) unbaked pie shell
    4 tablespoons butter or margarine
    ¼ teaspoon salt
    ½ cup sugar
    3 tablespoons lemon juice
    1 tablespoon grated lemon rind
    3 eggs, separated
    ¼ teaspoon cinnamon
    3 large sweet potatoes, cooked and mashed
    1 cup cream

Line pie plate with pastry. Cream butter until soft; add salt and sugar and continue to cream until sugar is well blended. Add lemon juice and rind. Add beaten egg yolks, cinnamon, potatoes which have been put through a sieve, and cream. Mix thoroughly, and fold in the stiffly beaten egg whites. Pour into pastry-lined pie plate. Bake in a hot oven (425°) for 10 minutes, then lower temperature to 350° and continue baking for about 40 minutes longer, or until a knife inserted in the center comes out clean.

ORANGE-GLAZED DATE CAKE

    ¾ cup soft butter or
        margarine
    ½ cup sugar
    3 eggs
    3¾ cups unsifted flour
    1½ teaspoons baking powder
    1½ teaspoons baking soda
    ¾ teaspoon salt
    1½ cups buttermilk
    1 cup chopped dates
    1 cup chopped walnuts
    1½ tablespoons grated orange
        peel
    2 tablespoons flour

Orange Glaze
    1 (6-ounce) can concentrated
        orange juice
    ¼ cup water
    ½ cup sugar

Using large mixer bowl, cream butter and sugar; beat in eggs one at a time. Sift together flour, baking powder, soda and salt. Blending at low speed, add flour alternately with buttermilk. Combine dates, nuts and orange peel and dust with flour; stir into batter. Bake in buttered 9 or 10-inch tube pan at 350° for about 1½ hours, or until cake begins to pull away from side of pan. Remove from oven. Make glaze by blending juice, water and sugar and bringing to simmer. While both cake and glaze are hot, slowly spoon over cake until all glaze is absorbed. Cool thoroughly before removing from pan. Serve with whipped cream (optional).

Yield 12 servings

COCONUT CHEWS

¼ pound butter
1 cup sugar
2 eggs
7 ounces coconut, flaked
1 cup nuts

1 (12-ounce) package
vanilla wafers, crushed
2 teaspoons baking powder
½ can sweetened
condensed milk

Cream butter, sugar and eggs, added one at a time, beating well after each additon. Add coconut, nuts, wafer crumbs, baking powder and milk. Chill mixture in refrigerator for ½ hour. Drop by teaspoon on greased cookie sheet. Bake 15 minutes at 350°. Sprinkle powdered sugar on top while still hot.

Yields 4 dozen

Microwave
Spread half the mixture in a 9 × 13-inch glass baking dish. Cook on simmer 15 minutes, rotating dish after 8 minutes of cooking. Repeat for second batch. Cut into squares.

MEXICAN SUGAR COOKIES

1 cup butter
½ cup powdered sugar
1 teaspoon vanilla
2¼ cups flour

1 teaspoon cinnamon
¼ cup granulated sugar
⅓ teaspoon cinnamon

Cream butter and powdered sugar. Blend in vanilla. Sift flour and 1 teaspoon cinnamon together; stir into creamed mixture. Roll into 1-inch balls. Flatten between palms to ¼-inch. Bake at 400° for 8 to 10 minutes. Mix granulated sugar and ⅓ teaspoon cinnamon. Roll cookies in sugar-cinnamon mixture while still hot.

CHOCOLATE CHIP RUM AND PECAN CAKE

1 yellow cake mix
1 small package instant vanilla pudding mix
1 cup sour cream
½ cup oil
1 tablespoon vanilla
4 tablespoons rum
4 eggs
1 (12-ounce) package chocolate chips
1 cup pecans, chopped

Beat the first 7 ingredients together for 7 minutes. Fold in chocolate chips and pecans. Spray bundt pan with Pam. Bake at 350° for 1 hour. Turn over immediately on your favorite cake plate.

This is a hit everytime. Super for the holiday parties. Terrible on your waistline.

GINGER CUTOUTS

½ cup molasses
½ cup sugar
½ cup soft butter or
  margarine
2¾ cups sifted all-purpose flour

2 teaspoons ground ginger
½ teaspoon salt
1 teaspoon baking soda
½ cup buttermilk

Mix first three ingredients well; add sifted dry ingredients alternately with buttermilk and mix until smooth. Chill for several hours. Roll out on floured board to about ¼-inch thickness. Cut with floured cutter. Place on ungreased cookie sheets. Bake in preheated moderate oven (375°) for about 15 minutes. Cool and decorate as desired.

Yields 5 to 6 dozen

HONEY FRUITCAKE

2½ cups flour
½ teaspoon salt
3 teaspoons baking powder
1 teaspoon soda
½ teaspoon cloves
½ cup butter
1 cup milk

2 cups honey
4 egg whites
1 pound dates, cut
1 pound white raisins
1 pound figs, cut
2 cups chopped nuts
2 cups candied citron

Sift flour, salt, baking powder, soda and cloves together; set aside. Cream butter and honey. Blend in milk and dry ingredients; beat well for two minutes. Add egg whites, one at a time, beating well after each addition. Continue beating for two minutes.

Fold in fruits and nuts. Pour into tube pan. Bake at 300° about 3½ hours.

ROAST PUMPKIN SEEDS

Scoop seeds from pumpkin with a large spoon and separate them from the strings and pulp. Do not wash. For every two cups of seeds, add two tablespoons melted butter or oil and two teaspoons salt. Toss well so that all seeds are coated. Spread on an oiled baking sheet and bake 45 minutes at 225°, or until seeds are crisp. Cool and store in clean, airtight jars or plastic bags.

CURRIED FRUIT

1 (20-ounce) can peach
  halves
1 (20-ounce) can sliced
  pineapple
1 (20-ounce) can pear halves

½ cup margarine
¾ cup brown sugar
1 tablespoon corn starch
1 teaspoon curry

Drain fruits. Place in a greased casserole. Melt margarine, blend in sugar, cornstarch and curry powder. Spoon mixture over fruits. Bake at 350° for 45 minutes.

DECEMBER

It's beginning to look a lot like Christmas every where you go. This is the time for family. I love every minute of this month from the baking, shopping, the family get togethers. The quiet of Christmas. I want to share the happiest times of my life from my kitchen to yours.

WINE CELLAR GIFT SELECTIONS

12 bottle cases to please the collector and the hostess.

Collector case

2 Cabernet Sauvignon
1 Pinot Noir
1 Zinfandel
1 Gamay (or other dry red)
1 Rosé
2 Chardonnay (or White Burgundy) Pinot Blanc
2 Reisling
1 Chenin Blanc
1 other dry white (Semillon, Fumé Blanc, Sauvignon Blanc)

Sociable Case

2 Sherry (selected from Dry, Cocktail or Cream)
1 Dry Vermouth
1 Sweet Vermouth
1 Port
1 Haute Sauterne
1 Light Sweet Muscat
2 Champagne
1 Pink Champagne, Sparkling Burgundy or Spumante
1 Fruit Flavored Wine
1 Brandy or Fruit Flavored Brandy

MINT YULE PUNCH

1 cup fresh mint leaves (can use more if you like)
¼ pound sugar
3 oranges
3 lemons
3 limes
1 quart Canadian whiskey
1 quart gingerale

Crush together the mint leaves and the sugar. Cut fruit in half. Scrape centers and put fruit and 1 each of the rinds with the mint mixture. Mix well. Chill. When ready to serve, place mint mixture, whiskey and gingerale in a punch bowl over a chunk of ice. Garnish with mint leaves. Enjoy!!!!

Serves 16

TRANQUIL TEA

Instead of synthetic tranquilizers and dangerous sleeping tablets, try this old fashioned remedy. Mix 1 ounce peppermint leaves (nature's digestive), 1 tablespoon rosemary leaves (nature's tranquilizer), and 1 teaspoon sage leaves (nature's sleep producer). Keep in a tightly closed jar. Use 1 heaping teaspoon of mixture to 1 cup of boiling water. Let steep for one minute, strain, sweeten with honey, now sip. Amazing tranquilizing effect, without a hangover.

ANGELS ON HORSEBACK

    24 large fresh oysters, drained
    12 slices bacon, cut in half
    ½ teaspoon onion salt
    ¼ teaspoon pepper
    ¼ teaspoon paprika
    2 tablespoons parsley, chopped

Place an oyster on each piece of bacon and sprinkle with seasonings and parsley. Roll up bacon to enclose oysters and secure with toothpicks. Place on barbecue grill over medium heat 4 to 5 minutes, turning often with tongs. When bacon has browned, serve hot as an appetizer. May also place on rack in shallow baking pan and bake at 450° until bacon is crisp, about 10 minutes.

Serves 6

CAVIAR PIE

    4 hard-cooked eggs
    4 tablespoons butter, softened
    1 medium onion, finely chopped
    1 can flat anchovies, drained
    1 tablespoon mayonnaise
    2 tablespoons chopped parsley
    1 (4-ounce) jar caviar
      Juice of a half lemon
    1 cup sour cream

Mash hard-cooked eggs and mix with butter and half of the chopped onion. Spread evenly on the bottom of a 9-inch pie plate and refrigerate for at least ½ hour.

   Mash anchovies and blend with mayonnaise and chopped parsley. Spread on top of egg mixture. Combine caviar and remaining chopped onion and add lemon juice. Spread on top of pie, then frost with sour cream just before serving. Serve with crackers or bread rounds.

(Can be made ahead of time except for adding sour cream.)

Serves 8 to 10

CHEESE APPLE

    4½ to 5 ounces blanched almonds, chopped fine
       Water to cover almonds
       Red and yellow food coloring
    ½ pound mild cheddar cheese
    ½ pound sharp cheddar cheese
    ¼ pound bleu cheese
    4 ounces smoked cheese

Color water red, adding a little yellow to make a good apple color. Soak almonds in colored water until desired color, drain and dry on paper towels. Best to do this serveral hours in advance. Grate the cheeses and blend together (hands do the best job). Form into apple shape. Chill several hours until firm. Spread soft butter thinly over apple and cover with red almonds. Add stem and leaves from lemon or other suitable foliage.

HOLIDAY MOCK OYSTERS

    1 eggplant, cooked and mashed
    ¼ pound butter or margarine, melted
  1½ cups cracker crumbs
    1 egg, beaten
    2 cans minced clams, drained
      Salt and pepper to taste

Mix all the ingredients. Place in a buttered casserole and bake at 350° for 30 minutes.

Serves 6

HERBS DE PROVENCE

    One part marjoram
    One part oregano
    Two parts thyme
    One part savory

Although the cooks of the region rely on the same basic ingredients they of course, like all artists, treat them in different ways. This recipe is a little different from the coarsely textured herbs de Provence that uses crumbled leaves that include lavender, rosemary and fennel, the powdered version of this recipe can be a little more subtle and is wonderful added to any dish.

APRICOT SALAD

   1 (1-pound, 14-ounce) can peeled apricots
   1 (1-pound) can crushed pineapple
   2 (6-ounce) packages orange jello
   2 cups hot water
1½ cups syrup drained from fruits
   ½ cup chopped pecans
   ½ teaspoon vinegar
   ½ cup sugar
   3 tablespoons flour
   1 egg, beaten
   1 can syrup from fruit
   2 tablespoons butter
   1 cup cream, whipped
   ¼ cup longhorn cheese, grated

Drain fruits, reserving syrup. Cut apricots into small pieces. Dissolve gelatin in hot water. Add 1½ cups syrup from fruits. Cool. Add fruit and nuts. Pour into lightly oiled 9 × 13-inch pan. Chill until firm. Mix sugar, vinegar, flour, egg and one cup syrup. Cook, stirring constantly, until thickened. Add butter. Cool. Whip cream and fold in. Spread over gelatin layer and sprinkle with cheese. Refrigerate. Can be made days ahead. Cut into squares and arrange on lettuce on large tray for buffet.

Serves 16

FROZEN FRUIT SALAD

   ¼ cup lemon juice
   1 (14-ounce) can sweetened condensed milk
   1 cup whipping cream, whipped
2½ cups small marshmallows
   3 bananas, cut in bite-sized pieces
1½ cups pineapple chunks
   1 cup chopped walnuts
   2 (10-ounce) packages frozen raspberries
   Maraschino cherries
   Fresh mint leaves

Add lemon juice to condensed milk and mix until thick. Add whipped cream and fold in other ingredients, folding in raspberries last so that they will not mash too much. Put in a large glass baking dish and place in freezer to freeze solid. Take out of freezer about 15 minutes before serving. Arrange maraschino cherries and fresh mint leaves on top.

BLACK CHERRY SALAD

2 (6-ounce) packages black cherry jello
2 (20-ounce) cans pitted black cherries
1 small can crushed pineapple with juice
1 teaspoon Knox gelatin
2 cups Mogen David Concord wine

Drain cherries, reserve the juice. Dissolve Knox gelatin in ¼ cup of the cherry juice. Heat the remainder of the juice. Dissolve the cherry jello and the Knox gelatin in the hot juice. Cool, add wine, cherries and pineapple. Place in a large ring mold and chill.

Wonderful with Poik Lorn or maybe turkey or ham. . . . . Loverly.

Serves 10

FRITZI'S MOLDED BEET SALAD

2 (1-pound) cans pickled beets, reserve juice
2 large packages orange jello
¼ cup onion, minced
3 tablespoons lemon juice
⅛ teaspoon allspice
2 teaspoons horseradish

Drain beets, add water to beet juice to make 3½ cups. Bring liquid to a boil. Add jello and stir until dissolved. Add remaining ingredients except the beets. Chill until syrupy. Add beets, pour into favorite large mold and chill. Serve with sour cream dressing.

Dressing

½ cup sour cream
½ cup mayonnaise
1 tablespoon horseradish

This feeds the large family gathering and can be cut in half for smaller gatherings with no problem. . . . .

ORANGE SAUCE FOR GAME BIRDS OR POULTRY

1 cup sugar
½ cup butter
½ cup frozen orange juice concentrate
1 (11-ounce) can mandarin oranges
½ cup lemon juice
Juice and grated rind of 1 orange
1 tablespoon Galliano

Bring sugar, butter and orange juice to a boil, add remaining ingredients and simmer for a few minutes.

This is wonderful with duck as well as pork, poultry and ham. May also use as a basting sauce.

SHRIMP ARNAUD

    2 tablespoons red wine vinegar
    6 tablespoons olive oil
    1 tablespoon paprika
    4 teaspoons Creole Mustard (see below)
    ½ teaspoon salt
    ½ heart celery, chopped
    ½ white onion, chopped
    1 tablespoon parsley, chopped

Mix all the ingredients together and serve over chilled shrimp.

Note: The Creole Mustard has a distinctive taste and can be ordered from:
    G. B. Rotto & Company
    821 Washington Street
    Oakland, CA 94607
    1-800-228-3515

If you do not want to order the mustard, you may use a Dusseldorf mustard.

PARSLEYED RICE

    1 cup uncooked rice
    1 cup fresh parsley, chopped
    1 onion, finely chopped
    2 egg yolks
    1 cup Parmesan cheese,
       grated

    1 cup milk
    ¼ cup butter, melted
       Salt and pepper to taste
    2 egg whites

Cook rice as usual. Add all other ingredients except egg whites. Fold in beaten whites. Bake in 350° oven for 45 minutes.

Serves 5

MOM'S SUPER POTATO CASSEROLE

    6 potatoes
    2 cups cheddar cheese, shredded
    ¼ cup butter, melted
    ⅓ cup green onion, chopped
    1 teaspoon salt
    ¼ teaspoon pepper
    2 cups sour cream, room temperature
    2 tablespoons butter

Peel cooked potatoes and coarsely shred them. Add cheese and melted butter. Mix lightly. Add onion, salt, pepper and sour cream. Mix lightly. Dot with butter. Bake for 25 minutes at 350°.

This is a lovely Holiday Buffet Dish.

Serves 8

BURGUNDY BLEU CHEESE DRESSING

½ cup bleu cheese, crumbled
½ cup oil
4 tablespoons burgundy
4 tablespoons wine vinegar
1 teaspoon Worcestershire sauce
Salt and pepper to taste

Blend ingredients together with a fork, leaving a few lumps of cheese. Chill in the fridge overnight to let the folks get to know each other. Dynamite on mixed greens, citrus fruits, sliced cucumbers and tomatoes. For variety I use crumbled Roquefort or Gorgonzola cheese.

CHRISTMAS MORNING BRUNCH

10 slices day old sourdough bread, cut into halves
Dijon mustard
½ pound grated cheese
2 cups diced or crumbled cooked meat or seafood
½ cup fresh mushrooms, sauteed
1 cup onions, sliced and sauteed
2½ cups milk
Salt and pepper to taste
5 eggs

Choose cheeses and meats to compliment each other. Butter a 9 × 13-inch casserole. Spread mustard on bread slices. Make 1 layer of bread in bottom of casserole, top with cheese, meat, mushrooms and onions. Repeat layer. Beat eggs, milk and seasonings together. Pour over all. Refrigerate overnight. Christmas morning pop this in the oven at 350° for 1 hour. Serve with favorite coffee cake or any Holiday goodie you have. Simply super.

Serves 12

HOLIDAY PILAF

½ cup cream sherry
¾ cup golden seedless raisins
3 tablespoons butter
2 cups converted rice
3½ cups beef bouillon
1 cup pine nuts, toasted
Chopped parsley

Plump raisins in the sherry for about 10 minutes. Heat butter in a skillet, add rice and stir fry for about 5 minutes or until rice turns a golden brown. Add remaining ingredients. Bring to a boil, lower heat, cover skillet and cook for 20 minutes or until rice is tender. Garnish with chopped parsley.

Serves 6

VEN RICE

    butter or margarine (melted)
    onions (minced)
    condensed bouillon
2 cans condensed consomme
2 cups converted rice (uncooked)
2 cans of sliced mushrooms
    (depending on how well you enjoy mushrooms, will determine
    the size of the can!)

This is easy to prepare

Just combine butter or margarine, onion, converted rice, sliced mushrooms, condensed bouillon and condensed consomme. Pour into casserole dish and cover. Bake at 350° for about 1 hour. Fluff before serving.

Serves 12

POTATO KUGEL

    5 pounds potatos
    1 large onion
    1 medium carrot
    9 eggs, beaten
    1 cup of oil
        Salt & pepper to taste

Grate first three ingredients. Add rest of ingredients. Pour in a greased 9 × 13-inch pan. Bake at 400° 1 hour.

MATZO KUGEL

    5 matzohs
    5 eggs
    1 carrot, grated
    1 large onion, grated
        Salt & pepper
        Oil for frying

Beat the eggs. Add grated carrot and onion. Add salt and pepper to taste. Soak matzohs in this mixture until soft. Fry kugel on each side until golden brown.

CROWN ROAST OF PORK WITH CRANBERRY STUFFING AND MUSTARD SAUCE BALCHAN

1 crown roast of pork, trimmed of any excess fat (approximately 18 chops). Cover the bone ends of the crown roast with foil to prevent burning in the oven. Place a piece of foil around the bottom of the roast so the stuffing will not leak through. Place the roast on a rack in a large roasting pan. Roast in a preheated 350° oven 20 minutes per pound.

One hour before the roast is cooked, fill the middle of the crown with Cranberry Stuffing, piling it quite high. Extra stuffing can be put in a buttered baking dish, covered, and baked with the roast for 30 minutes. Return the roast to the oven and roast an additional 1 hour. If the stuffing becomes too brown, cover it with foil. Place roast on a platter, remove the foil tips, and decorate with paper frills. Garnish with orange slices or spiced peaches and watercress. Pass Mustard Sauce Balchan separately.

CRANBERRY STUFFING

4 cups cooked wild rice	½ teaspoon dried marjoram
2 cups raw cranberries, coarsely chopped	1 clove garlic, finely minced
	½ teaspoon pepper
½ cup melted butter	½ teaspoon mace
3½ tablespoons sugar	½ teaspoon dried thyme
2 tablespoons grated onion	½ teaspoon dried dill weed
1 teaspoon salt	

To prepare stuffing, in a large saucepan combine the stuffing ingredients and cook over medium-low heat about 10 to 15 minutes, or until heated thoroughly. Stir the mixture often. Allow the stuffing to cool.

MUSTARD SAUCE BALCHAN

4 tablespoons pan drippings or 4 tablespoons butter	¼ cup heavy cream
	3 tablespoons Dijon mustard
4 tablespoons flour	1 teaspoon dry mustard
1 cup dry white wine	Salt and pepper to taste
½ cup chicken broth	

To prepare sauce, in a medium saucepan blend the 4 tablespoons pan drippings or butter with the flour. Cook the roux over low heat 3 minutes. Add the white wine and cook until thickened, approximately 3 minutes. Add the chicken broth and cream and cook an additional 5 minutes. Stir in the Dijon mustard and dry mustard. Salt and pepper to taste.

The roast can be kept warm in a 200° oven while preparing the mustard sauce.

Makes 8 to 10 servings

CHICKEN IN CREAM

      4 whole boneless chicken breasts
        Bottled lemon juice
        Garlic to taste
 ½ pint whipping cream
 ½ bottle Worcestershire sauce

Halve chicken breasts. Combine lemon juice and garlic. Marinate chicken for at least 2 hours. Drain chicken, place in a casserole. Combine cream and Worcestershire sauce pour over chicken. Bake, uncovered, at 350° for 1 hour. Lovely served on cooked wild rice.

Serves 4 to 6

ROCK CORNISH GAME HENS WITH WILD RICE STUFFING

Stuffing
      1 cup uncooked wild rice
      7 cups water
      1 teaspoon salt
      1 cup uncooked white rice
      4 tablespoons butter, melted
      1 medium onion, chopped
 ½ pound mushrooms, sliced
 ⅓ cup slivered almonds

Wash wild rice and drain. Bring 7 cups water to a boil, add salt and wild rice gradually. Lower heat, cover pan, and simmer for 15 minutes. Add white rice, bring back to a boil, then lower heat and continue to simmer for 30 minutes or until all liquid is absorbed. Add melted butter, onion and mushrooms. Cook for 5 minutes, then stir in almonds.

Rock Cornish Game Hens
      8 Rock Cornish game hens
 1½ cups butter, melted
 1½ teaspoons salt
 ¼ teaspoon pepper
 ½ cup Bourbon
 ½ cup red currant jelly, melted

Preheat oven to 425°. Stuff hens with wild rice stuffing, truss them, and place in a shallow baking dish. Pour ½ cup of the melted butter over the hens and sprinkle with salt and pepper. Roast for 20 minutes. Add Bourbon and melted jelly to remaining butter. Reduce heat to 350° and roast for another 30 minutes, basting often with Bourbon mixture.

Serves 8

ROAST PHEASANT WITH APPLE STUFFING

    ¼ cup butter or margarine
    2 tablespoons finely chopped onion
    2 large apples, chopped
    4 slices toast, cubed
    1 teaspoon salt
    ¼ teaspoon pepper
    1 teaspoon sage
    1 egg
    2 to 4 pound pheasant
    2 thin strips salt pork

Preheat oven to 350°. Prepare apple stuffing. Melt butter or margarine in medium skillet. Saute onion and apple for 5 minutes. Remove from heat. Stir in toast, salt, pepper, sage and eggs. Mix well. Spoon stuffing lightly into neck and body cavities of pheasant. Truss bird. Place pheasant in roasting pan. Top with pork. Roast in preheated oven for about 1 hour, basting occasionally with pan juices. Untruss.

Yield 2 to 4 servings

LAMB RUB

Rub uncooked leg of lamb with:

    1 tablespoon dry mustard
    2 teaspoons soy sauce
    1 teaspoon garlic powder
    Enough oil to form a paste

Oven roast, uncovered, at 325° until meat thermometer reaches 140° for medium.

Candy canes, popcorn, cranberries strung
Candle glow, mistletoe
Stockings are hung
Carolers, snowflakes, cedar and pine
Santa's sleigh bells,
Presents to find,
Families, friends, children
Bells chime
Bless our homes and Christmas time

SEAFOOD FETTUCINI WITH GARLIC AND MUSHROOMS

Mama Mia Is This Good

   1 pound fettucini noodles
   ½ cup olive oil
   ½ cup garlic, minced
   ¼ cup green onions, chopped
   ½ cup parsley, chopped
   ½ cup fresh basil, chopped (don't fudge get fresh)
   1 pound fresh mushrooms, sliced
   ½ cup dry white wine (I love vermouth)
      Dash of Tabasco
   ½ tablespoon chicken stock base
   ½ tablespoon beef stock base
   1 cup Italian tomatoes, chopped (use canned they're better)
   1 cup cooked lobster, chopped
   1 cup cooked shrimp
   1 cup cooked crab, chopped
   ¼ pound sweet butter
   ½ cup parsley, finely chopped

In a large skillet, add olive oil and saute the garlic, green onions, parsley and basil. Add the mushrooms, saute for a few minutes then add the wine, Tabasco and the tomatoes. Bring to a boil, add the chicken and beef stocks. Let simmer gently. Add seafood, simmering until just heated through. Boil fettucini until al dente. Drain. Add butter, then sauce and top with parsley. Serve immediately.

Serves 8

This is so good it should be against the law. The marriage of fresh basil, garlic and mushrooms make this a memorable occasion, then add the seafood now you have a fabulous dinner.

Serve with a Cabernet, crusty bread and a green salad. For dessert a little sherbet with liquer over the top and Italian cookies.

APRICOT BREAD

    1 cup dried apricots
    1 cup sugar
    2 tablespoons shortening
    1 egg
    ½ cup orange juice
    ¼ cup water
    2 teaspoons baking powder
    ¼ teaspoon salt
    2 cups flour
    1 teaspoon salt
    ½ cup chopped nuts

Soak apricots in warm water for ½ hour. Drain; cut into small pieces. Cream sugar, shortening and add egg. Combine orange juice and water; add alternately with dry ingredients. Add nuts and apricots. Pour batter into one standard-size bread pan or two small-size pans that have been greased. Let stand 20 minutes. Bake for 1 hour at 350°.

ORANGE MUFFINS

    1 cup sugar
    ½ cup orange juice
    ½ cup butter
    1 cup sugar
    ¾ cup sour cream
    2 cups flour, sifted
    1 teaspoon baking soda
    1 teaspoon salt
    1 teaspoon grated orange rind
    ½ cup raisins
    ½ cup nuts, chopped

Mix sugar and orange juice. Set aside for dipping after muffins are cooked. Cream butter and sugar. Add sour cream alternately with the dry ingredients. Fold in orange rind and nuts. The batter will be very stiff. Use well greased muffins tins that are smaller so that these will be bite sized. Bake at 375° for 12 to 15 minutes. While still warm, dip them in the sugar and orange juice mixture. Cool on wire racks.

Makes 36 little guys

SUNSWEET HOLIDAY CAKE

     1 cup uncooked prunes
    ¾ cup uncooked apricots (dried)
     1 cup sliced citron
    ¼ cup sliced candied lemon peel
     1 cup candied cherries
    ½ cup sliced candied orange peel
    1¾ cups raisins
     1 teaspoon mace
    ½ teaspoon cloves
    ½ teaspoon allspice
     2 teaspoons cinnamon
     1 cup prune juice
    ½ cup orange juice
     1 cup strained honey
     1 cup shortening
     1 cup granulated sugar
     4 eggs, beaten
     2 teaspoons brandy or rum extract
     1 cup walnuts
     4 cups sifted all purpose flour
     1 teaspoon salt
    1¼ teaspoons soda moistened in 1 tablespoon water

Immerse prunes in boiling water for 10 minutes, drain and cut from pits in small pieces. Wash apricots, drain and cut in strips. Combine fruits and peels with spices, cover with prune juice, orange juice, honey, and allow to stand overnight. Cream sugar and shortening, add well-beaten eggs, extract, and combine with fruit mixture. Mix well and add nuts. Add flour and salt and mix thoroughly. Last add soda, and when well-blended pour into greased paper-lined large pan and bake 2½ hours in a slow oven (250° to 300°). A tube pan is preferable.

This recipe is from the Sunsweet book, copyright 1947. The recipes were developed by the California Dried Fruit Research Institute, for Sunsweet.

I prefer baking small loaf shaped cakes to give as gifts. I found this recipe especially easy for a working mother, because the work is split into two days. For about 15 years everyone had a small fruit cake in the boxes I mailed to family all over the country. When I stopped everyone moaned about the loss, so I baked large quantities once more and inserted the recipe! Now I bake only one batch.

Of course, it's doctored for a few weeks with a combination rum and brandy. For my teetotaller relatives, I spooned grape juice over it.

Dorothy L. Hufford

RUGELAHS

  1 cup flour
  ½ cup sweet butter, softened to room temperature
  ¼ pound cream cheese, softened to room temperature
  Sugar
  Cinnamon
  Chopped nuts
  Raisins (optional)
  Jam

In a bowl, cream butter, cream cheese and flour, forming a dough. Cover tightly with wax paper and refrigerate overnight.

The next day, divide dough into thirds, then roll each third out into a circle. Spread each dough circle with jam and sprinkle with any desired mixture of sugar, cinnamon, nuts and raisins.

Cut into pie wedges, then roll each wedge up from the outside in. Shape into crescents.

In an ungreased shallow baking dish, in a 375° oven, bake rugelahs for 30 minutes.

DATE LOAF

  ½ pound graham cracker crumbs
  1 pound dates, cut into pieces (about 2 cups)
  ½ pound marshmallows, cut into pieces
  ¼ pound nuts, chopped (about 1 cup)
  1 cup heavy whipping cream, whipped
  1 teaspoon vanilla

Combine half the graham cracker crumbs with the dates, marshmallows, nuts, whipped cream and vanilla. Shape into a roll, then roll in remaining crumbs. Wrap in plastic wrap and chill for 12 hours. To serve, cut into slices and top with a dollop of whipped cream.

Serves 12

QUICK CHOCOLATE MOUSSE

  1 can Eagle Brand Milk (sweetened condensed)
  1 (4-ounce) package instant chocolate pudding
  1 cup cold water
  ½ pint whipping cream, whipped

In a large bowl, beat Eagle Brand milk, pudding mix and water. Chill 5 minutes. Fold in whipped cream. Spoon into serving dishes. Garnish as desired.

Serves 4

CHEESE CAKE

    2 cups matzo meal
1¾ cups sugar
1½ teaspoons cinnamon
    ½ cup melted butter or margarine
    4 eggs
    3 tablespoons potato starch
    ½ teaspoon salt
    2 tablespoons lemon juice
    ¼ teaspoon grated lemon peel
    ¾ cup whipping cream
    3 cups cream style cottage cheese, sieved or whipped in blender

Combine matzo meal with ½ cup of sugar, cinnamon and butter. Save about ¾ cup of this mixture. Press the rest into the bottom and sides of a 9-inch spring form pan.

Beat eggs until thick. Gradually beat in remaining sugar. Beat in potato starch, salt, lemon juice and peel, cream and cottage cheese. Pour into prepared spring form pan. Sprinkle with remaining crumb mixture.

Bake at 325° for 1¼ hours. Turn off oven and leave cake in it for 1 hour. Chill thoroughly. Remove sides of pan to serve.

Makes 8 to 10 servings

KICHLACH (Basic Recipe)

1¼ cups flour
    2 tablespoons sugar
    ¼ teaspoon salt
    3 eggs

Sift together dry ingredients. Make a well in the center and add eggs. Beat with a fork till combined into a smooth paste or dough and drop from a teaspoon on a slightly greased cookie sheet at least 1 inch apart each way.

Bake 20 minutes at 325° or till lightly browned at the edges and puffed.

Yields approximately 36

Variation 1
Combine as in basic recipe, adding ½ cup melted shortening or salad oil. Beat till well combined.

Variation 2
For "Mohn Kichlach", add 3 tablespoons fine poppy seed to Variation 1 and follow same procedure.

MATZOS SPICE SPONGE CAKE (WINE CAKE)

12 eggs, separated
2 cups sugar
1½ tablespoons cinnamon
¼ tablespoon cloves
⅓ cup wine
1½ cup matzos cake flour
1 cup chopped, blanched almonds

Beat egg yolks and sugar until light and spices, wine, nuts and cake meal. Fold in stiffly beaten egg whites. Bake in a 325° oven for about 1 hour.

CREME CHANTILLY

½ pint whipping cream, cold
2 tablespoons sugar
1 teaspoon vanilla extract or 1 tablespoon brandy, rum or sweet liquer.

Pour the cream into a chilled bowl and whip it briefly before adding the sugar. Then whip until it is thick and fluffy. The whisk or beater will leave light traces on the surface of the cream and it will retain its shape slightly. Fold in the flavoring.

Rabbi Yale Butler's
ALMOND MACAROONS

4 egg yolks
1 cup sugar
½ teaspoon almond extract or ¼ teaspoon nutmeg
2 cups almonds, ground
40 almond halves

Beat yolks, sugar, extract and add ground nuts. Chill ½ hour. Roll out balls and top each with half an almond. Bake 10 minutes at 350°.

Yield 40 almond-topped cookies

CHRISTMAS CATHEDRAL WINDOWS

    1 (12-ounce) package chocolate chips
    1 cube butter or margarine
    1 cup nuts, chopped
    1 (10-ounce) package colored marshmallows
      Coconut or powdered sugar

Melt chocolate bits and margarine in a double boiler. In a large bowl mix nuts and marshmallows. Pour melted chocolate over marshmallows and stir until well coated. On waxed paper sprinkle coconut or powdered sugar. Divide dough and form into rolls. Roll in powdered sugar or coconut. Wrap air tight and refrigerate 24 hours. When chilled slice.

Easy and super duper------------

SANTA'S LEMON BARS

    ⅓ cup butter
    ⅓ cup brown sugar, packed
    1 cup flour
    ½ cup nuts of your choice, chopped
    ¼ cup sugar
    1 (8-ounce) package cream cheese
    1 egg
    2 tablespoons milk
    1 tablespoon lemon juice
    1 teaspoon vanilla

Cream the butter and brown sugar until light and fluffy. Add the flour and nuts and blend until crumbly. Reserve 1 cup for topping. Press remaining mixture into an 8-inch square pan and bake at 350° for 13 minutes. Mix sugar and cream cheese in the food processor or blender until smooth. Add egg, milk, lemon juice and vanilla. Beat until smooth. Spread over baked crust and top with the 1 cup of crumb mixture. Bake at 350° for 25 minutes. Cool and cut into squares. Makes approximately 16 squares.

HOLIDAY CRANBERRY KUCHEN
Batter
⅔ cup butter, softened
½ cup sugar
2 eggs
1½ cups flour
1½ teaspoons baking powder
½ cup milk
2 tablespoons sour cream
Grated rind of 1 orange
Fresh nutmeg to taste

Topping
½ pound fresh cranberries
½ cup sugar
¼ cup water
Juice from 1 orange

Preheat oven to 350°. Grease and flour an 8-inch baking pan. In a mixing bowl cream butter and sugar. Add eggs one at a time, beat well. Sift dry ingredients together and add to butter mixture alternately with milk and sour cream. Stir in orange rind and nutmeg. Pour in prepared pan. In a small saucepan combine all the ingredients for the topping. Bring to a boil, reduce heat, cook until cranberries are soft, about 10 minutes. Cool. Spoon cranberries over top of batter mixture. Bake for 20 to 25 minutes or until done. Can serve with butter in the morning or with vanilla ice cream or whipping cream in the evening.

Serves 6

FRUIT BLOSSOM COOKIES
1⅛ cups flour
1 teaspoon baking powder
Dash of salt
⅓ cup butter
½ cup sugar
1 egg, separated
1 tablespoon half & half
1 teaspoon vanilla
⅓ cup preserves (apricot, peach, etc.)

Sift together flour, baking powder and salt; set aside. Cream butter, sugar, egg yolk, half & half and vanilla. Blend dry ingredients into creamed mixture gradually, mix thoroughly. Shape dough into balls, using a heaping tablespoon for each cookie. Place on lightly greased non-stick cookie sheet; flatten slightly and brush with unbeaten egg white. Bake at 350° for 12 minutes. Remove from oven. Top each cookie with ½ teaspoon preserves. Bake 3 minutes more.

Yields 1 dozen

CHRISTMAS MOLASSES CRINKLES

   1 cup shortening
   1 cup brown sugar
   1 egg
  ¼ cup dark molasses
  ¼ cup milk
 2½ cups flour
   2 teaspoons soda
  ½ teaspoon ground cloves
   1 teaspoon cinnamon
   1 teaspoon ginger
   1 (6-ounce) package chocolate chips
     Granulated sugar

Cream shortening, brown sugar, egg, molasses and milk until light and fluffy. Sift dry ingredients together and blend into shortening mixture. Fold in chocolate chips. Chill dough. Roll into walnut-size balls. Dip into granulated sugar. Bake at 375° for 10 minutes.

CANDY CANE COOKIES

   1 cup shortening
     (may be part butter or margarine)
   2 cups sifted confectioners sugar
   1 egg
 1½ teaspoons vanilla
 1½ teaspoons almond extract
 2½ cups flour
  ½ teaspoon salt
   1 teaspoon red food coloring
  ½ cup crushed peppermint candy
  ½ cup sugar

Cream shortening, confectioners sugar, egg, vanilla and almond extract until light. Sift flour and salt together, stir into creamed mixture. Divide dough in half. Color one half the dough with red food coloring, leaving the other half white. Add peppermint candy to white portion of dough. Roll 1 teaspoon of dough into strips about 5 inches long. Place 1 red strip alongside 1 white strip, press together lightly and twist like a rope. Place on cookie sheet. Sprinkle candy canes with ½ cup granulated sugar. Bake at 375° for 8 to 10 minutes or until firm. These candy cane cookies will delight young and old alike at Christmas.

GREAT-GRANDMOTHER'S SUET PUDDING

       Presifted flour
 1 teaspoon salt
 1 teaspoon cinnamon
 1 cup seedless raisins
 1 cup currants
 1 cup ground suet
 ½ teaspoon baking soda
 ½ cup molasses
 1 cup milk
 ½ cup butter or margarine
 2 cups sugar
 2 eggs

Grease and flour 1½-quart mold with tight fitting lid. Into mixing bowl sift together 1¾ cups flour, salt and cinnamon. Stir in raisins, currants and suet; mix well. Dissolve baking soda in molasses; stir into batter. Stir in milk; mix well. Pour into mold. Cover. Place in large saucepan; add boiling water to saucepan to come halfway up side of mold. Cover saucepan; steam for 4 hours. Just before pudding is ready, prepare Custard Sauce. In top of double saucepan combine butter or margarine and sugar. Cook over hot water until butter is melted. Stir constantly, until thickened and smooth. Serve pudding with sauce.

Makes 6 to 8 servings

CLOVE CAKE

 ½ cup butter
 ½ cup milk
 ½ cup molasses
 2 cups flour
 2 eggs, whole
 3 cups seedless raisins
 1 teaspoon soda, in the molasses
 ½ teaspoon cloves, cinnamon and allspice
 1½ teaspoons nutmeg
 ½ pound crystallized ginger and butter, for decoration

Mix butter and milk; add eggs, beating well. Add molasses and soda, milk, and flour that has been sifted together with the spices. Beat well. Add raisins. Bake in a greased 8-inch tube pan at 350° for 45 to 55 minutes. Brush the top with a little butter, and garnish with overlapping slices of crystallized ginger.

FLUFFY WHIPPED CREAM FROSTING

½ cup unsalted margarine
½ cup sugar
½ cup milk
2 tablespoons flour

Cook milk and flour together until thick paste. Chill thoroughly. Put in small bowl of mixer with sugar and margarine. Whip at high speed for 7 minutes or until it looks like whipped cream. Will frost top and sides of 8-inch cake. Recipe may be doubled for a layer cake.

BUTTER CREAM FROSTING

½ cup margarine
½ cup shortening
1 cup sugar
¾ cup lukewarm milk
1 teaspoon vanilla

In mixing bowl cream margarine and shortening. Beat in sugar and milk alternately. Beat vigorously until granules cannot be felt between fingers, (on high speed with electric beater for 10 minutes). Blend in vanilla. Sufficient to fill and frost 8-inch layer cake.

WHIPPED CREAM CAKE TOPPING

1 envelope gelatin
2 tablespoons Kirsch, rum or water
2 cups heavy cream
¼ cup sugar

Dissolve gelatin with Kirsch, rum or water. Stir in cream and sugar. Chill for 30 minutes. Then whip until heavy peaks form. This frosting will hold on a cake very nicely for a day or two.

MIRACLE ICING

This recipe is sufficient to frost an 8-inch layer cake.

1 cup sugar
1 egg white
¼ teaspoon cream of tartar
½ cup boiling water
2 tablespoons strawberry gelatin
1 teaspoon vanilla

In mixing bowl combine all ingredients except vanilla. Beat vigorously until peaks form (on high speed with electric beater.) Stir in vanilla.

CHOCOLATE ALMOND SPONGE CAKE

    8 extra large or 9 medium eggs, separated
1½ cups less 2 tablespoons superfine sugar
 ½ teaspoon salt
   1 tablespoon almond extract
1¼ cups cake flour
 ¼ cup cocoa

Beat egg whites just until soft peaks form. Gradually beat in ¾ cup sugar. Add salt and almond extract. In large mixing bowl, beat egg yolks until lemon-colored. Gradually add remaining sugar; continue beating until very light in color. Gently fold egg yolks into egg whites.

Sift flour and cocoa together 5 times; gently fold into egg mixture a little at a time. Pour into ungreased 10-inch tube pan. Cut through batter several times with a knife or scraper to break up air bubbles. Bake at 275° for 45 minutes then increase temperature to 325° and bake 15 minutes more, or until lightly browned and center springs back when lightly pressed with fingertips.

Invert on wire rack or inverted funnel until cold. Remove from pan.

THE BEST CHRISTMAS COOKIES I EVER TASTED

 ½ cup butter
 ½ cup brown sugar, packed
   1 cup sifted cake flour

Blend together the butter and the sugar, blend in the cake flour. Press into an 8 × 8-inch cake pan, that has been greased. Bake in a preheated 350° oven for 20 minutes. Remove from oven and cool for a few minutes.

   2 eggs
   1 cup brown sugar, firmly packed
   1 teaspoon vanilla
 ½ cup shredded coconut
   2 tablespoons flour
   1 cup pecans, coarsely chopped.

Beat eggs and add sugar. Beat until thick. Blend in coconut, flour and nuts. Pour mixture over crust and bake at 325° for 20 minutes. The mixture will be soft in the center. Place pan in frig to cool before cutting, however not too long. Sift 1 cup of powdered sugar into a bowl to roll your cut bars into.

This recipe is from Blanche Stenberg and it is the best cookie I've ever tasted. . . . .

Merry Christmas

INDEX

APRIL

Asparagus, with Sauce Maltaise, 61
Banana, Split, 70
   Baked in Orange Juice, 74
   Baked with Honey, 74
   Baked in Currant Jelly, 74
Beans with Mushrooms, 61
Bloody Marys, 55
Burgers, Pork, 62
Cake, Nut, 67
   Strawberry Spice Loaf, 66
   Strawberry Cheesecake, 67
   Lemon Angel Food, 68
   Zucchini Chocolate, 70
   Amaretto Cheesecake, 71
   Carrot, 72
   Strawberry Shortcake 73
   Coffee Cake, 74
Carrot, Tsimis, 60
Cheese Puffs, 56
Chicken, with Wine Sauce, 64
   with Mushrooms, 65
Coffee, Continental, 56
Cookies, Lemon Zucchini, 69
Derma, Passover, 59
Dip, Sheepherders, 59
Frosting, Cream Cheese, 66
Gin Fizz, 55
Ham, Baked, 62,
   with Sauterne, 63
Herbs, Fines, 58
Kichlach, 73
Kugel, Vegetable, 60
Lamb, Roast, with Stuffing, 64
Moo Goo Gai Pan, 65
Pie, Fig, 68
   Sour Cherry Pudding, 69
Pork, Roast Loin with Sauce, 63
Punch, Mardi Gras, 55
Rolls, No-Knead, 66
Salad, Spinach, 57
   Tostada, 57
   Crab Louis, 58
   Seafood Rice, 58
Sauce, Maltaise, 61
   Artichoke, 63,
   Cherry Wine, 64
   Herb & Mustard, 64
   Dessert Fruit, 71
Soup, Bean & Beef, 56
Strawberry, Fantasia, 68
Stuffing,
   Wild Rice, 59
   Rosemary, 64

MAY

Artichokes, Stuffed, 89
Bread, Zucchini Spice, 91
Cake, Lemon Coconut, 93
   Strawberry, 94
Casserole, Tamale, 86
Chicken, Wings, 78
   Salad, 80
   with Yogurt-Nut Sauce, 81
   BBQ, 90
   Croquettes, 90
   Sesame with Mushrooms, 90
Chili, Quick, 79
Cucumbers, Baked, 85
Eggs, 83
Eggplant, 86
Dressing, Sesame Seed, 82
Filling, Lemon, 93
Frosting, Strawberry Buttercream, 94
Grapes, Cheese Wrapped, 77
Ham, 88
Hash, 81
Peach, Sabayon, 91
Pie, Strawberry, 92
   Peanut Butter, 94
Pork, Chinese Red, 87
   Chops Florentine, 89
Pizza, Strawberry, 92
Potato Salad, 79
Punch, Lemon-Strawberry, 77
Quiche, Crustless, 84
Ribs, 87
Salad, Chicken, 80
   Avocado, Asparagus, Artichoke, 80
   Cantaloupe, 82
Sauce, Parsley Butter, 82
   Asparagus, Mushroom & Cheese, 85
   Cheese, 88
   Strawberry Dessert, 92
Sherbet, Peach, 93
Shrimp, Micro, 91
Soup, Strawberry, 78
Wine, Strawberry, 77

JUNE

Beans, Bourbon Baked, 107
Bread, Zucchini Nut, 111
Brisket, with BBQ Sauce, 108
Burgers, Teriyaki, 102
Cake, Champagne, 113
   Wedding, 115
   Groom's, 116
   Peach Shortcake, 111
Casserole, Squash, 107